ON THE
PLEASURES OF
LIVING IN GAZA

ON THE PLEASURES OF LIVING IN GAZA

Remembering a Way of Life Now Destroyed

MOHAMMED OMER ALMOGHAYER

OR Books

New York · London

This book is dedicated to John and Yetta. John's passing leaves a legacy defined by his dedication to creating a world where justice and change are not just ideas, but actions. His humor, resilience, and belief in the human spirit continue to resonate in the lives he touched, a reminder that one can challenge even the most powerful forces in the quest for a better world.

Yetta, who survives him, carries not only his memory but also the spirit of their shared fight for justice. Her quiet strength and compassion have been the heart of their work, a shining example of the power of love in action. Their love for Gaza and all of Palestine crosses borders, reaching from their hearts to every part of the world. In Yetta's continued commitment to the Palestinian cause, I find inspiration and a call to continue their work—a call that, even in sorrow, is rooted in hope.

Contents

Introduction

As a fresh-faced research fellow at Columbia University's School of Journalism in New York, a secret smile danced across my lips when I overheard a whisper like, "He was born and raised in a refugee camp, you know. Must have been so rough."

I had to stop myself from laughing, astounded by the way folks fixate on the sad side of the story, blind to the myriad treasures I know are also at play in Gaza. The region's rich cultural heritage, spanning centuries, finds expression in music, dance, theater, film, fashion, sport, gastronomy, and poetry. Influenced by its vaunted place as an ancient trade route, Gaza has a distinct character, archaeological treasures, and a cuisine that includes delectable seafood dishes and some of the best strawberries in the world. Gaza's Mediterranean beaches, with golden sands and cerulean waves, show the coastal strip as it once was and still could be—a seaside paradise. There is a fleeting stillness every day at sunset and dawn, with views reminiscent of coastal Greece, Spain, Thailand, Mauritius, Cornwall, Brazil, New Zealand, or the Bahamas.

There is beauty, too, in Gaza's streets. Neighbors prop each other up, joining hands in celebrating holidays, weddings, and other extraordinary moments. If you find yourself short on cash, you are forgiven by a taxi driver. If you lose your cellphone, a brigade of searchers emerges within moments, combing each nook and cranny until it's found. In Gaza, friendship blooms in minutes, not months. Before you know it, you've been invited into a new friend's home and offered a feast fit for kings.

In the company of farmers, every dish is a testament to the hard work of cultivating the bounties of the land. Imagine, if you will, the appetizing aroma of *qalayet bandora*, a mouthwatering concoction made with freshly plucked tomatoes, piquant onions, and fiery serrano peppers, with rich local olive oil and a sprinkle of salt, all simmered over a crackling campfire. As the magic unfolds in the frying pan, a symphony of scent teases the senses with each sizzle. Served alongside freshly baked bread and just-picked garden greens, it is a feast that would be the envy of the world, if only they knew about it. What some of our Gazan dining experiences might lack in cosmopolitan flair, they make up for in their charm, which stems from their authenticity. And that's to say nothing of the warmth of the welcome and the quality of conversations that often go long into the warm, starry nights.

Gaza is a diamond in the rough, a hidden gem the media does not know how to polish. In this book, I will tell you some of the intriguing and inspiring secrets of this most misunderstood and hidden territory, only twenty-five miles from top to bottom, home to more than 2.3 million people, half of them children. Roughly 70% are refugees driven from their homes in cities and villages surrounding Gaza in 1948. They persevere in finding solace and delight in the simplest of pleasures as their lives and their passionate pursuits entwine.

One connecting thread in this book is Naji, a man from a war-torn village in northern Gaza. A photo of him blindfolded, zip-tied, half-buried, and presided over by armed Israeli soldiers appeared in a news image that captured the concern and imagination of a family from Houston. They happened to see it in an airport in Dubai and wanted to help, motivated by a sense of duty, frustration, anger, compassion, and guilt. I was tasked with locating the man and connecting him with the Americans. For Naji and his family, this proved to be a turning point, opening up greater financial freedom and a path toward a brighter future.

Another recurring character is my good friend Hassan, proprietor of a medical laboratory nestled in the heart of Rafah, my native city located on the Egyptian border in the south of Gaza. I met him when I was a teenager donating blood to help victims of Israeli invasions. He was intrigued by my decision to help at such a young age, and despite our notable age difference, a strong and enduring friendship was sparked. I learned a great deal from him about life, witnessing his everyday work as well as his life-altering interventions for people dealing with fertility struggles—whether his clients were too fertile or had trouble conceiving.

Later in the book, there is a sudden interruption. The author mysteriously disappears from the scene, kidnapped by unknown assailants. The story of my torture and interrogation raises questions that still need answers.

It must be noted that I made a pact with my publisher to write this book two years ago. As we stand on the precipice of publication, we witness the ongoing mass destruction of nearly everything Gazans have worked to build for themselves over decades of occupation and siege. Not everything—you can find occasional whimsy and joy even in camps full of displaced and hungry children, with teenagers leading Dabka dances and men dressed as clowns entertaining young kids. Or you may see the sky swarming with kites, the Palestinian answer to F-16 fighter jets. When the fire ceases and the dust settles, we will see what can be salvaged.

Don't be deceived—the people of Gaza are not a defeated people. Gazans possess an incredible level of determination that ignites the entire community. The stories in this book are a testament to this strength and resilience that defines true human dignity.

Nowhere else have I experienced such exceptional compassion and solidarity. When a home crumbles under the weight of bombardment, the entire community rallies together, hastening first to the bombed-out buildings to search for survivors, then to their own dwellings (if they still stand) to gather provisions for the displaced families. No hardship escapes a cascade of supportive words, heartfelt prayers, and compassionate actions.

This land has, after all, been the stage for countless battles throughout history. From the conquests of Alexander the Great and the Romans, to the clashes between early Muslim armies and European crusaders, Gaza's soil has witnessed the ebb and flow of great powers. The land has seen the footfalls of Napoleon's troops in 1799 and the confrontation between British expeditionary forces and Ottoman troops in 1917.

But nothing in Palestine's history has been quite this savage. Gaza finds itself regressed to an epoch reminiscent of the Stone Age amid a barrage of relentless strikes and a medieval-style blockade of food, water, electricity, and medicine. More than two million Palestinians are left grappling with acute dehydration, starvation, homelessness, disease, and indiscriminate bombings, with nearly all infrastructure crippled or destroyed, including Gaza's medical system, universities, and water treatment plants. Most homes, businesses, archaeological sites, and historic mosques and churches have been damaged or destroyed.

Innocent people are killed in such overwhelming numbers, the idea of a solitary grave has become a luxury. Gaza has become a garden of mass graves holding entire families along with neighbors and strangers, their individual identities entwined in a common shroud. And they are the lucky ones not buried in the rubble of their homes or picked apart by scavenging dogs until they are mere skeletons. Some characters in this book are accounted for, dead or alive, while the fate of others is unknown, with many likely dead, injured, or starving as I write. Nearly all have been uprooted from their homes and chased again and again from places where they've desperately sought refuge.

There is much more to say about this. For now, let's travel back to Gaza as I knew it. Even though it sometimes feels like a dream, Gaza was and is a real place full of poets and musicians, athletes and pharmacists, doctors and lawyers, farmers and fashionistas, entrepreneurs and dancers, a Christian man who plays Santa Claus in a (mostly Muslim) town decimated by Israeli airstrikes and a blind sheikh who champions women's rights. Even under years of siege, with catastrophic poverty and unemployment, people find joy in sharing food, strolling on the beach, chatting with neighbors in the street, walking their dogs (a new Gaza fad), and using the ruins of previous Israeli assaults as their own personal parkour arenas.

Every day they discover renewed significance and drive, defying the challenges of chronic illnesses, amputations, and trauma. Observing Gazans, seeing their boundless enthusiasm and resolute commitment, can leave an indelible mark on one's soul. As they walk me through their stories, I am amazed how much I can learn from my people born into chronic distress and violence. An inner fire fuels them and gives them hope that seems to last across the generations. I meet amputees who receive understanding and compassion that many people with all their limbs intact will never experience. They have been through the worst of the worst and yet remain strong, hopeful, and above all, kind.

I write most of the book in the present tense to make Gaza feel alive once more—an illusion, a resurrection, a magic spell. A chance for you to feel, as so many of us have, what it's like to see it all before you... and then to wake up from the dream and see it laid waste.

Join me and see my friends and so many inspiring people and places live again, if only on the page and in the mind of you, the reader. Join me in getting to know some of the big personalities and small moments of inspiration and beauty that most people outside of Gaza have never seen, and that all of Gaza's residents know so intimately. After reading this, perhaps you will begin to understand what Gaza means to so many people, and why its people have remained steadfast in their dreams of freedom and their refusal to leave their homeland.

Let us remember these names, faces, and places, even as so many are wiped off the map. When Gaza is rebuilt, it will be in their loving memory.

Chapter 1

Walking Gaza's Streets

You are now in Gaza, where the warm embrace of hospitality starts with a humble cup of tea or coffee and an invitation to relax and feel at home. What sets Gazans apart is our knack for reveling in life's simple pleasures. In the confines of the tiny Gaza Strip, a deeply-rooted appreciation for the mundane, the everyday, has blossomed. From savoring a simple meal with friends to witnessing the sun's descent over the tranquil sea, Gaza's denizens discover pure bliss in these tiny fragments of life on earth.

As I make my way to the post office through the bustling streets near Al Awda Square in the center of my hometown of Rafah, every step is met with a smile, a wave, or a cheerful greeting. This is a place where a simple trip to collect my mail can turn into an unforgettable experience. Everyone is eager to share what they have, from ice cream and pastries to paper cups of coffee or buttered corn, and make you feel at home. In this place, it's not about what you can buy but the connections you make along the way.

For example, there's always something going on at the Al Awda Pharmacy[1] in the city center. There's the woman who waits outside until the pharmacist is alone because she's too shy to ask her question in front of others. There's the friendly banter and laughs between the staff and the regular customers. That sense of community and warmth makes the pharmacy feel like more than just a place to pick up medication, and I always look forward to my visits.

One day I bump into my old friend Hassan as I make my way out of the pharmacy. He beams with delight, envelops me in a bear hug, and invites me to his small medical lab across the street. We chat as I pile my mail on the edge of his desk and he busily prepares a pot of our favorite thyme tea, which clears the throat and calms the mind.

Hassan knows I enjoy nothing more than collecting the newspapers I have written for. Some may arrive a year later, as mail service is extremely unreliable in Gaza. But it still feels good to touch Norway's *Morgenbladet*, *The Nation* from the US, UK's *New Statesman*, and magazines from Japan, Brazil, and Sweden. Hassan's eyes alight on an envelope covered in Montana, USA stamps and birthday stickers. I open it and discover it's a birthday card from a friend sent a year and a half ago. We both have a good laugh about the slow delivery.

By coincidence, the postman arrives at that moment. I joke with him about promoting national shipping. He says two clients make his job worthwhile: the local telecom company and me, with all the magazines and newspapers sent to me in Rafah.

Lab specialists elsewhere are known for relying on Google searches. Hassan relies solely on his experience and verified knowledge. He knows his limitations and sometimes advises people to seek a more advanced lab for a second opinion. But for basic tests such as blood tests, urine tests, tissue biopsies, and pregnancy tests, he is unmatched in Gaza.

He asks me about the state of the world and how Gaza appears from the outside. He often tells me, "You are the one who gives me hope." His two incredibly bright daughters and five sons are consistently at the top of their classes. His eldest daughter, age seven, scored a remarkable 99.1 percent average across all her classes. Hassan himself obtained a modest diploma in diagnostic testing from a local college, but with grades like these, his daughter can become an astronaut or brain surgeon or something equally impressive.

Still, he worries about the future. We discuss gender equality and empowering young women for leadership roles and how these changes will require a real change in mindsets. We don't have to verbalize our unspoken hope for an end to the occupation, peace and calm, freedom of education and travel, and space to breathe and think positively about future trends for Palestinian society.

A young teenaged girl arrives with her older brother. Due to limited seating in the waiting area, her brother waits outside. The girl hands over her urine sample for pregnancy testing. Her tears flow as her anxious brother paces outside.

A street vendor boy barges in selling popcorn. Hassan's lips, usually curved in a gentle smile, quiver with suppressed emotion. No one answers the popcorn boy. He takes the hint and exits to search out a more receptive crowd.

Hassan gently probes, "How did your brother become so concerned?"

She confides that her mother became alarmed when her periods suddenly ceased. Hassan assures her there could be various reasons for such irregularities.

Her eyes are fixed on the lab's entrance, where her brother still paces restlessly, mindful that their family's reputation—quite unfairly—hangs in the balance. With tension thick in the air, Hassan prepares to deliver news that could alter the girl's life forever.

He takes a look at the test strip, and his solemn intake of breath gives away the result.

Her facial expression is one of terror, and she is shaking as Hassan notes the test result on his ledger. She confesses that in a whirlwind of passion and naïveté, she was entangled in a relationship with a teenaged boy, their immaturity evident in their unpreparedness for the consequences of their illicit connection. The girl pleads with him to provide a second pregnancy test result showing she is not pregnant to placate her older brother. This puts Hassan in a difficult position. He refuses to compromise his professional integrity. But he has an idea.

With a subtle nod, Hassan excuses himself under the pretext of fetching papers from the neighboring bookshop. Stepping into the shop, he discreetly signals Karam, the proprietor. Along with paper goods, Karam sells a variety of gifts and knickknacks: red stuffed teddies, perfume, cologne, engraved items, lingerie, and occasionally fresh flowers. He knows most of the love stories in the schools and probably knows this one, but he's discreet about it, understanding these are sensitive matters that can ruin lives.

"Karam," Hassan murmurs quietly, "We need to stall. Can you arrange a brief power outage in the lab?"

If Hassan simply waits for some time, he may not need to bother, because rolling power cuts in the afternoon are the norm. But he needs a sure thing, and fast.

Karam nods, grasping the urgency of the situation. With practiced efficiency, he contacts another shop owner to coordinate a temporary disruption to the electricity supply.

A fleeting darkness descends upon the laboratory, and Hassan moves stealthily, with practiced finesse, to slip a note into the girl's trembling hands. In hushed tones, he says that since his printer isn't working at the moment, she should come back after his siesta to get the results.

Hassan never told me what the note said or how he helped the young woman resolve her problem. The teens were certainly not ready to be married, and the other options seemed to be termination or talking with the family about raising a child with an unacknowledged father. Hassan himself is against ending pregnancies, believing every human being is a blessing and there is nothing called an "illegitimate child." But perhaps he did not believe it was always his place to choose.

What I do know is that she was not the first or the last young woman who went to him for help and support.

Hassan's network includes everyone from judges, high-ranking military officials, engineers, and doctors to farmers, fishermen, mothers and children from every walk of life. He has earned respect for his professional skill and expertise, but it goes beyond that. Like the local pharmacist, Hassan has a strict policy of never turning patients away regardless of their ability to afford the tests they need. This principle is deeply ingrained in him and passed down from his mother. People come to see Hassan knowing they will be treated with dignity and respect regardless of their financial circumstances. In a world where medical care is out of reach for so many, Hassan is a beacon of hope, his kindness and compassion thriving in the heart of a city under blockade.

He uses his lab not just for tests but to encourage his patients to discover a newfound appreciation for life's simplest pleasures, such as spending more time with loved ones, strolling on Gaza's Mediterranean beach, or spending time on a favorite hobby, even in the face of difficult or chronic illnesses. He helps them recover a sense of purpose, joy, and meaning, which supports them to heal and cope.

He has a particularly remarkable way of comforting patients diagnosed with markers of organ failure, infections, or rare disease. Through his compassionate approach, he creates a safe space for self-reflection, prompting some patients to use serious illnesses as a catalyst for positive change in their lives and the lives of those around them.

His patients are often inspiring in their own right. I witnessed a woman known for having lost her three sons in war reach out to another woman who had just received a diagnosis of a rare blood disease. We all expected a woman who had lost her children to be shattered, but instead she radiated hope, speaking passionately about love and the power of perseverance in life, and it brought joy and surprise to the woman receiving the difficult diagnosis. It was an awe-inspiring moment that humbled us all.

We will meet Hassan again later with more stories from the lab, a microcosm of Gaza. For now, we will take our leave from Rafah, my hometown in the south of the Gaza Strip, and travel to the far north of Gaza where I'm given a mission to solve an intriguing mystery.

Interlude: The Half-Buried Man

The media generally has little to say about Gaza except in times of major crisis. But they do part of their job when they expose moments of brutality.

In the middle of the second Intifada, during a period of heightened violence and attack, Israeli soldiers launch a ground invasion with tanks and bulldozers into Beit Lahia, a northern village with fertile soil and relatively warm winters, known for its production of plump and delicious strawberries. Danny Salomon, a photographer embedded with the Israeli military, snaps a photo showing several Israeli soldiers and two bound and blindfolded Palestinian detainees, one of them wearing a dark grey collared shirt and inexplicably buried to his navel in a sandy ditch. A soldier in the photo gestures tiredly toward the half-buried man as if it's simply another day's work.

The image and its clear and chilling power dynamic makes its way to *Agence France-Presse* (AFP), the Israeli newspaper *Yedioth Ahronoth*, and Palestinian and other Arab newspapers, traveling to multiple capitals in the region. The world has become accustomed to images of injured and arrested Palestinians, but a half-buried Palestinian civilian is something new. The image becomes the "Pick of the Editor" at Getty Images, capturing the aftermath of the sleepless nights of Israeli incursions affecting innocent farmers.

An American family returning from their summer vacation, transiting through Dubai, stumbles upon the image in a newspaper at the boarding gate. Curiosity and compassion drive them to search for details about the "half-buried man." They want to help, motivated by a sense of duty to bring humanity closer together.

The family finds Palestine's first blog, *Rafah Today,* where I connect with the world, telling stories of the life around me and documenting incursions, shootings, home demolitions, and other attacks by the Israeli military, mostly against innocent civilians. I was with Rachel Corrie, a young American woman, a few weeks before she was run over and fatally crushed by an Israeli bulldozer as it destroyed an innocent family's home. I later guided her parents around the neighborhoods—some of them destroyed—where she spent her last weeks in Rafah. This and other tragic stories are documented on my blog.

The Texas family finds my blog and reaches out via email. I respond from my usual local internet café. Their interest puzzles me, since it seems like everyone has become accustomed to such daily humiliations. But the photo seized hold of their consciousness, the man's agony etched into their souls, igniting a determined inquiry into the grim realities depicted in the image.

Unfortunately, I cannot tell them anything about his name, his exact location, or how to get in touch with him. That will require some detective work.

I begin by asking journalists, thinking one of them must have taken the photo, but my friend Firas informs me that he saw it in Palestinian newspapers some time ago. It's a challenge to find the archives. I ask around and learn that the only institutions that maintain newspaper archives are the Palestinian president's office or the municipality library. I end up searching through one newspaper after another in Rafah's municipality until I finally find it and take a photocopy.

If *Al Ayyam* newspaper had provided a detailed photo credit, I could have contacted the AFP news desk, as they owned the photograph. But I have no such luck, and the location only says "north Gaza."

So, I end up searching in random places east and north of Gaza City. I show the image to countless people in supermarkets, schools, universities, and community centers, and still, nobody recognizes the blindfolded, half-buried figure.

Finally, someone tells me he looks similar to someone he knows from a village in the far north. I go there on a painfully cold winter day and meet Khalil, a man in his late fifties, the cousin of a journalist I know from the same village. He has short, practical hair, a thick, dark mustache, and streaks of grey in his beard. He is accompanied by his shadow, his youngest son, who is ten. Khalil is a compact man, not much taller than the boy, and has deep brown almond-shaped eyes and a hint of a smile that radiates calm, confident kindness. He wears a worn kuffiyeh and a fleece-lined black jacket, his face weathered and bronzed from long hours in the sun.

Khalil transports vegetables between farms and packing houses. He knows almost everyone and is always on the move, so I move with him in his pickup truck. Each farm has a story, some food to offer, new tastes, and new hospitality. Most people I meet know my uncle Salah[2] (from my mom's side) who works as a water expert in the north.

A gathering spontaneously develops at one farm along the way after I start asking questions, and it grows cozier than anticipated as someone offers us desserts. My new friends hungrily await the sizzling knafeh, a sweet pastry roasting over an open flame, but I'm eager to take the intel I've gathered so far and continue the search.

Khalil kindly insists on giving me a ride to my next stop. I'm trying to reach another neighborhood in Beit Lahia, and I feel we're getting close. We also seem to be getting closer to the dangerous Israeli fence.

We make a series of stops at his cousins' farms. At one of these, he presents me with freshly picked strawberries. Dutch experts say Gaza strawberries have a richer taste than those imported from Spain and Morocco. I agree—I've tried all three, and Gaza's are the best. Most Gaza farmers hold the prestigious Good Agricultural Practices (GAP) certification, an internationally recognized set of standards dedicated to ensuring food safety, sustainability, and quality that allows them to export their products. Yet it always remains up to Israel whether and when the strawberries are actually allowed to leave Gaza.

In the bustling packing house, brimming with produce ready to be hopefully transported to the Netherlands and sold in other European markets, the sweet abundance is overwhelming. But I've been taken in by the Americans' enthusiasm, and I am as eager as they are to see what happened to the man after the image was taken. I urge Khalil to press on.

First, he says, we must visit more of his cousins. They are diligently harvesting green peas. My host knows my weakness for this small, spherical seed, the prized yield of the *Pisum sativum* plant. He insists I sample one, and the taste exploding in my mouth when I crush a pod full of peas is nothing short of magical. But I need to follow up on the clues gathered so far, and my host seems not to grasp that I cannot carry bags overflowing with enough strawberries and peas to feed a small army.

As he drops me off, he introduces me to Ibrahim, another cousin, who emerges selling goods at a bustling road junction. Before bidding me farewell, Khalil kindly bestows upon his cousin the generous offering of strawberries and peas that I sadly could not carry and adds a refreshing bottle of water and a handful of fresh green almonds, which he also shares with me. These fuzzy, light-green orbs harbor soft, jelly-like, skinless almonds. They are delicate, wholly different in texture from mature almonds, with a satisfying crunch and hint of tartness, reminiscent of unripe peaches or fresh dates.

Once Khalil leaves, Ibrahim, still stationed at the road junction, invites me to sit and puts half the bottle of water to good use, heating it up on a small gas cooker. He brews a steaming pot of fresh mint tea, a robust infusion with an abundance of sugar, a taste I know so well. We each enjoy a warming cup before I set out on what I hope is the last leg of this journey.

As I stand to leave, Ibrahim pauses briefly, fixing his gaze on me.

"Take some strawberries," he offers, his voice laced with determination.

"Really, it's enough, I've had my fill," I reply, nodding in gratitude.

"Have some more," he insists.

This is Gaza. In media accounts, Gaza is a 'sacrifice zone,' one of the lost places on the planet, pulsating with conflict, despair, and wasted lives. Yet the gory and depressing headlines cannot erase a thriving, rich, and generous culture, even if it is rendered largely invisible to the outside world.

Finally, at my next stop—yet another random farm—a man peers at the photo and says he knows the distinctive soil clinging to the man's half-submerged body. At first, I dismiss him as delusional. He can identify a location based on its dirt? But it turns out he is a seasoned worker who digs deep in the earth to find water sources in areas plagued by scarcity, and he possesses an intimate knowledge of the terrain. Sitting beneath a sprawling tree, pushing a fresh cucumber into my hand, he tells me the photo was likely taken in an area called Umm Al-Nasr Village, also known as the Bedouin Village, on the outskirts of Beit Lahia. This place and the Swedish village near Rafah are the worst places one can live in Gaza. Umm Al-Nasr is wedged between a sewage plant and the Israeli fence, and few dare to go there even to provide public services.

I push on to Umm Al-Nasr Village and ask around, and I'm told that someone bearing a striking resemblance to the man in the photo might be stuck in a restricted buffer zone, where a security clearance is required to enter. Buffer zones are lands near the border that Israel has largely bulldozed and cleared of buildings and trees. Farmers are often prohibited from accessing their lands, with Israel citing various security reasons. The zone extends around all of Gaza's borders, including the border with Egypt, where Israel demolished thousands of Palestinian homes. Even the sea is hemmed in. Israel imposes severely limited fishing zones and frequently fires on Palestinian fishermen whether or not they wander past whatever nautical "border" Israel is imposing at a given time.

Every movement is observed in the buffer zone. The only vehicles allowed in without fuss and scrutiny are ambulances and vegetable or food supply trucks. Even the UN requires permission to enter, and of course it's that much more difficult for Palestinians to get a permit. I decide not to bow to this bureaucracy and instead call

Khalil and ask him to smuggle me into the area in his vegetable truck.

Walking within the isolated, empty buffer zone feels
like navigating a treacherous dance atop jagged shards of
glass. Khalil and I trudge along a muddy road, its surface
slick from rainfall. Clutching the worn remnants of the print-
out in my hand, we approach a woman seated with a basket, cracking open nuts for her livelihood. I show her the
photo and ask my usual question for what feels like the mil-
lionth time. My heart is in my throat. Could this finally be it?

On another street in Rafah, a ten-minute walk from Hassan's lab,
a man takes his stand outside a local bank, his grip on the cash
machine unyielding. Hesham is determined to be at the front of
the queue should news arrive that the salaries of public employees have finally been deposited. Others sit on the dusty street
or lean against the wall of the bank, refusing to yield their place
in line. Explosions a few hundred meters away generate clouds
of dust as Egyptian troops demolish the homes of their own
people to create a wider buffer zone between Gaza and Egypt.

A young man perched on a donkey cart remarks, "That cash
machine won't sprout wings and fly away, Hesham."

Another quips, "Really, who knows when the ATM machine
might grow wings and take flight?" as he gives up and takes
his leave.

A man stationed outside the bank showcases a collection of
new shoes for sale. He hopes that upon receiving their wages,
the men standing in line will purchase his unsold stock so he
can get back home with some funds to feed his family for Eid.
Winter is on the horizon, and sturdy footwear is needed to with-
stand the chill. As the shoe salesman diligently polishes each
pair to perfection, he shouts the prices amidst a cacophony of
taxis, cars, tuk-tuks, motorbikes, and donkey carts.

This neighborhood enthralls me with its ceaseless human activity and the ingenuity with which people defy adversity. From the Sheikh en route to the mosque to the teenager yearning to spread his wings beyond the border and the mother standing in line, awaiting a bank transfer from her son in North America and anticipating her daughter's wedding, each person has their own story. All are intertwined in the rhythm of life here, beckoning people to share their tales and jokes over steaming cups of coffee.

Fragments of my childhood still linger on this street, which I first trod as a young boy in second grade, next to the remains of the Palestine railway station. Until 1948, it connected Gaza with Egypt, Jordan, Syria, and Lebanon. The railway played a crucial role in trade and travel between Palestine and its neighboring countries, and parts of the tracks are still visible today.

I vividly recall our neighbor, Abu Raed, erecting the building that now stands before me. As an eight-year-old child, I was consumed with curiosity about what it was for.

"This will be Rafah's inaugural bank," Abu Raed proudly told me.

"A bank? What is a bank for?" I asked him.

He responded patiently, "Well, you come here with your money to safeguard it and utilize it for your needs and desires when you grow older."

Even now, this wonderful and bewildering answer reverberates within me. Abu Raed's words etched themselves into my consciousness, and I never forgot the promise held within the building, which symbolized hope for our close-knit community's future.

Three decades later, I walk this same street, standing in the same spot, and observe Ashraf, the bank's retail supervisor, trying to organize this multitude of people awaiting their turn outside. A young man pleads with Ashraf for a loan of $25, which he promises to repay as soon as his salary arrives.

Ashraf has to say, "I'm sorry, but I can't fulfill these requests anymore." The man persists, explaining he cannot even afford a gas cylinder he needs for cooking without an upfront payment. Ashraf repeats that a loan is not possible. Another man approaches, seeking permission to use Ashraf's phone, as his own battery has gone down during the long wait.

Later I find out that not only is the man allowed to make his call and to charge his cellphone in the bank, but Ashraf also ensures that the exceptional loan for $25 is approved until the young man is paid.

Adjacent to the bank is the local wheat flour mill. The miller, alongside his cousin, the carpenter, joins the queue at the bank. I catch a glimpse of the miller, whom I last encountered as a teenager, when I would see his daughter daily on the way to school. I wonder what has become of her. He still sports the same crimson beard but has aged quite a bit. Flour coats his hands, and I'm sure the machines in his mill are still adorned with the fine white dust produced by his tireless efforts to grind wheat for the entire neighborhood. The donkey stationed outside the mill may not be the same donkey I saw all those years ago, but the unchanging fragrances of the street evoke a sense of nostalgia in me.

In the dusty, bustling animal market, where owners still bring their sheep, cows, camels, and goats for sale, the serene and melodic strains of a violin impart a rustic and pastoral ambiance to the surroundings. In some ways Gaza is timeless, the smell of ground wheat still mingling with the rich aroma of freshly ground and brewed coffee. These familiar scents are comforting, transporting me to an era filled with warmth and tradition, which actually still remains in Gaza. In most other places, all this would have disappeared, eaten up by that greedy monster, progress.

I catch sight of a shepherd boy standing amid his flock of sheep and realize he is the one playing his violin. The dust swirling about him adds a touch of romance to the scene, a kind of rustic charm in the middle of town. A radiant smile illuminates the shepherd's face and he loses himself, completely absorbed in the music. The sheep are as captivated by the melodies as we humans are, and they follow in the boy's footsteps along the lively street.

The symphony of sounds intensifies as cows emit mournful lowing, sheep release plaintive bleats, chickens cluck, and roosters crow. It is a chorus that defies the passage of time. Yet occasional detonations at the border remind us of the precarity of it all.

Approaching the Rafah border, the clamor subsides and a sense of tranquility rules the land as troops pause for their midday rest. Faiz Abu Taha, the proprietor of a small convenience store, reclines next to his humble abode, savoring a simple yet satisfying meal of zucchini in tomato sauce with bread and hot green chili peppers. A kettle brews fragrant tea nearby. In a gesture of spontaneous hospitality, he extends an invitation for me to join him. He tells me his earnings are enough for his family's needs, and he has fostered good connections with local merchants and distributors who supply his shop with essential goods. His intricate web of relationships has been woven over time, and it benefits his entire neighborhood. He seems to feel a sense of peace as he tells me about it. It is truly remarkable how a modest enterprise like this elicits such a strong sense of belonging within Gaza communities.

Walking Gaza's streets, I feel rich in the warmth of human connection, in a timeless culture, and in the sounds, smells, tastes, and colors of a land with a long and storied history and—hopefully—a promising future.

In the pages that follow, I invite you to partake in a literary banquet, from beaches and cafes to bookstores and theaters and back to the hidden gems of everyday life. With each chapter, you will draw closer to the heartbeat of Gaza's cities, villages, and refugee camps. Let the feast commence, and with each turn of the page, I invite you to take another step into the captivating enigma that is Gaza.

Chapter 2

Labor and Merriment

When the eminent Special Envoy for Peace in the Middle East arrives from Norway on a field mission, I find myself in the noble role of guiding him as we traverse the teeming streets of Rafah. Official visitors to Gaza seldom carve out moments for informal rendezvous, yet I discern a distinct hunger within the Envoy, an appetite for experiences beyond the norm. This grants me space to guide him into places where the essence of Gazan life can be found, unveiling the untold narratives that reside in their midst. He is received as a revered guest, embraced wholeheartedly by local denizens who exude an unbounded enthusiasm that fosters a profound sense of belonging.

With each interaction, I perceive an enchanting spell cast upon him as he becomes captivated by the pervasive warmth and genuine hospitality that permeate every gesture of the populace, from the far north to the far south. This embattled nation possesses precious endowments of time and human vigor, commodities often lacking in more regimented capitalist societies. In Gaza, life unfurls as a treasury of daily surprises that many Westerners miss in their hurry to get through their days.

The barbershop is the best place to meet young people and understand non-elitist thinking. Conversations flourish as local men convene, exchanging tidings and immersing themselves in current affairs while awaiting a rejuvenating shave and haircut. The Envoy soaks in the aspirations of the younger generations of this land who yearn for a brighter tomorrow.

A stone's throw away, nestled in the heart of Rafah, more tales unfold within the walls of a beauty salon—an unspoken narrative of resilience and determination amid the cacophony of hairdryers and the lively hum of conversation. A sisterhood emerges, steadfast and hopeful. In the sweltering embrace of Rafah's summer, the oppressive heat intertwines with the heady aroma of styling products while the hum of a generator tells the tale of the relentless scarcity of electricity.

The envoy can only poke his head in and receive greetings and offers of tea before it's time for him to make his way out of Gaza and back to Norway. But if he could speak Arabic and stay longer, he would witness that in this sanctuary of femininity, conversations unfurl like delicate threads weaving together the intricate tapestry of their lives. Amid the warm camaraderie, women find not only fresh hairstyles but also moral support and guidance, acceptance and understanding.

Today's focus shifts to the salon owner's compassion as she lends her support to a woman named Leena. A loyal client at Hassan's lab for the past ten years, Leena comes in every month for the same pregnancy test, and every month she gets the same answer. Hassan says nothing when he gets the results—he simply bows his head kindly—and she understands it is negative once again.

Hassan is aware of this intense family pressure on the woman to get pregnant. He knows that if she is divorced, she will have no option but to go and live with her older brother and his wife and seven children. She is jobless and has nowhere else to go. After years of futile visits to his lab, Hassan poses a question to the woman that hints at a possible breakthrough: "Can you bring your husband along next time?"

The husband arrives a few days later dressed in a dark blue and white training suit. He was formerly a customs official at the now-defunct Gaza International Airport. The airport lingers in the recesses of my childhood memories as a phantom of dreams unfulfilled. It was damaged by Israeli warplanes and bulldozers in 2001 and shut down after only a couple years of limited operation. Though I never set foot within its hallowed halls, the notion of a direct connection between Frankfurt and Gaza kindled a fervent desire within the hearts of many Gazans. Perhaps one day, the phoenix of Gaza International Airport will rise anew, casting its majestic shadow over the land, offering a gateway to the world for generations to come.

The husband tells us he is on early retirement and spends his days at home subsisting on a pension. This is his second marriage, as his first wife was unable to conceive, leading to his divorce and remarriage. Yet, mysteriously, the problem persists.

Hassan holds his peace and treats the man with respect and compassion, kindly explaining that tests need to be conducted on the man as well as his wife if they wish to conceive, especially after a decade of disappointment. Hassan knows it is a delicate case, and the man might well take offense and walk out the door, or worse. Or Hassan's hunch might be wrong, and the woman may be the sole cause of their fertility issues after all. He is swimming through hot soup; his path is uncertain. But he knows the stakes are high for the wife, and he takes a chance.

Hassan sighs after the man leaves. "We can only wait and see now." Leaning back in his chair, he closes his eyes, preparing himself for the next steps. "Women are capable in so many ways," he says, "but our society expects them to be like Spider Man and perform miracles."

Thankfully the man does take Hassan seriously and comes back to the lab with a sperm sample. Unfortunately, it has been in a cup for over an hour on the way to the lab, rendering the sample useless. The man gamely makes another special delivery, more quickly this time, but admits he feels a bit out of place. "After all, isn't it women who usually come for these sorts of tests?"

Hassan knows he has a hill to climb to both educate this man about reproductive biology and deliver what may be difficult news. He politely tells the man to come back in two hours for the results.

Barely forty minutes later, the man parks his motorcycle outside and walks back in, anxious to know. Hassan is still watching the swimmers under the microscope. He motions the man to wait in a chair and says reassuringly, "Just give it a little more time." But the man is increasingly impatient, and nervous. The waiting feels like an eternity.

Finally, Hassan takes a deep breath and faces the man. "I believe your wife is fertile and capable of conceiving a child."

The husband looks confused, surprised, and shaky as Hassan pulls out his notebook to write down the result of the test. Hassan then sits down opposite the husband and settles in for an informal biology lecture. He rolls up his sleeves and offers a patient lesson on the science of fertility and how both partners play a role—how a baby is conceived when a sperm from the male fertilizes an egg from the female. The fertilized egg then implants in the uterus and begins to develop into a fetus. With Hassan's guidance, he believes they may yet be able to welcome a child into their home.

"Am I okay?" the man asks.

"You are okay," Hassan answers. "The issue is with your sperm count, which unfortunately is not enough to fertilize an egg."

The man's face falls, but Hassan is quick to let him know there is hope. In most cases, he says, medications or diet changes may be enough, but in the worst-case scenario, some patients opt for assisted reproductive technologies like in-vitro fertilization (IVF). Hassan does not believe IVF is worth trying at this point. The man looks more confused. He is in disbelief. It's clear he has barely been listening.

"Surely it is a woman's issue to conceive a child."

Hassan gently insists that this is not the case. I admire how Hassan is protecting the wife, but I also wonder how he can be so sure she has no issues. When I ask Hassan about it later, he says he's been doing this job for long enough to know what the issue is.

The husband is uncomfortable with the idea of telling his extended family that all this time the problem with conceiving a child lay with him, not his current wife and probably not his ex-wife either. Hassan assures him that nobody needs to know. But he also remarks that it is unfair for his wife to carry the burden alone.

The husband finally relaxes a bit, realizing the truth behind Hassan's words. "And what kind of family can we create when all the pressure is on the mother?" he muses.

Hassan puts the teapot on, which is unusual unless he considers the patient a special friend. Some people accuse Hassan of being stingy, but I understand why he limits this. He can't socialize with all his patients or he'd be overwhelmed and unable to do his job.

But this is a man who clearly needs a warm cup of tea. He sits down heavily, cradling a cup in his hand.

"In some cases," Hassan begins gently, "lifestyle changes can improve sperm count. This may include maintaining a healthy weight, quitting smoking, and avoiding certain drugs," he tells the husband, who falls silent. Something Hassan has said strikes a chord with him, and he wants to hear more. They both agree, in the end, that the first entry point is nutrition, and that a possible blockage could also be affecting sperm production. In some cases, surgery may be needed to correct the issue, but Hassan prefers to keep surgery and medication as a last resort.

The real starting point for success, in Hassan's view, is being clear on who you are as a human being, defining what you stand for and what matters most to you. He asks the man to choose a peak moment from his past when he felt he was doing something extraordinary.

Hassan helps him recognize that feeling of being fulfilled and present in his own life, a feeling of true happiness and feeling like his old self, before all the stress and unhappiness of not having children. The psychological boost works wonders and the man looks rejuvenated, asking eagerly how long it will take to address the sperm count issue.

Hassan works with a network of traditional healers, and he knows exactly what to suggest for cases like this. He recommends two places the husband can go. The first is the home of a 65-year-old man who works between 5-7 pm and typically has two or three clients per day. This man uses olive oil and gentle groin massage to open up any possible sperm blockages. This healer will know from the first few minutes if there is any blockage and whether he can help. Massage therapy can also improve blood flow and reduce inflammation in the genital area, which can improve a man's sperm motility and shape. Hassan says surgery could also treat the issues at hand, but he prefers finding a good massage therapist over waiting for a hospital specialist and painful surgery.

The second place is an *attar* (herbalist shop) where he can buy honey mixed with nuts and black seeds (*Habat Al Baraka*), which is also believed to help with fertility. Hassan explains that infections are a common cause of infertility in both men

and women and can lead to inflammation or scarring of reproductive organs. This mixture with locally produced honey
includes antioxidants and other nutrients containing antibac-
terial properties that seem to prevent infections such as chla-
mydia, gonorrhea, and prostatitis that are common culprits for
fertility issues in men.

The husband's face lights up with hope as Hassan assures
him this will improve his chance of fathering children. "Patience
is key," he tells him. "Patience with yourself and with your wife.
The miracle will come, and you will see the magic."

The husband agrees to go and see the masseur. In fact, he
jumps on his motorbike and heads there right away, picking up
the honey mixture along the way. Hassan's words seem to have
lifted a great weight of doubt from his shoulders.

I can't help ask about the woman's side of things. Hassan
assures me she's in good health. I ask, "What happens next if
the treatments don't work? What if there's more to the problem
than just infections?"

Hassan remains preternaturally confident. "There should be
no 'if.' We just have to knock on these doors and see what lies
on the other side."

Hassan is not rewarded by medals or financial bonuses for
his tireless work but by small, private triumphs that he keeps
close to his chest. He does not brag about how many couples
he has helped, but he does take quiet pride in spotting and cor-
recting misinformation.

The next client comes in and I take my leave. I should have
left much earlier, but the cup of thyme tea was too good to
pass up.

It's already dark when I step out of the lab and into the bustling
activity of the busy street, and I ponder how time seems like an

illusion when one is not in any hurry. The voice of Sheikh Hassan Jaber fills the air, starting the *Isha*, the last prayer of the day. It has a deep, resonant, melodic quality with an unmistakable aura of gravitas. The words are stretched and elevated in a captivating rhythmic pattern to call the faithful to prayer. The loudspeakers from the minarets of Al Awda Mosque amplify his voice, creating a powerful echo that reverberates through Rafah's city center.

After prayers, I hear the deeply evocative voice of the blind Sheikh, a large man who always wears dark glasses. His iconic voice embodies Rafah traditions and values. The Sheikh also serves as a moral compass for many. He offers his conflict resolution services after each of the five daily prayers. Disputes range from commercial matters to divorce or a misunderstanding over a purchase or sale. Once the prayer is over, the crowd heads towards Sheikh Hassan, who sits in his designated spot ready to offer guidance and counseling.

Everyone knows he is not just an Imam but also a skilled mediator. The tradition of promoting peace, harmony, and justice in all aspects of life is deeply rooted in Islamic culture, and this moderate Sheikh is a living symbol of that tradition. The community looks up to him with respect and trust; he is known to bring people together in a spirit of unity and cooperation to help maintain social cohesion and promote a culture of peace and tolerance.

On this day I walk into Al Awda Mosque and see him in his usual black sunglasses with his grandchild directing him. He moves slowly through the mosque, an iconic place of beautiful and functional design. The chandelier, suspended in the central prayer hall, creates an intricately patterned and awe-inspiring ambiance. Crystals, glass, and other decorative elements reflect and refract the light in beautiful ways. To look upwards is to see beauty shining back at you.

A man is following the Sheikh, trying to persuade him to change a decision he has made. But changing the mind of a stubborn and revered Imam is not an easy thing.

"She is my wife!" the man insists.

"But this is wrong," the Sheikh says. "It is her hard-earned money and you have no authority over that."

The man is clearly unhappy the Imam has ruled that he cannot take his wife's salary and spend it as he sees fit. But the Sheikh has spoken. The husband is well aware that if he takes the matter to court, Sheikh Hassan is also the mufti of the Rafah court (that is, an Islamic scholar who interprets Muslim law and issues legal opinions), and the court will again likely rule in favor of the wife. I laugh to myself as I see this man learning the hard way that justice is blind.

The mufti seeks to end the discussion by reminding the man that Islam emphasizes the importance of "treating women with respect and kindness and prohibits any form of violence or abuse towards women."

The man cannot resist a retort. "Isn't a woman and her money for her husband?"

Sheikh Hassan says with measured confidence that this interpretation may be convenient to him but is incorrect. "Islam encourages women to work and earn a livelihood and recognizes their right to own property and engage in business transactions. In Islam, women are highly regarded and honored."

The Sheikh's grandson chuckles, used to his grandfather's firm conclusions. After exiting the mosque, he holds the Sheikh's hand in the crowded late summer evening. Every taxi driver and motorcycle comes to an immediate stop as the Sheikh and his grandson cross the street to let the respected blind man with his white turban pass.

Interlude: Finding Naji

The woman cracking nuts in the buffer zone peers at the worn photograph of the half-buried man. Her eyes meet mine.

"What do you want with him?" she asks.

Khalil explains that some people from abroad want to assist the family.

"This is Naji," she says. "You can tell from his dark hair and mustache. That day is etched in our memories."

"Who is he?" I ask eagerly.

"He used to earn a small living leasing farmland and selling whatever vegetables he could cultivate. But since that day," she nods toward the photograph, "he stays at home. He has not ventured outside for months."

Curiosity burning me up, I ask, "Where does he live?"

The woman gestures toward a modest makeshift dwelling nearby constructed of wooden poles and plastic sheets. Strangely, the entrance is guarded by a solid metal door. I approach and knock. The door swings open, revealing a woman adorned in a flowing, intricately-patterned dress and headscarf. Two young children peer out at me from behind her, curious. We introduce ourselves, and she confirms she is Naji's wife.

I ask if we can meet her husband. In a few moments Naji himself silently exits the house and joins us in the rain. There's no doubt about it. I want to jump up and down and hug him, but I manage to contain my excitement as I take a brief, silent moment of pride in accomplishing my mission after months of tireless searching for the man whose photograph is fading in my hands.

Naji fixes his gaze on me, and my excitement is put in stark perspective. Meeting him for the first time is like stepping into a room heavy with unspoken stories. His dark hair frames a mournful face, as if life has etched pain and hopelessness into his features.

Warily, he extends an invitation to enter his house. We can shelter there from the rain, he says. We step inside, and my eyes catch sight of three pots on the ground catching rainwater dripping through the roof in an attempt to keep their children's mattresses dry. The roof of Naji's family home, composed of worn and tattered cloth, provides meager defense against the biting winter elements.

The younger child, we learn, is a four-year-old girl named Malak, and her brother Mohammed is six. The family owns nothing but this humble dwelling on dangerous land that many Gazans won't dare to enter. They live side by side with farms producing top-quality, export-ready fruits and vegetables, yet they never ask for handouts. Families in this area are particularly proud and fiercely independent. They refuse to compromise their dignity for the sake of a meal. As my mother, that great feeder, often reflects, "We are a nation ready to starve rather than beg." Yet we can give, and we can receive freely, without asking or being asked.

The specter of war, occupation, siege, and brutality are ever-present in all of Gaza, hovering like a dark sword over the life and color of our existence. Palestinians are made to know, in ten thousand ways—from being put "on a diet" with blockades to being bombed relentlessly in "wars" that are more like shooting fish in a barrel—that everything we know and love can be destroyed in an instant if Israel chooses, and we have no one who can protect us. We have no freedom, no human rights, no citizenship, no ability to plan our futures or create a functioning independent economy, and extremely limited ability to travel outside the Gaza Strip—even to the West Bank, much less the rest of the world. Most children in Gaza have never seen a mountain, a lake, a river, or our holy places in Jerusalem, just an hour's drive away.

But in the heart of the buffer zone, Naji and his family shoulder an even heavier burden than the rest of the Gaza Strip. Each step they take is monitored by the omnipresent specter of the Israeli military and its sniper towers, cameras, and automated defenses.[3] Attacks on buffer-zone communities are both more frequent and more rarely reported, given the difficulty of entering these areas at all, much less with filming equipment.

As I sit in Naji's humble abode, I am struck by the dignified generosity of this family. Despite their limited means, they offer me and the farmer a warm cup of tea and slices of dry bread—the only sustenance they have in the home.

We ask gently about the day in August when the soldiers invaded. The sight of their father, partially buried amid the turmoil, still weighs heavily on Malak and Mohammed. They also recount the terror they felt from the intimidation inflicted by a military dog after all the males of military age were rounded up. Some were released immediately, but Naji and three other young men in their twenties and thirties were detained for days with no word about why they were taken, or where, or for how long they would be gone.

This was, of course, completely 'normal.' Palestinians of all ages are regularly kidnapped by the Israeli military with no charge or trial, frequently beaten and tortured, and often intimidated into signing confessions in Hebrew. But these men were the lucky ones. Adel Ghaben, a 22-year-old neighbor and the son of a prominent strawberry farmer, was killed by an Israeli sniper bullet to the head on that same day.

Naji rarely says anything unless directly asked. During this first meeting, there are odd silences punctuated by flickers of pain in his eyes. There is a fragility to his demeanor, as if the scars of his experiences influence the way he moves and gazes. Thankfully little Malak is more talkative, and I can always shift to her if I feel stuck.

Naji tells us he doesn't know why the soldiers dug a hole and forced him into it. It wasn't clear if it was an act of humiliation or to use him as a human shield or what. There was no active fighting at the time.

When I tell him I searched him out because an American family was curious about him after seeing his photo in the newspaper, fear flashes on his face. I can tell a part of him wants to say he doesn't buy it, wants us to leave him alone.

So, I don't stay long. In any case, thinking about the transformation of their lives that will be possible thanks to a little bit of financial support makes me impatient to leave and tell the family in Houston that I have finally found Naji.

The bustling city of Rafah wakes up each morning to the countless challenges of life in Gaza with renewed determination. People make their way to work and school and run morning errands to the lilting voice of the Lebanese singer Fairuz. The beach stretches out beside the road, a reminder of another world beyond the horizon.

Conditions in Gaza change the way teachers teach, hunters hunt, farmers farm, doctors practice medicine, painters create art, gamers play games, and parents raise children. This is a new model of creativity—of people with limited resources who can invent new ways of experiencing pleasure and connection and enjoy themselves with almost nothing. Give a Gazan three seeds and she will transform them into a flourishing kitchen garden.

Gazans may not adhere to all the norms of the outside world—cold bread and warm soft drinks are more our style, given the long hours of power cuts—but there's always a silver lining: these hours without electricity and television have led to a veritable baby boom. Electricity cuts cause immense

hardship but also force families to rely on each other for enter-
tainment and social connection as they gather in the evening
to chat on doorsteps and in courtyards. In the absence of electricity, people cherish friends, family, and neighbors as the sun
sets. They play board games, share stories on the sand dunes
in Rafah, build sand castles, play tag, hide-and-seek, or soccer,
and fly kites to say hello to family members on the other side of
the border. Or they simply sit and enjoy each other's company.

A music enthusiast holding a battery-powered device
relaxes on the sand and listens to the latest pop hits from artists like Ariana Grande, Taylor Swift, Billie Eilish, and Justin
Bieber. Thanks to an online friend from Santa Barbara and
an online radio show that features new music, she often gets
access to music before it's released in the US. She loves sharing her finds with local kids in the music market.

Not far away, four lawyers have found a way to escape the
stress of court hearings by camping in a tent and pretending
they're not lawyers for a while. I am not a lawyer, but they occasionally extend an invitation to a respected engineer, politi-
cian, poet, or writer. This week I'm the lucky guest. The sound
of the waves is drowned out by the bubbling of *harira* soup on
the wood fire Ibrahim is tending. It's a wonder where he gets the
talent for making such a delicate soup, but then I remember his
Moroccan wife who insists on staying with him in Gaza along
with their two children, even after a fifty-one-day Israeli assault.

Thanks to her, Ibrahim makes a perfect Moroccan soup with
lentils, chickpeas, and fava beans. He seasons the soup with
ginger, pepper, and cinnamon before adding a generous amount
of fresh cilantro, parsley, celery, and onion for additional flavor
and body. His fellow lawyer Lutfi holds his mobile phone light
over the pot as he adds broken vermicelli as a filler.

We have eaten this soup many times, but the best time to
enjoy it is during Ramadan after we break our fast with fresh,

hand-picked arugula from the garden. Ibrahim is always eager to experiment with new flavors and has another surprise for us: he also brought seabass filled with fragrant spices and herbs to grill over the open flame. The aroma makes our mouths water, and when it's cooked to perfection and portioned out, the dish is both tender and juicy, every bite bursting with flavor.

Listening to their anecdotes and experiences of interacting with judges in court provides me with invaluable insights. While they scrupulously maintain confidentiality, the collective narrative paints a vivid picture of the society we live in. But eventually we forget about legal matters and politics. This is a time of wild laughter, enjoying the last drops of a late summer evening by making *knafeh* over the remains of the flame. Gaza makes its own version of *knafeh* that melts in the mouth, made with shredded phyllo dough, cheese, and sweet syrup. The flavors come together to create a crispy, creamy dessert with a delicate texture, sweet and satisfying. As we eat, the lawyers are no longer lawyers but connoisseurs. They will not be billing for the hours spent cooking and eating, and the night ends listening to the soulful voice of Umm Kulthum.

Chapter 3

At the Shoreline:
Quail, Surfing, and Pizza

The first light of dawn illuminates Gaza City's Mediterranean shore as Maher Shamalakh, a 19-year-old quail hunter, shivers in the cool sea breeze. Maher dedicates his autumn days to catching wild quail as their migration route passes through Gaza. He spreads his fifty-meter nets along the seashore and waits patiently for the guests to arrive. Maher inherited this job from his grandfather, who did it for forty years. (His family is known in Gaza for their expertise in quail hunting, fishing, and farming.) Despite the hard work and long hours, Maher takes pride in his family's tradition and feels grateful for the opportunity to feed his family.

The common quail has streaks of brown and white around the eyes and is common in Europe. It is quite similar to the Japanese quail, though the male has a distinctive call often described as sounding like "wet-my-lips." It is used by males to establish and defend territory and communicate with females during breeding season. The loud and clear sound carries long distances. It is this distinctive call that signals the quails' arrival.

Clad in a white Adidas pullover in the dim light, Maher sits in silence on an empty flour sack adorned with the logo of the United Nations Relief and Works Agency for Palestine Refugees (UNRWA). This agency has been vilified and defunded on multiple occasions, but the organization is crucial in supporting the health, education, social services of over six million eligible Palestinian refugees.[4]

Maher watches the horizon for the shadows of birds. He leaves only for dawn prayer in the nearby mosque of Sheikh Ijlin, then returns to his nets. Gaza City is silent. The traffic has yet to commence, and the tranquility is interrupted only by murmured prayers emanating from the mosque and the steady rhythm of donkey hooves on the road as farmers travel to harvest grapes.

"It is all a matter of luck," says Maher. "Sometimes they land on my shore nets. Other times they fly over and head toward high buildings or land further down the shore in my friend's nets. It's a matter of destiny whether these birds coming from so far away end up on my family's dinner table, or whether they continue on to make more of themselves. Their destiny and ours are intertwined."

Though still a teenager, Maher is responsible for feeding five brothers and four sisters. This resonates deeply with me, as my own father's absence loomed large in my childhood. As the oldest child, at only six years old, I began working after school and late into the evenings in a factory that made school bags. Later I worked amid the looms and threads of another factory that made jeans. I embraced the challenge with a resilience born of necessity and considered it an opportunity to hone my strength and ability to navigate the unpredictable currents of life.

For Maher, this is the only work he can rely on, lasting just a few weeks each year. He considers the quail a gift provided by God and nature.

"Other people sell their catch in the market," he says, "but I choose to take them home for my family to eat."

Quail mostly breed in Europe and parts of Asia and over-winter in Africa. Their migration through the Mediterranean peaks around September, when some flocks number in the tens of thousands. Migration patterns are influenced by factors such as tides, weather patterns, breeding and wintering locations, habitat loss, and pressure from hunting. As such, the timing and intensity of quail migration varies from year to year and place to place.

Maher finished his secondary school education but knows that university education is out of his reach due to his family's poverty. His siblings urge him to continue his education, as he has always been a good student, but he knows he must focus on supporting them. Quail is one of Maher's favorite topics, perhaps because they only come once a year. The annual arrival transforms this season into something akin to a festival for Maher's family and other quail hunters. "I love quail soup," Maher says as he seems to imagine the warm broth before him. He's confident he'll catch enough birds this year to provide for his family.

For the rest of the year, the family relies on vegetables they can grow in their garden as well as seasonal fruits, including figs and cactus fruit and the popular Sheikh Ijlin grapes, believed to be the best in the region alongside those grown in Hebron. Markets are expensive, and consumers have little money to pay. The majority of the population is out of work while costs continue to rise. Maher's grandfather hunted quail when Gaza's borders were still open and living conditions were better. Now the family depends on this activity for survival.

Quail meat is a delicacy in many cuisines because of its tender, mild flavor, similar to chicken but slightly more gamey. The meat's firm texture and relatively low fat content make it a popular choice for grilling, roasting, or sautéing. In the West, quail is served in expensive restaurants. In Gaza, it is the poor man's substitute for chicken, goat or beef, which are out of reach for most people for all or much of the year.

Maher chats with Abu Ehab, a father of four who also relies on the migratory season to provide meat for his family. The World Health Organization has expressed concern at rising malnutrition indicators in Gaza, including stunted growth, wasting, underweight children, and high rates of anemia among children and pregnant women. For Maher and his family, the quail migration holds the promise of a few good meals and stocking up on iron and protein.

Recently, however, local authorities have sent written warnings to people like Maher that soon they will no longer be allowed to hunt quail. New restrictions aim to preserve migratory species and protect their habitats so the populations can recover. Of course, Maher wants and needs to ensure the quails' long-term survival. But he worries about his family's health and wellbeing, too.

As the rising sun breaks through the clouds on the horizon, tiny shadows flutter about. Maher senses this movement. His intuition is confirmed as four pairs of exhausted common quail suddenly come to rest in his nets. "Got them!" he whispers triumphantly.

Most of the birds that pass through the area survive, finding only rest and solace on Gaza's shores, a welcome stopover on their long journeys. Blissfully unaware that a blockade has been imposed upon the territory, they continue to fly unauthorized through Gaza. Some get caught. Most carry on. For the human residents of Gaza who cannot fly away, they are a delicacy.

"Welcome, my sweet little ones," Maher says with joy. His excitement is palpable as he cradles the warm feathered bodies in his cold hands. His friend helps him retrieve the birds from the nets and he gently places them into his sack with a wide grin on his face.

Suddenly a merchant appears. He offers Maher fifteen Israeli shekels (around $4) for each quail. Maher declines, despite the tempting offer. He still prefers to take the birds home for himself and his family to eat. The merchant, an experienced quail breeder, explains these birds can fetch a good price in local bird markets, with each pair selling for at least $5. But Maher has no interest in selling his precious catch.

"We must eat, too," he says, "and right now, this is all we have." As more quail land in his neighbor's nets, Abu Ehab sings out in celebration. Maher and the merchant gaze at the horizon, watching the sun rise above the sea, revealing patrolling warships that enforce naval restrictions as part of the blockade. These ships are always on the lookout, prowling and often harassing or even firing on the small fishing boats that seek to sail a small distance from Gaza and catch some food for their family from the sea.

Against all odds, Maher is optimistic. He knows Gaza remains a crossing point between the two great continents of Africa and Eurasia, situated along ancient avian and human migratory routes. Unlike his feathered quarry, he knows he has almost no prospect of going beyond the fences surrounding Gaza or further than three or six nautical miles into the sea. (The distance depends on Israeli policies at a given time.) But for Maher there is comfort in the simple pleasures of catching quail at dawn and sharing them with his loved ones. He looks forward to the celebratory feast in the evening and can't help but feel grateful for the blessings that have come his way.

An eight-minute drive north from the quail-hunting nets, surfers are hanging ten toes on the nose, charging into the waves.

Despite Gaza's wild waves and temperate climate ideal for surfing, for years Gazans could only surf virtually, through photographs and imagination, or with improvised materials. That started to change when a young fisherman named Ahmed Abu Hassan managed to buy an old surfboard from someone who had dragged it into Gaza from a second-hand shop in Israel.

Volunteering as a lifeguard, his whistle around his neck, scanning the waves for anyone in distress, he explains that surfing came naturally to him. "I learned how to surf by watching it on TV. It always attracted my attention whenever I used to see it."

On the water, a solitary figure glides effortlessly atop silver waves, glistening sun-kissed diamonds of water splashing around him. The waves seem to reach skyward, and the young man disappears for an instant, reemerging as the water crashes on the sand, gathering pebbles as it goes. Families seated on the beach pay rapt attention, fascinated by his performance.

With his surfboard slung under his right arm, 33-year-old Mohammed Abu Jayyab emerges from the ocean. Tanned, lean, and wearing a wet t-shirt featuring his favorite Spanish soccer team, he is the first surfer most Gazans have ever laid eyes on. After placing his board securely in the sand and shaking the water out of his hair, Mohammed strolls over to his friend Ahmed trailed by a throng of children who encircle him. Both Mohammed and Ahmed are self-taught surfers, bound together by their passion for the sport.

"For the past few years, I've been searching for my own board," Mohammed explains, "but I couldn't find one, so I borrow Ahmed's. Surfboards are available in Israel, but they're very expensive."

Like most men in Gaza, Mohammed is unemployed. Together with his wife and three children, he struggles to make ends meet in Al Shati, Gaza's most densely-populated refugee camp.

Asked why he surfs, Mohammed's eyes light up like a man describing a woman he loves. "Surfing allows me to experience true freedom," he enthuses. "It's like an addiction."

Ahmed agrees. "I love it. Surfing has become my favorite thing."

"We live in Gaza," Mohammed says with sober intensity. "It's a vast prison. We endure sieges, occupation, electricity shortages, poverty, and harsh psychological conditions. Surfing allows me to breathe, to forget the worries and pain of our lives, and enjoy freedom and fun, if only for a few moments."

"Unfortunately," Ahmed notes, "in Gaza we don't have any schools or places to train."

But once again, a newspaper photo is about to change history in Gaza.

One day in 2007, not long after Hamas takes over the Gaza Strip after an attempted CIA-backed coup,[5] a Jewish-American doctor and surfer noticed a picture in the *LA Times* of two young Palestinian surfers with one dilapidated board between them.

Dorian "Doc" Paskowitz had been surfing for nearly all of his eighty-six years. Growing up in Galveston, Texas during the Great Depression, he taught himself to surf as a young teen and convinced his family to move to Southern California. In 1955, nursing wounds from two failed marriages and a career that no longer inspired him, he happened to meet the consul general of Israel on a Jewish retreat and accepted his invitation to move to Israel,[6] where be began teaching surfing lessons in Ashkelon.

A year later, Egyptian president Gamal Abdel Nasser announced he was nationalizing the Suez Canal. Though he offered full economic compensation to the British and French governments, they were outraged. They weren't about to allow upstart local ruler to foil their plans or go against their interests.

In collusion with Britain and France, Israel attacked Egypt's Sinai Peninsula in October 1956, advancing to within ten miles of the Suez Canal. Under the pretext of "protecting the canal," Britain and France invaded a few days later.

The US Eisenhower administration was trying to distance itself from European colonialism, especially at a time when they were condemning the Soviet Union for meddling in Hungary. The US voted for a UN ceasefire resolution and the creation of a UN peacekeeping force and pressured the warring parties to accept it, which they grudgingly did.

Doc Paskowitz rushed to Tel Aviv when hostilities first broke out to volunteer with the Israeli military, but he was rejected. Still, his time living in the desert near Gaza, catching and eating fish from the sea, surfing, walking for miles every day, and sleeping under the stars rejuvenated him. He returned to the US a changed man, married again, had nine children, and traveled the world surfing with them. He opened a successful surfing school in San Onofre (near San Diego) that still operates today.

When he saw the photograph of the two young men surfing in Gaza, he decided to do something about it. In the process, he became a local celebrity.

Within hours of seeing the photograph, Doc reaches out to Arthur Rashkovan at Surfing 4 Peace, a community he founded two years earlier to bring together Palestinian-Israeli and Jewish Israeli surfers in friendship and peace. He asks if they can gather used surfboards from Israeli surf companies to donate to Gaza. They manage to convince four Israeli surfing equipment companies to donate fourteen boards, and Doc comes to Israel to deliver the boards to Gaza personally.

The two surfers who share one board know about the special delivery and nervously await news of its arrival. Israeli authorities will not allow the Palestinian surfers to travel out of Gaza to meet with the Americans, so the doctor has to work out how to transport the surfboards through the walls around the impenetrable fortress of Gaza. Every day after landing in Tel Aviv, he goes to the Erez checkpoint and finds it closed.

Finally, they manage to secure the necessary permits to deliver the boards to Gaza through the Erez checkpoint. But when they arrive at the agreed upon date—Doc Paskowitz, his son, and the S4P volunteers—with all fourteen boards and extensive international media in tow, an Israeli soldier bluntly informs Doc Paskowitz, "You cannot go in."

Doc refuses to take no for an answer.

"I traveled 12,500 miles from the US to the Gaza border," the doctor tells the soldier. "You are not going to keep me from seeing those men when I'm only fifteen meters away from them." At first, the soldier remains unimpressed. So, the American doctor turns to Plan B, grabbing the soldier jovially and kissing him.

Shocked, the soldier protests, "Don't hug me! Don't kiss me! I'm a soldier!"

Doc Paskowitz chuckles as he mimics the horrified soldier. Then he walks around the guards and heads for the crossing. "You can shoot me in the back if you want to," he says over his shoulder. "I have friends waiting for me on the other side who need these boards."

Doc's stubbornness prevails and both he and his son David are permitted to deliver the boards to the waiting Palestinian surfers. As Doc Paskowitz passes through the border with the surfboards and his team, happiness surges through his body like a wave.

Ahmed and Mohammed feel the same when they finally meet face to face. After trying out the beautiful new boards in their familiar stretch of the Mediterranean coast in brand-name T-shirts donated by surfing legend Kelly Slater, the surfers overflow with gratitude. Back ashore, they beam as they thank Doc Paskowitz for his kind and genuine concern. "We feel privileged to have met such a loving man," Ahmed tells me later. "He really cares about us."

When I ask Doc Paskowitz about his motives for his gifts, he says he imagines that Palestinian children can share their love for surfing and make it a point of contact with others in the Arab region. Doc learns that the only Israelis Ahmed and Mohammed ever met were soldiers stationed at the border. He believes Palestinians and Israelis can one day surf together and even live together and care for one another.

Ahmed fervently agrees. "All religions call for forgiveness and peace, not wars," he says. "Sport is the mother of nations. It unites us all."

Scores of newspapers, journals and magazines around the world cover the inspiring story. The two friends hope they can fulfill a dream of establishing the first ever surfing school in Gaza.[7]

Doc Paskowitz's act is a shining example of human solidarity in action. People in Gaza often feel overwhelmed and isolated, but support and solidarity from friends around the world, from all walks of life, make a real difference in their ability to cope and recover and feel enough space in their psyche to hope and dream of a better future.

Interlude: A Surprise for Naji

My mind races as I plan what to say to the family in Houston. They've been searching for Naji for months. Knowing they'll be anxious to hear that I've found him, I manage to find an internet cafe and send a message with an updated photo of Naji and his family. Soon I receive their reply, which fills me with joy and relief. The father wants to sponsor Malak, and the mother will sponsor Mohammed.

As soon as I am able, I plan a second visit to Naji's family. I hadn't wanted to overwhelm or over-promise during my first visit, but this time I sense Naji's kindled curiosity, and I can't hold back any longer.

"An American family wants to help you and your family," I announce to him.

"Me and my family?" he asks doubtfully, as if trying not to foster any false hope.

"Yes, you and your family."

"But we're confined to this buffer zone. We have no connections beyond here. We don't have a clue what life is like outside this place."

"But that man, his wife, and his kids know about you. They live in Houston, USA."

He stays silent for a long moment. "Maybe the person you're looking for is someone else, not me," he finally says.

"It is you. They came across a photo of you featured in the news."

He looks at the photo and confirms it is himself. He ponders silently while Malak also peers at the image and fiddles with her fingers.

We agree to swap phone numbers. Naji has forgotten to charge his cellphone and has no electricity in his home. His phone dies just before we get the chance to exchange numbers, so I write his cellphone number on the palm of my hand.

I tell Malak and Mohammed that we'll start with English lessons so they can communicate with their new friends in Houston. A US-based surgeon will arrive soon in Gaza carrying stacks of English-language children's books for them to get started on, sent by the American family. As we say goodbye, I promise Naji and his family that I will be back.

Driving through the village of Beit Lahia, I take in famil-iar scenes: a female farmer selling nuts, an elderly man and his children harvesting tomatoes and cucumbers, a young man selling fresh corn. Workers load boxes of eggs onto a truck at a small chicken farm at the edge of town. I reflect with joy on the fact that one family is about to embark on a journey of renewal. Naji will finally have a good reason to keep his phone charged and to stay connected.

From surfing diplomacy, we turn to kitchen diplomacy. The aromas of tomato sauce, cheese, springy dough, and fresh toppings waft in the air. The spectacle of a world-class chef visiting Gaza has drawn a crowd that eagerly awaits a taste of Domenico Maurizio Loi's authentically Italian pizza. Domenico and his team are in Gaza as part of a cooking exchange program funded by the Italian government. They are here to introduce locals to the gentle art of Italian pizza making while learning about Palestinian cuisine from local chefs. Domenico calls out for more tomato sauce and extra cheese to make the perfect slice.

The atmosphere is filled with excitement and energy. Chatter and laughter fill the air as men, women, and children snap pictures and share them with friends and family on social media. Everyone is thrilled to participate in this first-ever pizza festival in Gaza.

Asaad Dawaas, a Palestinian restaurant owner, hopes that one day he will be able to travel the world with his Palestinian culinary skills, building bridges to different cultures. "I hope this is just the first step toward more food exchanges. We learn how to make pizza and they will learn about our traditional *maqluba* and other delicious Palestinian food," he says as he stretches out a ball of pizza dough. *Maqluba* is a flavorful dish consisting of layered meat, vegetables, and rice sprinkled with toasted slivered almonds, traditionally served flipped upside-down.

For Domenico, this journey to the heart of Gaza means far more than exchanging recipes. It is a mission steeped in profound significance, supported by the Union of Italian Chefs and entrusted with a weighty message of solidarity, hope, and love. Food, in the culinary haven of Italy, means more than eating; it is symbolic of a welcoming identity. The pizza festival, rolled out in the confines of this war-torn enclave, symbolizes respite, a fragment of bliss for those trapped in the clutches of a relentless siege. It is a breath of fresh air for people whose hunger for freedom has been starved for so long.

"We come to Gaza with a message of solidarity for the besieged people and to learn more about their suffering," he says, deftly stirring a pot of bubbling lasagna sauce. "We've met so many good people here looking for freedom, not the terrorists they've been made out to be. We're happy to teach them the art of Italian cuisine and to learn the secrets of Palestinian food as well."

The crowd watches in anticipation, wondering what the Italian chef has in store for them next.

A waiter approaches with a piping hot pizza. The first bites are taken and a warm wave of satisfaction and contentment leaves everyone grinning foolishly. Waiting for the pizza has been a delicious moment of anticipation, but the food itself is even better.

Israa Salah, a 21-year-old student, rushes to the port the moment she hears about the cooking demonstration. "We need more of these events, as trapped Palestinians," she exclaims. "It allows us to practice our rights and duties as part of human civilization." A chef offers Israa a slice of fresh pizza covered in melted cheese and tomato sauce, and she savors it with delight.

Domenico, who learned to make pizza at the tender age of thirteen, uses a ladle to spread the tomato sauce in a circular motion, leaving just the right amount on every square centimeter. He closed his restaurant in Sardinia for two months to participate in this food exchange festival.

The visiting chef delegation will travel to the West Bank next. Unfortunately for people like Israa, the prospect of visiting this other piece of her nation remains elusive due to travel restrictions imposed by Israel. These restrictions inhibit personal and professional growth and cut people off from discovering the diversity within their own country, leaving the territories largely estranged from one another, like brothers caged in separate prisons.

The Gaza-based Palestinian Ministry of Culture praises the Italian chefs for bringing not only culinary skills but also cultural and humanitarian values. "This delegation is here to exchange knowledge with our besieged Palestinian people," explains Samir Mutair, Deputy Minister of Culture. He cannot resist the grin spreading across his face at all the positive energy around him. The chef's hands move with practiced grace, deftly sprinkling shredded mozzarella for the next masterpiece, ensuring an even layer that melts to perfection in the oven.

"Today's pizza festival is a message to the entire world that here on this land, there are people who deserve to live freely, in dignity," adds Mutair. Peppers and tomatoes are chopped and mixed with fragrant herbs, filling the air with a tantalizing aroma that draws in yet more new arrivals. Palestinian mothers gather to learn about the Italian methods of pizza making, eager to see the process unfold before their eyes.

Umm Abdel Aziz traveled from Deir Al-Balah in the central Gaza Strip. "We have seen Italian pizza making on YouTube videos, but seeing it with my own eyes and smelling the herbs makes a big difference," she says excitedly.

A young Palestinian chef expertly adds pepperoni, mushrooms, and onions to a pizza, carefully ensuring each slice has balanced toppings. At the Castillo restaurant, Palestinian chefs watch a demonstration of pasta layered with cheese, Bolognese and white sauce to make a mouth-watering lasagna. The restaurant was already a favorite among Gazans, but the owner admits their culinary knowledge and skills have been enriched by the visiting Italian delegation.

"Simplicity," says Domenico, "is the key word of my native cuisine." His Gazan audience knows this about their own cuisine, and now they know it applies to Italian cuisine as well. He tells an audience at Al Taboon, one of the best-known pizza restaurants in Gaza, "For every two kilos of flour, you need two liters of water. Then we let the flour and water breathe."

As everyone moves back to the tables, Umm Abdel Aziz is savoring the taste of the delicious lasagna. "It's savory, cheesy, and rich. I wasn't sure what to expect. But I love its comforting taste and satisfying texture."

At another restaurant, assistant chef Maria Rita Pirastu expresses her joy as the Italian chefs gather to learn to make *musakhan*. "We are so happy to have the chance to pass on our skills and to learn a little from our hosts in return." The sumptuous dish of roasted chicken served on *taboon* flatbread, topped with caramelized onions, sumac, and pine nuts, is a perfect representation of the warmth and generosity of the Palestinian kitchen. As Maria savors the tangy and zesty flavor of Palestinian comfort food, the Italian chef can't help but admire the resilience of the residents of the coastal enclave amid the hardships they face.

"The people of Gaza are just like us, seeking happiness and joy in life, despite the sadness that surrounds them," she observes, watching the Palestinian chefs work their magic. *Musakhan* and pizza are both eaten communally. Both bring people together around the table sharing food, laughter, and conversations. With *musakhan*, tearing off pieces of bread and scooping up juicy meat, sweet onions, and crunchy pine nuts makes for a fun, interactive way of eating together, much like pizza slices. Pizza and *musakhan* have united two nations that share the Mediterranean seaboard.

For the Italian and Palestinian chefs, the pleasure of dining is not just about taste and texture, but also about building social connections through shared experiences. As the Italians learn more and receive invitations to dine with local families, they realize their journey in Gaza is too short to fully explore the hidden marvels of Gaza, much less all the warm and laughter-filled homes that wish to invite them in. They visit the iconic fifteen-story Italian Tower on Gaza's skyline, erected by an Italian businessman in the 1990s, with dozens of shops and offices.[8] Walking through the streets of Gaza, Maria and Domenico are awed by the sight of Banksy murals painted on the walls of buildings, depicting the strength and resilience of the people of this land.

International solidarity comes in all shapes and sizes, like an Irish man who drove an ambulance through the desert to leave it behind in Gaza for a hospital in need. There are those who offer shelter, surf boards, medical care, or even something as simple as making pizzas. In their actions, these individuals embody human solidarity, and their efforts inspire others to follow in their footsteps and help the trapped population of Gaza sustain itself and remain hopeful in the hardest of times. Whatever they provide to us is not as important as the feeling that we belong to a wider world after all. We are not completely forgotten.

Chapter 4

Starry Nights: Jupiter and Venus from Gaza

Walking in Al Nazla, a suburb of Jabalia a few kilometers from Naji's home, I catch a scent of fresh paint that hints at the presence of Banksy, elusive and clandestine, around the next corner.

Al Nazla is described by historians as a "small hamlet" that has since merged with the sprawl of Gaza City. The ambiance is alive with a medley of sounds, including children playing in the dusty streets, as the sun climbs higher in the sky. Nazla was the site of the Byzantine-era town known as Asalea, home of Alaphion of Asalea, a fourth century monk and early Christian missionary.

On this fine spring day, my gaze is drawn to captivating Banksy murals that grace the walls of crumbling buildings, infusing the air with a sense of reverence that so captivated Maria and Domenico, the visiting Italian chefs. These vibrant expressions of creativity materialize overnight, their intricate details and vivid colors seeming almost like a call or a token from a brighter future.

Israel's campaign of mass killing and destruction in 2014 must have struck a chord with him. His publicist released a statement that said: "I don't want to take sides. But when you see entire suburban neighborhoods reduced to rubble with no hope of a future—what you're really looking at is a vast outdoor recruitment center for terrorists. And we should probably address this for all our sakes."

His purpose in coming to Gaza was to draw attention to the suffering endured by the people of Gaza and amplify the urgent need for peace and justice in the region.

I approach a new mural, in which children play amid the rubble of destroyed buildings, frolicking and laughing, their innocence defiantly reclaiming a sense of joy among the remnants of destruction. Nearby a Greek goddess cowers against a wall as if fearing a missile strike. It is a scene that stirs a bittersweet ache within me; a reminder of how much people in Gaza long for normal life where they are neither victims nor heroes.

Of course, even the best art can lead to unexpected controversies. One man in Gaza, a father of six, lost his home when Israel bombed his neighborhood, with nothing but its front door left standing.

Then, a miracle happened: an original Banksy appeared on that door depicting the Greek goddess Niobe weeping in a pose reminiscent of "The Thinker" by Auguste Rodin—but more hopeless than contemplative. It is a powerful image of the depths of despair, imploring viewers to engage in deep reflection on the human toll exacted by war.

This work of art was no doubt worth more, at least in monetary terms, than the home that had been destroyed.

But Rabei Darduna, the owner of the home, didn't know that. When Belal Khaled, a fine arts student, offered to buy the door for $175, he accepted the offer, only to realize too late the high market value of the work.

The image quickly became a powerful emblem of inspiration, resilience, hope, and defiance in the face of the horrible toll exacted by the bombings of Gazan homes. But the story of the sale caused outrage within the Palestinian community and even reached international media attention.

A battle rages on social media over questions of ownership and fraud as people name and shame the artist who covertly purchased the door. A trusted source close to Banksy tells me Banksy believes Rabei is the rightful owner of the door as he is the owner of the ravaged house. Some argue that it should be placed in a museum for the public it was created to represent.

Belal admits he understood the historical, cultural, and monetary value of the artwork, which is why he paid $175 instead of a mere $25. He believes the importance of preserving this artifact surpasses monetary considerations, as it holds a rich tapestry of history within its aged and weathered frame. He believes the door should be kept in a protected place.

"If the door remained where it was, it would have lost its value with reconstruction, or it would have faded away in the sun, or children would have painted over it," he says. "But the ethic of Banksy is that his art stays with the people it speaks out for."

Belal believes the door deserves to be showcased in Arab and international art exhibitions so the story of Gaza can be told.

On hearing of Banksy's wish for the door to be returned to Rabei, Belal insists that any financial revenues from exhibiting the door will be shared with the owner of the demolished home. He expresses the desire to establish a fund so that undiscovered Palestinian artists can showcase their artworks and build bridges with other international artists.

But social media campaigns against Belal continue to rage on, and the question turns into a legal dispute.

Despite these controversies, or maybe because of them, Gaza-based journalist Mohammed Al-Baba concludes that Banksy's artwork has done a great service to the Gazan people. The door has again drawn world attention to the besieged Strip.

"No one should buy or sell the work of a world-famous artist. He came from England in solidarity with Palestinians in Gaza, and we should treasure his message," he says.

I feel burdened by the weight of my obligation to persuade the buyer to return the door to its rightful owner, but I am grateful to Banksy for making this controversy possible in the first place.

Al-Baba agrees. "Whatever happens, I'm glad Banksy's artwork in Gaza shows how much the Palestinians want to preserve Palestinian heritage and continue the raising of awareness that Banksy reignited."

When I ask Belal about returning the door to the family if Banksy requests it, he replies, "I would first explain to him about the inappropriate location of the painting... If he asks me to return it, I will." He seems convinced of his legal ownership of the door and its importance as a piece of art.

Whatever the ultimate fate of this door, one thing is certain: Banksy's art has had a profound impact on the younger generation. His unique style of combining social commentary with humor and striking stencil imagery has renewed their passion for art, culture, and social justice. Banksy's enigmatic persona and aura of mystery bolsters the allure of his work, and his anonymity—and the question of how he gets in and out of Gaza—adds to the intrigue.

Banksy's art has become particularly popular among the digitally savvy Palestinians who grew up with social media platforms, allowing them to easily share and engage with the images. At an art exhibition at the Gaza Union of Cultural Centers, I meet a young woman who expressed her appreciation for Banksy's use of public spaces as his art canvas, which challenges traditional notions that art belongs exclusively in galleries and on the walls of the rich and famous. His art inspires many to think critically about the world around them, to express themselves more creatively, and to use their voices to effect change.

Interlude: A Home for Naji

As Khalil and I drive toward the packing houses, I remember Naji saying he wasn't sure how to open a bank account, and I decide to take matters into my own hands. I call the local bank branch and speak with the manager, requesting an exceptional approval for Naji to open an account, even though he is a poor man with no income. To my relief, the manager agrees, and soon Naji has his own account complete with a plastic card with a long string of numbers. I call Naji and tell him where to go and what to do to pick up his ATM card.

Sometime later, I receive an unexpected call from the bank branch manager.

"*Ustaz*," he says, using an honorific that means 'professor,' generously applied to any reasonably learned person. "Do you remember the guy you sent to us a few months ago?"

My heart skips a beat. "Of course. Is everything alright?"

"He's alright, but he had a fainting spell in front of the cashier."

"What happened?" I ask, concerned.

"He passed out when the cashier gave him the received amount."

"Did he not receive his $150 this month?"

"He did."

"So why did he have a fainting spell?" I ask, confused.

"He got a little more than usual," the branch manager explains with a chuckle, "and I don't think he believed his eyes. It was as if he'd received a gift from heaven."

Naji received thousands of dollars, enough to transform their living conditions from mattresses on sand under a plastic sheet to a proper two-bedroom house with a modest kitchen, a bathroom, a cement roof overhead, electricity and running water, and comfortable raised beds.

Mohammed Qraiqae is one of many young artists inspired by Bansky's legacy on the walls of Gaza. A fresh-faced youngster, barely a teen, he is known as the young Picasso of Palestine. He works in a wide range of mediums and styles, from painting and sculpture to printmaking and ceramics. His versatility is a source of inspiration for other local artists, and his paintings, varying from photorealistic to deeply impressionistic, belie world-class talent.

Mohammed was born and raised in Shujaiya, a residential neighborhood devastated by numerous wars and conflicts. Watching him at work, I see his pleasure in creating works of art. His work is not only skillful, it is also soulful and original. His oil paintings have a luminous quality while his sketches capture the truest expression of a subject with simple lines and gestures.

Whether he is depicting the curved wrinkles on the face of a Palestinian elder or making one of his more abstract pieces, his attention to detail and eye for interesting subject material are truly inspired. In his modest studio, he is surrounded by an array of various art supplies, including found materials. His expressive hands move as if they have a life of their own, crafting intricate masterpieces in front of my eyes, apparently with ease.

His passion for art started young, and Banksy is not his only inspiration. His older brother Malek Qraiqae also has a talent for painting. "I started painting when I was five," Mohammed recalls. "It's been a passion of mine ever since." He tells me his most meaningful painting is of a Palestinian woman raising her hands to the sky in supplication and lamenting, "Enough!"

"That painting means a lot to me," Mohammed says. "It's a reflection of the pain and suffering of the Palestinian populace, and I hope it can help bring attention to our struggle."

Social media has made it easier for Mohammed to expand his reach beyond the besieged Gaza Strip, and his art collection is in demand by people in the Gulf and Europe. Despite the challenges he faces as a young artist in Palestine, he remains determined to continue creating and sharing his unique vision with the world.

"I feel like I am painting the story of Gaza," he tells me.

His work has already been exhibited in several countries, from Turkey and Iran to Tunisia, where state officials welcomed him, eager to showcase the talent emerging from this under-represented region. The blockade makes travel abroad nearly impossible for most, but Mohammed has been lucky to have help securing entry visas through his supporters and friends.

"As a stateless Palestinian, every state on earth is your second home," he says wryly.

The many assaults on Gaza have affected everyone, and Mohammed is no exception. During one summer offensive, he was constantly worried about the safety of his artwork, which he feared would be destroyed by the relentless shelling and bombing.

Still, while the story of destruction and death is a big part of Gaza's history, he says it should not be the only one. Through art, he hopes to show the world that Gaza is more than a war zone. He paints images that restore the dignity of Palestinians and express their dreams of a luminous future for their homeland.

"Through art, we can be ambassadors to the world. One painting can capture the hearts of millions," he says over coffee in his house. We both fall silent, and I am struck by the power of his words and his belief in the transformative power of art. My eyes land on a painting that depicts a Palestinian farmer tending to his land, and I take a moment to admire it. Palestinian farmers are an icon of cultural identity and tradition and a reminder of the connection between the people and the land. The colors are vibrant and bold, the details intricately rendered.

The blockade has also made it difficult for him to obtain the materials he needs, and when they are available, they cost twice as much as they should and have lower quality. But he finds ways to do what he can with what he has.

"I love painting even when I have no paints. When paints are not allowed to come through, I used coffee, sand, and glue instead," he says with a shy grin.

Unfortunately, though he gets requests for his art from buyers across the globe, from Dubai to Chile, and even in the West Bank, it's nearly impossible for him to send his paintings out of Gaza due to Israeli restrictions. Shipping companies operate only for essential items, and artworks are not considered essential.

But the more he paints, and the more he creates a name for himself, the more art supplies he can afford, including by painting commissioned portraits of local people.

I make a habit of taking visiting diplomats and state officials to see Mohammed's work and that of other artists. They are allowed to buy artworks and take it out of Gaza in their diplomatic cars. This encourages Mohammed and his fellow artists to continue. He also takes part in art competitions, raising the profile of his hometown in the process. He wants his fans to love Gaza and become supporters of its liberation.

Artists also often present their works as gifts. I once knew a Palestinian fine artist who gifted a visiting European Foreign Minister an unusual present: a Palestinian passport covered in hundreds of needles sticking out all over, like a hedgehog's spines. The minister could not hold or transport the gift without risking damage to his pocket or his suitcase. It was a poignant symbol of the challenges Palestinians face in Gaza. The artist recounted that he had obtained many Schengen visas for his art exhibitions in Barcelona, Paris, Rome, Florence, and Berlin but had only been able to travel a few times out of the many visas granted.

The very same day, the Foreign Minister had a dinner scheduled with the Prime Minister in Israel. In jest, I suggested the passport souvenir could become a unique centerpiece and "talking point" for the dinner table. It could replace the traditional flower vase. As we got into the car, the Minister chuckled. "I don't think my dinner guests would appreciate a prickly centerpiece, although it's a unique symbol of Palestinian resilience."

"I see that fans can become defenders for our dreams and hopes," Mohammed Qraiqae tells me happily. One of his latest challenges is to create one hundred portraits in a single week, which would earn him a Guinness World Record. He is confident he can achieve this feat as soon as he obtains a visa to travel to a country where he can move more freely.

Despite many challenges, Mohammed dreams of inspiring the children of refugee camps with his talent. He believes every child in the blockaded Gaza Strip has talents that could take them equally far, and he wants them to know that. He hopes younger Palestinian artists will follow in his footsteps and make their mark on the international art world.

As he works on his latest piece, Mohammed's small fingers move in a magical way, effortlessly sketching the energy and movement of the subject. I regret that I will never know what it's like to grasp a paintbrush with the same finesse and mastery.

His creative aspirations go beyond art for art's sake. His artwork is intended to carve out a lasting legacy for the children and youth of Palestine, both at home and in the diaspora. He has a wisdom and talent at his tender age that astonishes me. He dreams of serving as an ambassador for Palestine one day. He is already engaging in cultural diplomacy through his artwork.

"Art is my way of expressing myself, of reflecting my happiness and pain," Mohammed says, his eyes intense. "Through my art, I can channel the pain and suffering of those around me and make it visible to the world."

Mohammed's remarkable success paved the way for him to settle in another Arab country where he can live and paint with more freedom and showcase and sell his artwork to admirers across the globe. Yet, in his heart, his gaze remains firmly fixed on home.

Another extraordinary journey is that of Professor Suleiman Baraka, a Palestinian astrophysicist and esteemed NASA scientist. From early childhood, Baraka gazed at the night sky, yearning to explore the vast expanses of the universe. "It's something I've always been very interested in, contemplating how and why things happen," he says.

Baraka received his bachelor's degree at Al Quds University in Jerusalem in 1987 followed by a master's degree at the Islamic University of Gaza, then a PhD in France. Later he moved to the US to work as a post-doctoral research fellow with NASA at Virginia Tech.

"That was a turning point in my life," he tells me. "To work with an organization that has developed some of the most extraordinary modern-day visions with a real capacity to change history… It was a dream come true."

His family remained in Gaza while he prepared to bring them all to the US for a new life of freedom, diversity, and friendship. After years of hard work and relentless pursuit of knowledge,

Professor Baraka immersed himself in groundbreaking NASA projects, pushing at the boundaries of humanity's understanding of space.

His American colleagues recognized his abilities as an astrophysicist and researcher specializing in the magnetosphere that surrounds the earth. Dr. David Sibeck, NASA's mission scientist for the THEMIS space weather project, praised Dr. Baraka's research:

"Dr. Baraka represents exactly the kind of researcher suited for research on space-age projects: energetic, ever curious, able to communicate with both the general public and the specialist. His talents lie in using numerical simulations to predict phenomena that can be confirmed with NASA's spacecraft observations. As such, he embodies the best in the long tradition of rigorous intellectual inquiry dating from the times when the Arabs were the leaders in preserving and enhancing our understanding of the world around us."

But everything changed after the bloody assault on Gaza that Israel called Operation Cast Lead in 2008-9. Dr. Baraka's 11-year-old son Ibrahim, the second oldest of his four children, sent him a message to let him know he was happy because he had received a new bicycle and to remind his father to take care of his health.

Then Dr. Baraka watched helplessly as violence continued to ramp up. One day, while he was in his NASA office in Hampton, Virginia, he got a call saying there was a bombing in his area of east Khan Younis. Then he got a message saying his own home had been bombed. Then all communications were cut for ten hours.

Frantic with fear, he did all he could to find out what had happened. Finally, he received word that Ibrahim was critically injured, his mother was moderately injured, and his home was destroyed by a one-ton bomb. Several of his brothers and their families also lost their homes to Israeli airstrikes, leaving twenty of his nieces and nephews homeless. His library, which he had collected over twenty years and his personal telescope were destroyed, too.

Tragically, the shrapnel in his son's brain proved fatal.

All his dreams to reunite with his family in the US faded after he lost his child. It wasn't long before a decision crystallized. "There was always a debate inside my head, tossing around the thought that the missile that hit my son could have been developed by colleagues I lived and worked with on a daily basis. I couldn't reconcile that thought," he says.

So, he followed the calling of his heart and returned home, leaving behind his high-powered job to live as an inspiration for others, including his own remaining children.

His return home was not only driven by the tragedy of Ibrahim, but also by a strong determination. Amid professional accolades and scientific triumphs, a void had tugged at Professor Baraka's heart. His thoughts and emotions perpetually gravitated toward his cherished family and Gaza, the land he called home. He had a deep longing to bridge the physical distance separating him from loved ones and a burning desire to share his passion for astronomy with them in person.

His homecoming was a bold move. Many of his colleagues and friends could not understand his decision. To Professor Baraka, it was the only choice that made sense. Once in Gaza, he wasted no time in reconnecting with family and friends.

He now spends hours sharing his love of the stars and planets with those around him. "Normally, if you ask a Palestinian child what they see in the sky, they will only say Apache helicopters and F-16 fighter jets," he explains. "I want to show them something beautiful beyond these weapons of war. And not just my kids. All Palestinian children."

He hopes to open Gaza's first university astronomy department, but a major stumbling block is that there is no space telescope in the Gaza Strip.

"Gaza is like a concentration camp, closed off from the rest of the world and economically isolated," he says. "In the USA or UK, you can purchase a telescope from any optics shop and simply take it home. But in blockaded Gaza, enthusiastic, intelligent students are deprived of that right."

Still, he manages to bring space science into local schools and universities, with hope of establishing a full astronomy department at a local university. He also organizes stargazing events for local schools and community groups and gives public lectures on astronomy to try to expand children's imagination beyond this prison called Gaza. He quickly becomes a dearly beloved figure.

He sits in his home office, making use of what little electrical power he has between blackouts to transmit his data to his scientific colleagues abroad. When I visit, he takes me on a brief tour.

"My son was killed here," he points out, walking around his rebuilt home, now surrounded by trees. "I used to take my kids on the roof and show them Jupiter and Venus through my telescope." He shakes his head. "But they destroyed my home, my roof, my telescope, and they killed my son. My home was not a military base. My eleven-year-old son never hurt anyone. He didn't need to be killed by a fighter jet."

As we talk for hours over homemade *maftool*, we begin reminiscing about our time as students in the US. Professor Baraka says with amusement, "One of my professors gave me the nickname 'PLO Guy.' It wasn't easy back then, but I can joke about it now."

"That rings a bell," I say, reminded of my own PhD experience. "Some of my professors weren't bad and were willing to listen to my experience and learn about the true cost of war. But many of my fellow students were influenced by media misinformation. I ended up engaging in deep discussions over coffee with them for many hours. Then I would finally get fed up and say, 'Can we please talk about laughter and peace instead of war and trauma?' It really caught them off guard."

He laughs wryly. "Then there was the time some American security agency contacted my supervisor because some parents said their children didn't feel secure with a Palestinian who they feared might blow everyone up." He shakes his head at the memory. "And now I have decided to move from the great expanse of the universe to a small pocket of land on earth. But I have no regrets. I share my passion for astronomy with those I love most, and I inspire countless others to follow their hearts and pursue their dreams, no matter where they may lead."

Professor Baraka is so easy to talk to, such a good listener with a calm personality, I lose track of time as we talk. I suddenly realize it's getting close to midnight, and I have a thirty-minute drive ahead of me. His last thoughtful gesture is to offer me a cup of coffee to perk me up before I depart.

A breakthrough comes in February 2010: "After four months of contacts with diplomatic friends, we were able to get our first educational telescope into Gaza to view the stars, planets, and near galaxies," he tells me with a grin and invites me to join his first "open telescope" night a few days later.[9]

The professor is stunned to see hundreds of people arrive, mostly mothers with their children. All are eager to examine the stars and planets using Gaza's first telescope.

"A telescope is an important tool. It can give us a sense of freedom and mobility from our tiny place on the earth," he tells the assembled crowd. He also explains the long ancient history of astronomy and its historical place in the Arab region and shares his belief that Gazans should look to the stars and remaster the science of space.

Ten-year-old Sabrina says to her mother in a hushed tone, "It's bigger than the borders around us." She came with her younger brother Adam after hearing about the event from their cousin, a student at the university where Professor Baraka teaches. The sight of distant stars, planets, and galaxies sparks her imagination and inspires Sabrina to ask questions about the cosmos. Looking through the telescope, a fascination for science and astronomy grows within her and encourages her to learn more about the world around her. Her mother holds Adam's hand at the head of the long queue as families wait for their turn. Professor Baraka seems to feel a sense of fatherly responsibility to the girl and shows her the cosmos with love, patience, and compassion. The mother's grin makes it clear how much she values this opportunity for her daughter, an experience likely to inspire a lifelong appreciation for the wonders of the universe.

"I want Gaza to contribute to the knowledge production of global science," he says as Sabrina gazes at red Jupiter, the Milky Way, hazy Andromeda, and Cassiopeia, eyes wide with amazement and curiosity. Sabrina tells him how excited she feels to share her new knowledge with her science teacher and classmates.

This community appreciates the privilege of welcoming home a scientific celebrity and treasures his actions in a land stripped of so many freedoms and resources. Professor Baraka brings kids closer to Mars and closer to realizing that he was once a kid like them—yet he made the move from Gaza to NASA and back again.

"Now I need to build new infrastructure for young scientists—men and women—who want to contribute to making a difference in human civilization," he tells me, then turns back to the children peering through the viewfinder, explaining what they are seeing. For him, every child represents his own son Ibrahim, who cannot see this.

The crowds only grow over time and get a boost when Professor Baraka becomes UNESCO's first Middle East chair-holder in recognition of the value of his work.

Later I join him again in his office after a full day of open exchanges with the public. He says with both love and exasperation, "Anyone who does not manage to fall in love with these people must have something wrong in their heart. How can one not see that these are ordinary and kind human beings who simply want to be able to live like anyone else on the planet?"

Professor Baraka still deeply feels the pain of losing his son. "I never forget Ibrahim," he says to me while filing his work for colleagues in France. "But I have enough strength to bear my loss and carry my soul forward into my research explorations. It is work, devotion, management and leadership that make the difference."

Part of his decision in coming back was to honor the school where Ibrahim was a student before the missile took his life.

"I gathered my son's former classmates together and, with the help of the telescope, took them closer to the moon. I want them to feel relief among the stars and heavens above, to scan the skies freely." He recounts hugging the children as they talked about his son, recounting their favorite memories of him. "I want to teach these children about peace and love— nothing else. We must look beyond the military drones and get them to reach for the stars."

He gives me a meaningful glance. "If you truly believe you are living in the land of prophets, then you must act as a messenger. I have my message, and that is to establish the educational infrastructure for astronomy in Palestine."

Maybe leaving NASA was Professor Baraka's way of drawing closer to the stars, albeit not in the manner he had once imagined as a child. He now sees Ibrahim among those stars. He tells his wife, "Come and I will show you Ibrahim," inviting her to look to the heavens through his telescope and see their child there.

His extraordinary trajectory is a testament to the indomitable spirit of Palestinians. Among Palestinians, he is seen as a hero who left behind a highly prestigious job and headed home to Gaza to bring back something beautiful.

Chapter 5

Wisdom and Strength

My two grandmothers steeped me in a profound appreciation for the enduring value of education, knowledge, and lifelong learning starting from a very young age. Their wisdom became an eternal source of guidance amid the chaos and unpredictability of life.

Yet there's an intriguing paradox in our modern era. In a time filled with awe-inspiring technological marvels, one would expect a collective appreciation for knowledge and innovative learning. Instead, there appears to be an unsettling shift in many societies away from progress and toward anti-intellectualism—a celebration and glorification of ignorance that would horrify my illiterate grandmothers. I often wonder, how did we arrive at a point where willful ignorance is so often preferred over the pursuit of knowledge?

At the tender age of five, I observe my grandmother in Jabaliya, the far north of Gaza Strip, engrossed in a game of Five Stones on the doorstep—a game I have yet to master—as she patiently tends to her okra stew simmering on the stove, eagerly awaiting my grandfather's return from work.

My grandfather is known as a real man of action. When the UN presence was established in Gaza in 1949, after the Nakba displaced so many Palestinians from the lands around the Gaza Strip, he helped set up operations, food distribution, water supplies and sanitation systems in the resulting refugee camps.

Even as a child, I'm impressed by his ability to communicate fluently in three languages: Danish, Arabic, and English. He learned Danish from his manager at the UN, a man he still speaks fondly of, and he often used English as it was an official language of the UN.

His wife, my grandmother, is a formidable force in my life and a kind ally. "One day, we will see you going to Al Fakhoura school and being one of those guys who graduate," she says with a penetrating stare. "You become a teacher, and no one will boss you around."

As we wait for my grandfather, I sit with her, enjoying the delicious aroma of okra stew with rice. The anticipation is almost unbearable.

My eyes catch sight of my grandfather's Renault R4 GTL, a remarkable white relic of a vehicle. Excitement courses through me and propels me toward the gate. I can sense his weariness; he looks exhausted. As he steps out the car, he removes his light blue shirt, the UN uniform, leaving only his white cotton undershirt. Since my mind is still attuned to okra stew, I bounce back toward the kitchen, wash my hands, and head to the kitchen table, where my grandmother stands with a large bowl of mixed greens. My grandfather follows and lays before her the fresh vegetables he bought on his way home. Wielding a sharp knife, she carefully chops them into bite-sized pieces with fluid, efficient movements. She has a way of focusing all her attention on whatever task she is doing at any particular moment.

As she chops lettuce, tomato, and cucumber with precision, I am reminded of how she plays Five Stones with similar grace and finesse. The sound of the knife against the wooden cutting board is rhythmic and fills the kitchen, followed by the scraping sound of vegetables being pushed into the bowl. It's a symphony that sounds like joy. As she turns to flip the cooking pan, rice bubbles and steams. The heat from the pot is palpable, even at a distance. I can see the sense of satisfaction in her eyes as she tends to each dish.

I help her set the low rounded table and carry the salad bowl as steam from the hot rice fills the air. More steam rises from the red okra stew, filling the room with its enticing aroma. It will be just the three of us for lunch, as the other aunties and uncles on my mother's side are still in college. The warmth of the kitchen, the smells and sounds of the cooking, and the anticipation of sharing this meal with my loved ones all come together generating a sense of comfort and belonging that I cherish.

The stew tastes so fulfilling in my mouth, with a rich, savory flavor and a slightly sweet and grassy undertone from the okra. The texture is thick and hearty with a velvety consistency. The flavors of okra are balanced with cumin, coriander, and thyme, adding warmth and depth to the dish. I love the combination of the rich hot stew with the fresh green salad. My grandfather was never fussy about food and taught me a valuable life lesson. He said: "If you have to dislike anything in food, then dislike an empty plate." This lesson stayed with me ever since, and I never reject or fuss over a meal.

Here, in this moment, I am fully immersed in the satiating experience of this home-cooked meal, and nobody needs to tell me to eat my food. The love and care infused into the meal is evident in each bite, and the warm sense of togetherness is a feeling I treasure.

My grandfather often repeats what my grandmother tells me, about how important quality education is for our entire family. Navigating turbulent waters their entire lives amid a conflict that forced all four of my grandparents to become refugees, they have invested in education more than anything else, recognizing it might create a better future by breaking cycles of violence and poverty. Education remains highly prized in Palestinian culture. Irrespective of weather or war, children make their way to school as unfailingly as they can, even if they don't enjoy the privilege of shoes. There is hardly ever an excuse to skip class. Access to higher education is deeply valued as well, even with youth unemployment at catastrophic levels. There's always hope things will improve and college degrees will have a chance to be put to use.

My grandfather believes that even if someone does not do well in school, they can still obtain trade skills and other practical knowledge to enable them to build a better future for themselves and their communities. Teachers also provide children with a sense of normalcy and stability in troubled times. Schools can become safe havens for children, offering a place where they can learn, grow, and sometimes shelter from attack.

I had the good fortune to meet a particular teacher whose passion for his pupils touched all those around him. Ahmed Sawaferi recalls how drastically his life changed in a split second. One minute he was heading home to study for an exam, and then a missile struck, severing both of his legs and one of his arms.

Instead of sinking into despair, Ahmed discovered an inner strength he did not know he possessed. He managed to turn his physical injuries into a source of strength. He wholeheartedly dedicated his life to the noble craft of teaching and continues teaching in a wheelchair, determined to inspire his students to learn and stay strong. Using his own personal experiences, Ahmed challenges them to understand that almost anything is possible with hard work, faith in oneself, and determination. And he makes learning fun, which helps pupils retain information and do better in exams. His energy is contagious, and his pragmatic optimism has inspired many of his students to achieve great things, both within and beyond the classroom.

I go to his house at 4:30 am and shadow him until he gets to his classroom. What I observe is miracles of will. He wakes up so early to allow himself extra time to get ready and reminds himself to appreciate the positive aspects of his life and express gratitude for them from the first moment of each day. This shifts his mindset away from pain and problems and makes him feel renewed and capable.

In his little apartment, he doesn't have a specialized adjustable bed or other accommodations. Nonetheless, he wakes up and moves swiftly but carefully around his tiny apartment in Gaza's old city, making his way to the bathroom, brushing his teeth, maneuvering his wheelchair, and placing a teapot on the fire, all using the same hand.

He takes a calm and loving moment to brush his four-year-old daughter Jana's hair and say goodbye to his ten-month-old baby boy Motasem before he leaves for Safad School in Al Zaytoun in the east of Gaza City—an area badly impacted by bombings of the local church and mosque in the 2014 onslaught.

As I walk with him, he suggests we can all learn to use our struggles as stepping-stones to transform suffering into a source of victory even in the toughest moments. He knows his children need him to be a pillar of strength and show that his disability will not be allowed to define his family's future. As he rolls his wheelchair to school, he must carefully navigate uneven road surfaces, potholes, cracks, and debris scattered along the way.

Every school day, Ahmed gets to class and pours his energy into the students—there is never a dull moment. He teaches how motivation can help turn pain into strength of purpose, an ultimate act of resilience. And it applies to all of us, disabled or not, Palestinian or not.

After class, eight-year-old Amjad Tafesh stands in front of his teacher and whispers shyly, "I am very proud of you, and I look up to you, Mr. Ahmed."

Ahmed looks proudly at me, and I can see how his pupils still see him as strong despite his pain and physical difficulties. His key message to his pupils is to love, respect, and value their education and their nation more each day. He knows the odds are stacked against them because of who they are and where they live.

Like many teachers in Palestine, Ahmed is paid only sporadically by the local education ministry, so his job is financially unreliable.[10] Yet, he is determined to continue to have a positive impact on his pupils' lives. Each day, he takes the first few minutes to talk about the principles and values of steadfastness, social cohesion, and survival. He thrives by these values himself, which means he also models what he teaches.

In the fingers that remain on his left hand, he clutches a piece of chalk and writes notes on the board. Today's lesson is about Islamic values and respecting the rights of neighbors and others around you. His voice is strong; he is louder than other teachers, and his students pay close attention.

During break time, Ahmed rolls his wheelchair to the soccer field, where he plays basketball with students using one hand. With his wide, bright smile and neatly trimmed beard, he attracts the attention of every student on the field. He is their hero, who has survived against all odds and continues to teach them about life and the rules of the game.

As he rolls his wheelchair with precision, he scores in the soft-floor open-air basketball hall. He continues to bounce the basketball while chasing his students, proving that the human will can be as strong as muscle and bone, and sometimes stronger. "My message to all disabled people is not to forget life or give in to despair. There is no life with despair, and there should be no despair in life."

Everything is surreal, he admits. "It is a strange feeling to sit in the same classroom where I was once a student. Now I am the teacher, and a colleague to my previous teachers." His voice is imbued with confidence. "I never thought I would be a teacher with challenged abilities. But my dream came true, and no one could stop me. Nothing should stop us, because this military occupation will end. We will be free."

As I walk with Ahmed after leaving the school, I am struck by how much attention and admiration he receives from people passing by on the streets. Disability does not define him; he is instead defined by being loved by the community that surrounds him. And I realize this is another reason why he starts out for school earlier than other teachers—socializing takes time!

Interlude: In the Mayor's Office

As I arrive at the usual road junction, Khalil is waiting with his young son to drive me into the buffer zone. I catch him in the middle of a conversation with his son, who looks at him adoringly. They have just finished a late afternoon drop-off for the next day's vegetable market, and they catch me up on the local chatter as he offers me some of the random produce sitting on his dashboard. He is close to the earth and always carries something to nibble on, whether it's fresh greens or a sweet or spicy pepper.

When we reach Malak's house, her mother answers my knock at the metal door. Disadvantaged families have a warmth that can't be bought with all the money in the world. Malak's shining eyes are beaming with happiness, a priceless currency that transcends all others, as she welcomes me into the house with a full spread of home-cooked food. It's so satisfying to see Naji's family break away from their usual diet of tea and bread twice a day and have richness and variety in their meals. The sharing of food is now international.

There's more good news: Naji has spoken with a construction contractor who gave him an estimate and said he was ready start building. However, he still needs a building permit from the local municipality, which takes time and requires municipal fees that can be quite costly, including an extortionate "rodent control fee."

Khalil waits for me outside Naji's home, as he prefers. He looks at me curiously as I exit the house. "Are we finished already?"

"Not yet," I reply, my mind busy working on how to get that permit.

We jump into the farm truck and start driving. He makes a stopover at his usual hideout, a metal hut where his farmer community hangs out between harvesting and driving between farms and packing houses. There is always someone inside tending a fire and preparing food or tea. Khalil has a habit of picking a handful of eggplants, chilis, lemon, and other fresh goodies and improvising a snack, and meals are typically prepared for the farmers during the lunch hour and sometimes at the end of the day.

Now several farmers are gathered toasting bread and preparing mutabal, a traditional mezze of the Arab region. The dip is made with smoky eggplant, yogurt, garlic, parsley, tahini, and virgin olive oil. It bears a strong resemblance to the better-known baba ghanoush and the Greek melitzanosalata.

"How far is the municipality?" I ask.

"It's about a ten-minute drive, but it might be closed to the public," he replies, his tone hesitant.

I shrug, reaching for a slice of bread. "Well, we won't know until we try, right?"

"Toasted bread can't wait," his brother says with a chuckle. "But go quickly and come back. We will keep the eggplant on the fire."

The municipality is closed, but Khalil knows there is usually a magic password for every institution. He doesn't expect to get a formal appointment with the village mayor, but he is determined to find some way to see him. He walks around the building searching for a way in.

Suddenly, his sturdy Nokia mobile phone rings. It is Abu Fadi, the head of communications for the municipality, who tells him to come in through the back door. We go in and explain our need for a permit to build Naji's house. Abu Fadi gives us an overview of how things will work. Within minutes, we have all the information we need to help Naji build a new home for his family.

Abu Fadi warns Khalil that this case is an exception. He is not supposed to give out such information without going through the proper channels. But he understands the urgency of the situation and wants to help in any way possible. With the map and the necessary paperwork, we leave the municipality feeling hopeful for Naji and his family.

"Nature provides an exception to every rule," I say happily.

"Yes, but to proceed with this exception, we must first obtain an administrative decision from either the mayor or the city council," Khalil says.

"Perhaps we can appeal directly to the mayor," I suggest.

Securing an audience with the mayor of Beit Lahia is no easy feat. As the chief executive of a busy border town, he grapples with innumerable challenges and responsibilities, including security hazards. Continuously besieged by requests, grievances, and appeals from constituents, officials, and various agricultural organizations, the mayor's schedule is tightly packed. But with help from Abu Fadi, we manage to find a sliver of time for an audience with the mayor.

My walk with Ahmed takes us to the Orthodox Church of Saint Porphyrius, one of Palestine's oldest Eastern Orthodox churches, which is not far from his house. From here, I bid him a fond farewell and move on to meet an inspiring figure, Sara Al Najjar, a young woman who lost both her legs in an artillery shell attack on her home in Deir Al-Balah.

She recounts the harrowing tale of how she lost her legs on that fateful summer day in 2014. A deafening explosion reverberated through the air, propelling her onto the balcony, where she witnessed her neighbor's home succumbing to the devastation of a tank shell. She called to her husband to seek refuge in the lounge, hoping for a shred of safety. But as she lingered behind for a moment, a tank shell struck her with merciless force. Sara was transported to the hospital by ambulance, only to be targeted again when a missile hit the operating room where she was having surgery.

Despite her tragic loss, Sara is brimming with hope for her life journey. Sometimes she feels alone, but her father never lets negative feelings creep in, and she receives overwhelming love, support, and acceptance from her family and community. Like Ahmed, she remains determined to channel her pain and use it to achieve even her wildest dreams.

Before her injury, Sara worked as an accountant for a local ice cream factory and was known for her energy and expertise in solving problems encountered by small-scale merchants and shopkeepers across Gaza. Thankfully she's been able to return to the job she loves.

"The greatest victories come from overcoming the most significant obstacles," she says. "As my life takes a new shape, I anticipate growth even without my own legs. Now I embrace the balance of numbers and the sweet flavors of destiny."

When I ask what her secret is, she pauses for a second. "The greatest battles are fought within ourselves, and victory lies in finding peace amid chaos." Before her injuries, Sara suffered from depression as wars raged on. She lacked any sense of hope for a better life. Yet after her injuries, she feels life has just begun.

Initially hesitant about having artificial limbs, Sara sees young friends wearing prosthetics and decides to give it a try. On a cold morning, she tries on new legs for the first time, excited to begin training with a physiotherapist at Gaza's Artificial Limbs and Polio Centre. She is aware that her brain is the key to successfully walking with the prosthetics.

Supported by her loved ones, including her husband, she also musters the courage to relinquish their rented apartment and return to the embrace of her family. She finds comfort and a renewed feeling of joy, knowing that family can provide the unconditional support she and her husband need to forge ahead.

She still faces the challenge of adapting to her new limbs and training to regain her ability to navigate stairs, hills, and corners. With support from her family and friends, she feels confident she can overcome these obstacles and the traumatic memories that haunt her. Life remains difficult for Sara, but her prosthetic legs have set her on the path of progress, as her skilled mind and fingers continue to manage finances and settle accounts with ice cream vendors across the coastal enclave.

A twenty-year-old Palestinian woman, Aya Masoud, sits on a wooden chair and gracefully bends her back as she threads a needle using only her toes. Unlike others injured by war, she was born without arms. She discovered a passion for creating art using embroidery and, after years of practice, displays astonishing precision and skill. Her work showcases Palestinian patterns, colors, and designs and merges drawing with embroidery. Aya is also determined to pursue her education without limitations. She embraces the challenge of performing her school duties and exams using only her toes. Her strong commitment pays off as she excels beyond expectations and achieves remarkable academic success, graduating from university with distinction.

There is a surprisingly competitive spirit among many people with physical disabilities in Palestine, and I am amazed to witness their speed and agility. The Al Jazeera Sports Club supports athletes with disabilities to take part in various sports including soccer, basketball, swimming, and volleyball, and the club achieved a remarkable feat by securing a place in the Guinness Book of World Records for the largest marathon exclusively for individuals with disabilities, boasting an astounding participation of over 2,400 resilient athletes.

Some of the athletes have taken part in international competitions. Khamis Zaqout won five international gold medals in discus throwing, javelin throwing, and shot put, coming home to great celebrations.

Another remarkable person is Yasmine Alqatta, a 23-year-old who lost her leg in an airstrike in east Khan Younis. Yasmine shares with me how her life was transformed and how she is acquiring digital skills to build a more inclusive future for people with disabilities.

"I may have lost my leg, but I haven't lost my spirit. I'm determined to overcome this and achieve my dream of becoming a coder. I am so grateful to have discovered a new passion for digital skills and technology. It's opened up a whole new world of possibilities for me, and I'm excited to see where it takes me."

She dreams of working for a tourism agency to ensure that people with disabilities have full accessibility and can join in all touristic activities.

"I'm lucky to have the support of my father, who has always been there for me," she says. "The love of a father is the first foundation upon which a daughter builds her world, a source of strength and confident support that shapes her into the person she becomes. I want to use my passion for technology to make a difference in the lives of people with disabilities. I want to empower them to travel and explore the world without limitations." She grins brightly as she sips a cup of tea behind her laptop. "My father has shown me anything is possible, and I want to pass on a message of perseverance and possibility to others like me around the world."

Yasmine has formed a close-knit community of friends who understand her needs and experiences. For her, disability brings people together in a unique way by fostering deep bonds and a sense of empathy otherwise hard to find. Their shared experiences create a special feeling of camaraderie that goes beyond any physical limitation. Not every person with disabilities can meet in person, but they have become more aware of each other's inspiring journeys through social media groups.

There was a time in the past when physical disabilities were stigmatized and even viewed with shame by most families. Now, a shift has taken place in the dominant cultural perspective. People like Ahmed, Aya, Khamis, and Yasmine are part of a community taking root in Gaza that champions the rights and unique skills and wisdom of people with disabilities.

One of the most striking stories I've come across is the story of two disabled men who became like one.

On a beautiful spring day in Gaza, Adli and Mansour are in need of a new pair of shoes. Their economic backgrounds are quite divergent, but they have been close since their school days. They pull up on their shared motorcycle outside a local shoe shop and make their way inside on their crutches. Both are excited to try on the latest styles and quickly settle on a pair they both love. They split the cost. Adli pays for the left shoe, which is all he needs, and Mansour pays for the right. They love that they have the same taste in shoes and the same-sized feet, and they laugh and joke with the shop owner, who has never before seen two customers come in to buy a single pair of shoes.

They tell him about a chilly afternoon when Adli noticed Mansour's shoe looked worn out. He offered to give Mansour his other sneaker, since he didn't need it and they had lost opposite legs in successive Israeli attacks. Mansour was hesitant, but Adli assured him they had the same shoe size and that the shoe would be comfortable and supportive. After trying on the shoe, Mansour realized it was indeed very comfortable, and he accepted Adli's kind offer. They've been sharing shoes ever since.

I later meet them at a fálafel shop, and as they wait for their food, Adli shares his story of fearlessly acting as a first responder during an Israeli attack, only to become a victim himself in a second strike.[11] He was brought into the hospital in a coma, and a medical crew pronounced him dead. His broken body was transferred to the morgue.

Adli looks disturbed as he recalls what he was told of these events. Mansour sits silently, listening to his friend tell the story. Adli's father arrived at the morgue to say a final farewell to his son only to feel Adli's hand and realize it was warm; his son was still alive. His screams of joy echoed through the hospital as he embraced his son. Miraculously, Adli regained consciousness in the morgue and was returned to the hospital.

The doctors were astonished. Adli needed several operations in various Gulf states to fully recover, with Mansour by his side. Little did Mansour know that he, too, would lose a leg just a few months later.

Mansour's younger brother witnessed the bombing that maimed Mansour but did not know his own brother was among the victims. He ran back to his house, breathless and shaking, saying, "Someone has been killed!" His mother's face turned pale and she whispered a solemn prayer for the victim's family, wishing them patience during this difficult time. Hours later, she learned that the victim was her own son, who had lost a leg and some fingers and had shrapnel in his head.

After recalling such sad memories, the two men eat their falafel sandwiches—Adli's favorite—in pensive silence. "The only positive thing about being injured has been how it's strengthened my friendship with Adli," says Mansour. "We share everything and split expenses—after all, we are one soul with two bodies."

"My other leg is over there," Adli jokes, pointing to Mansour.

Mansour laughs and responds, "Yes, and that's my other leg, and I can't even think of going anywhere without it, or without Adli."

Adli grins. "Together, we are better than before we were injured."

Mansour nods, his eyes lively.

They enjoy spending time together, whether it's shopping, eating, relaxing, strolling along the beach, running errands, or riding their one motorcycle. Living in Shujaiya, in East Gaza City, a region heavily impacted by war, the two men like to walk together from the far eastern border to the seafront in the far west, passing through Gaza's fishing hub. Despite their physical challenges, the friends continue to do their daily activities together, taking pleasure in the simple joys of life.

Both men get on their motorcycle and head back home, laughing once again and sharing stories that never seem to come to an end.

In this town, people with disabilities are supported and understood in ways often hard to come by elsewhere. They don't have to fight for access, inclusion, or representation because everyone has sympathy for people whose bodies have been dismembered by Israel's military hardware, and because the situation is so common. Disability has been normalized. When Adli and Mansour sit on the seafront to chat for hours, people stop and greet them as they watch the rhythmic motion of the waves in the ocean. They find joy in daily life and inspire others in the community to do the same.

Years later I catch up with the two men as we walk under a sycamore tree on Al-Mintar Hill, an area near their homes that overlooks Gaza City. Despite the city's changes, it still retains a serene beauty, and Gazans try not to let an atmosphere of defeat take hold. In Shujaiya, people's mode of resilience is to stay, stand firm, and try to enjoy life as best they can despite the odds stacked against them.

Mansour is now married to a wonderful woman named Neda. To his great joy, they are expecting a baby, and his wife is thrilled to have found a job selling homemade sweets online. She's also happy her husband has the support he needs through his friend Adli.

"We are able to find joy by sharing all we have and continuing to care for one another even through pain," says Mansour.

As for the motorcycle: Mansour handles the gears and Adli steers. Everyone who sees them fly by on the street is amazed by their degree of cooperation.

"When we share a ride, I feel like a whole human body with nothing missing," Mansour says with a lighthearted laugh as they head toward home with the sunset behind them.

Chapter 6

Ramadan and Santa Claus

Making my way from west to east in Gaza City—from the marina to the Old City—I catch sight of Adli and Mansour and their marvelously coordinated maneuvering of the motorbike up ahead, zipping through crowded streets like synchronized swimmers on wheels. Dodging through the maze of streets filled with bustling vendors, honking cars, and chatty pedestrians, I feel I'm playing an epic real-life game of Frogger. The Church of Saint Porphyrius catches my eyes, a beautiful ancient monument in the heart of Gaza City. Dating back to the fifth century, the church exudes a peaceful atmosphere and a sense of awe at the passage of time.

Continuing toward the Christian quarter of Gaza's Old City, one senses the harmonious coexistence of Christian and Muslim families. Families of both religious persuasions exchange meals and friendship, especially during holidays and special occasions. This tradition of shared humanity and hospitality is deeply ingrained in the culture and history of Gaza and in the entire Arab region, where people of different religions have lived together for centuries.

Both religions value sharing food as a testament to their generosity, kindness, and respect for one another. Christian families prepare traditional dishes like roast lamb and baklava while Muslim families make dishes such as *maqluba*, shish kebab, and *knafeh*, and everyone has their own recipe for *waraq enab*, the famous stuffed grape leaves. As families engage in lively conversations, they share stories and laughter and learn about each other's worries and hopes.

Approximately 3,000 Christians still call Gaza home, with the majority living in Gaza City near the three main churches: the Greek Orthodox (St. Porphyrius), the Roman Catholic (Holy Family), and the Gaza Baptist.

Inside the Church of Saint Porphyrius, the Byzantine architectural style with a central nave and two aisles leaves me feeling a little dizzy. We are in the presence of holy relics and the tomb of Saint Porphyrius, the fifth-century bishop of Gaza. The walls and floors feature beautiful mosaics and colorful frescoes depicting scenes from the Bible and the lives of saints. Outside, the church looks modest enough, with a simple stone facade and small courtyard. Inside, there is a sense of peace, tranquility, and spaciousness. The Church of Saint Porphyrius signifies the perseverance of the local Christian Palestinian community in the face of the turmoil this region has witnessed over the centuries and especially in recent decades. It serves as an active site of worship and a place of pilgrimage for those who can reach it from within Gaza and occasionally from beyond.

For Muslims in Gaza, as elsewhere, the month of Ramadan has special significance. It is a time for spiritual reflection and devotion to God. Fasting from dawn until dusk is a way of purifying the soul and cultivating empathy for those in need. The *iftar*, the breaking of the fast, is a cherished tradition where families, friends, and neighbors gather to share meals and prayers. The spirit of Ramadan extends beyond the dinner table, as it is also a time of charitable giving and acts of special kindness. Many organizations in Gaza hold food drives and other initiatives to help those in particular need during Ramadan.

During the biggest festival in Gaza, the three-day *Eid al Fitr* holiday at the end of Ramadan, the streets reverberate with the symphony of animated conversations and joyous laughter. The warmth is almost indescribable as everyone goes out of their way to shake hands with every neighbor and acquaintance during the Eid days, whatever their religion, and it nurtures an environment of harmony in the communities. Families embark on leisurely strolls together, paying visits to aunts, siblings, grandparents, and sisters, punctuating their journey with frequent pauses to exchange affectionate greetings, hugs, and cheek kisses. These interactions serve as a balm for those with broken social bonds.

Yet each stop on the way burdens the digestive system. In my own case, I am compelled to eat or drink something in each of nineteen separate houses when I break my fast on the first day of Eid, visiting aunts on my father's side, my grandmother, and a small group of orphaned and displaced individuals I visit at least once during Ramadan to check up on them, among others. Drinking so many cups of soft drinks, juices, teas, and coffees and sharing so many meals, fruits, and confections during the marathon of visitations makes the fasting seem like a distant memory.

Hundreds of Christians and Muslims share traditional dishes at this time, creating a true feast for the senses. It's a foodie's dream come true, a gastronomic celebration worth traveling across the world to experience. If only people could get into Gaza to be here.

A microcosm of Gaza's interfaith harmony and compassion is the friendship between Kamal Tarazi, a 55-year-old Christian, and his blind neighbor, Hatem Khries, 45. During the holy month of

Ramadan, Kamal wakes up early and takes Hatem to the Al-Burno Mosque five times a day, every day, so the blind man can pray. Kamal patiently waits for prayers to finish so he can escort his neighbor safely home, from the dawn prayers until *Taraweeh* evening prayers. He insists he does not mind this grueling routine. They also share *iftar* together after sunset, though Kamal does not fast.

"We have been friends for fifteen years and have always shared our joys and pains," he says, patting Hatem on the shoulder. "We are never separated. Everyone knows I am Christian and he is a Muslim, and they see how deep our friendship is."

They stay connected throughout the year, not only during Ramadan. Kamal goes to the mosque with Hatem every Friday and Hatem goes to church with Kamal on Sundays. Hatem is a pharmacist who lost his sight five years ago following a work-related accident at his pharmacy. His bond with his Christian neighbor, he says, has "helped him hugely" ever since. Over the years they have helped one another overcome a host of other problems including poverty, imprisonment, and war. Their entire families have become close.

Kamal tells me nothing external distinguishes a Gazan Christian from their Muslim neighbors. "A Christian in Gaza protects a Muslim and a Muslim protects a Christian—we are one body," he says.

The neighborhood of Al Zaytoun where Kamal and Hatem live is steeped in history and is known for being one of the oldest parts of the Middle East, where Muslims and Christians have lived side by side for centuries. The church stands next to the mosque, and people of different faiths have lived next to each other for as long as they can remember.

Kamal says he personally has always felt welcome in Gaza, his home. "We, the people of Gaza, have a relationship that is grounded in mutual love and respect," he states. The Orthodox church organizes food parcels for Muslim neighbors, and during a recent Israeli assault, as artillery and air strikes hit Gaza's population hard, the church opened its doors to all who needed shelter.

Kamal is also a political activist and spent nine years in prison before being released as part of the Oslo Accords. He lives on a meager pension. Other friends may be too busy getting on with their own lives, but Kamal has all the time in the world for Hatem. They love shopping together, as they both enjoy the sensory delights of Al Zawya market. Kamal reads books and newspapers to Hatem and they naturally debate politics, one of the well-established pastimes of the Arab region. When the sun sets, the two friends continue their conversations about Gaza and the future of Palestine long into the night.

The two friends remind me of a conversation I had with my good friend Monsignor Father Manuel Musallam, head of Gaza's Roman Catholic community. In his office one day in a school he manages, I told him about Western media reports that Gaza's Christians are considering emigrating because of Islamic oppression.

Father Musallam sighed. "If Christians emigrate, it's not because of Muslims. It is because we suffer from the Israeli siege. We seek a life of freedom—a life different from the life of dogs we are currently forced to live."

Christians and Muslims are equally devastated by the hardships of the blockade, and some say the two communities have been brought together by the adversity they face rather than divided. They share the problems of the constant shortages of food, water, medicine, and medical supplies.

"Friendship goes beyond religion—if we suffer, we suffer together. If we flourish, then we will also be together," Kamal says, and Hatem nods in agreement with a pearly smile.

"If I knew there was one doctor in the world who could guarantee a high success rate for bringing back my friend's sight,

I would donate one of my eyes," says Kamal. "I would live with one eye if I knew my friend would see again and enjoy the sight of his five children and look in their eyes."

Two eyes, like two legs, can be enough for two in Gaza.

Interlude: Bureaucratic Benevolence

The mayor is a stout former construction engineer with a distinguished mustache. He is sitting behind a desk framed by shelves that hold more than ten trophies of appreciation from agricultural organizations and international partners involved in farming, sanitation projects, and initiatives such as breast cancer awareness campaigns. Pen in hand, surrounded by senior advisors, he is signing a stack of papers in front of him. Khalil is sitting beside me, waiting patiently as I watch the mayor at work.

"There's something I need to get off my chest," I jump in. "If I share it with you, would you be willing to assist me?"

"I'll have to hear what it is first before I make any promises," he replies, his words measured and precise.

One of his advisors blurts out, "You look familiar."

"I suppose so. I spent some of my childhood not too far from here," I reply.

"Where?" the mayor asks.

"Tal al Zaatar."

My grandparents on my mother's side live in Tal al Zaatar. Administratively, it is part of the Jabalia refugee camp, north of Gaza City, run by UNRWA. It is built on a hill ("Tal"), the highest elevation in Gaza, with newer, larger homes and wider streets. Relief services aren't available there, so only people who work hard or get lucky can afford to buy land and build in this area. All residents are refugees from villages surrounding Gaza, including my own family from Yibna. When I was a child,

I lived with my other grandparents in Rafah in the south. After their home was destroyed by the Israeli military, the ICRC offered us a tent to live in. My grandfather up north insisted we refuse the tent and move in with them instead. So, I spent three school years in with my mother and siblings in Tal al Zaatar.

The mayor looks at me with sudden interest and says, "Ah, Salah is your uncle?"

"Yes, that's correct," I affirm, impressed how quickly he made the connection.

The mayor bows his head in acknowledgment. "Your family has always had a good reputation, including your grandfather at the UN."

My Uncle Salah from my mother's side is employed at this municipality, and the thought of being found by him here makes me nervous. If he spots me, I will have no choice but to abandon the delicious mutabal and toasted bread waiting for us in the tin shack. My uncle will no doubt invite me for a meal, demanding to know why I didn't tell him I was in the area. Then my grandmother will start in, first subjecting me to her own righteous wrath at my sneaky ways, then busily making her famous *waraq enab* (stuffed grape leaves). She'll insist that all she needs to do is to stand on her tippy toes in her garden and pick the leaves, stuff them, and two hours later we'll be eating. Then I'll no doubt be invited to spend the night. It's impossible to turn down any invitation from my grandmother.

Even more than that, I'm still a university student and need to get home and study for my linguistics exam. Normally, the journey home would take about an hour. But the Abu Holi and Al Matahen checkpoints, manned by Israeli soldiers, divide the north from the south and often remain closed for days (or more), impeding the free movement of people and goods. I've spent weeks stranded due to arbitrary changes in checkpoint rules. It always makes me nervous being on the "wrong" side of a checkpoint. I was "lucky" enough last semester to be stranded "only" a few days at the checkpoint and make it to my final exam in Shakespearean literature after I spotted a neighbor who was an ambulance driver. I asked if I could hitch a ride with him, and he agreed. Only after the crossing did I realize that the woman on the stretcher was a dead 64-year-old mother being transported to her relatives.

My Uncle Salah's name seems to unlock a flood of stories and anecdotes from the mayor and his advisors, all eager to show off their friendship with him. He's popular due to his outstanding work ethic and extensive knowledge of water pipe engineering. Gaza is a small, crowded place—families are connected.

As I convey Malak's family story to the mayor, his eyes well up with tears that strangers from afar would be so concerned about the welfare of some of his town's people.

"Is it safe to assume the exception for Malak's house can be approved?" I ask hopefully.

"Absolutely. And we're granting a hundred-percent waiver of all fees," he replies with a grin. I later learn this includes the ludicrous "rodent control fee."

Without hesitation, the mayor orders his head of engineering to dispatch a team of engineers to aid the family with a simple, strong design at no extra cost. I am overjoyed.

As I prepare to leave, the mayor urges me to come to his house for lunch. I know he is serious because he calls home to check what they have cooked.

Khalil mutters, "You won't be disappointed with our homemade farm mutabal," and nods toward his truck.

I'm on edge, caught in the cozy but sometimes exasperating web of Arab hospitality. I managed to evade Uncle Salah, and now this. I rack my brain for any excuse I can think of, bid good-bye to the kind mayor, and scurry off to indulge in the cozy ambiance of a roaring fire and delicious mutabal.

It does not disappoint.

But I have one last favor to ask.

"Malak's family?" Khalil asks.

"Yes, please."

Raindrops cascade down the dusty surface of the old vegetable truck, tracing paths on the worn window glass and cracked windshield. They sound like a million tiny drums as we make our way to Naji and Malak's place. After a quick update to the family about the mayor's exceptional administrative approval, we are back on the road, drenched and happy.

Christians join the *Eid al Fitr* celebrations that mark the end of Ramadan, and there are similar heartwarming displays of interfaith harmony, respect, and compassion at Easter and Christmas. Christian families come together to attend church services, exchange gifts, and share meals with loved ones, and the Christian community organizes initiatives to bring joy to children, especially those living in refugee camps.

But sometimes Palestinian Christians don't feel like celebrating while everyone in Gaza is mourning their dead. "I have restricted our celebrating this year to church services and Christmas trees at home," Ibrahim Jahshan tells me after a particularly devastating Israeli onslaught. Ibrahim is a thirty-year-old Christian friend, slender and youthful, with a strong jawline, a well-groomed beard, and expressive eyes. He is in charge of social activities for his community and lives in Al Zaytoun, the same neighborhood where Kamal and Hatem live. The neighborhood is the largest in Gaza City by area and the second largest in terms of population. It is located in the heart of the hilly old city and named after the abundance of olive trees, which still cover most of its southern lands, and it is known for its many charming cafes and shops as well as ancient markets, like the gold market and the carpenters' market, that still function today. With minarets and steeples punctuating the skyline and the marble below inscribed with writing that goes back hundreds of years, it's a wonderfully charming part of town.

Walking with him, I realize it is impossible to reliably distinguish Christians from Muslims. Ibrahim wears a Santa Claus outfit around Christmastime, but he also recites Quranic passages with serene fluidity in everyday speech. He is happy to explain, with evidence from both faiths, why the killing of innocent people is banned.

For decades, shops in Gaza City have kept to the traditions of setting up Christmas trees and displaying Christmas gifts for sale. But during particularly tough years, a shopkeeper acknowledges that Gaza's Christians do not buy Christmas gifts at the normal rates. He looks forlorn but resolute as he cleans some dust that has settled on red Christmas bags.

Ibrahim Jahshan tells me that as a Palestinian Christian, born and raised in Gaza, he enjoys life and has never felt any kind of religious oppression. "We are united as one nation, one land, one blood," he says, adding that during assaults, both Christians and Muslims go to the hospitals to donate blood, and hundreds of newly homeless Muslim families took part in the funeral procession of Jalila Ayyad, an elderly Christian woman who was sitting at her home in Gaza City when an Israeli airstrike killed her.

Through Ibrahim I meet the Patriarch of Jerusalem, Fouad Twal, who often visits to meet with Gaza's Christian community. Twal tells me, "Christmas is the holiday of peace and love. We hope that everyone will live in peace. Peace always comes with justice, and there is no peace that comes through force or fighting. Only with justice can we live in peace. From Gaza we ask the whole world to feel with us and look at our situation. Do not forget Gaza."

Community members come together in Gaza to support local charities and non-profit organizations working tirelessly to bring some festive magic to children during the holidays. These efforts involve hundreds of people working tirelessly to bring hope and cheer children who otherwise have little to celebrate. Various organizations collect donations to purchase toys, sweets, and other treats for the children.

Once a year, Santa Claus comes to give gifts to poor children, especially those whose homes have been destroyed. Santa's bulky red (fake) belly wobbles as he passes through the ruins of Shujaiya dragging a huge sack. Standing on the wreckage of demolished homes, he signals his arrival to the children with ringing bells.

"Baba Noel [Father Christmas] is here for all of you: the poor and those injured and maimed in the war. I'm here to shake hands with all of you!" he says. The children are fascinated. Many of them have never met someone dressed up as Santa Claus, whose giving and kindness reflects the true meaning of the Christian holiday season. Ibrahim really gets into his role, playing the part with gusto and props galore, spreading cheer that reflects in the eyes of the children.

While these efforts may seem small in the grand scheme of things, they make a real difference in the lives of children and their families. For an instant, they can forget their hardships and enjoy a little bit of happiness and hope for the future. Ibrahim says his church chose Shujaiya, a place with no Christians, for the Santa visit because it was the worst affected by recent devastating air assaults. I feel in these moments that Ibrahim represents the heartbeat of Gaza.

"We are all under siege," he says, "Christians and Muslims. Both our bodies and our graveyards were hit during the war."

According to UNICEF, the United Nations Children's Fund, 1.1 million children in Gaza face inadequate access to some combination of mental health care, psychosocial support services, medical care, and food and water. That's 92 percent of all children in Gaza. But it doesn't stop Ibrahim.

"For those who want to learn the true meaning of coexistence between Christians and Muslims, Gaza is the perfect example," he says as he decorates his Christmas tree with his wife and four-month-old baby. "This is the time for the world to remember the origin of Christmas. If Jesus was alive today, he would be just like any other Gaza Christian who is not allowed to make the journey to Bethlehem."[12]

Chapter 7

Fashion and Flips

In another corner of the city, a vibrant junction teeming with students from three major universities, a hub of intellectual fervor and urban energy decorated with graffiti by local artists, I meet a young woman who challenges all societal norms.

28-year-old Nermine Demyati was born and raised in Khan Younis, the second largest city in the Gaza Strip, located in the south near Rafah. She has had an eye for fashion since childhood. At the age of twelve she began designing her own clothes, altering the shape and cut of whatever she had on hand and adding personalized touches to suit her taste.

"When I was 16, I learned about all the latest world fashions on YouTube," Nermine shares with me. "I wanted to be a designer but couldn't find a college that offered training. So, I decided to learn myself via the internet."

She's not the only one. The fashion industry in Gaza has undergone a dramatic transformation in recent years, blending global fashions with locally-made designs and time-honored Palestinian styles. Traditional embroidery patterns and woven textiles take center stage, with silk and wool fabrics weaving contemporary masterpieces. Social media and e-commerce have boosted the fashion industry in the Arab region generally, and Gaza is no exception. Several Gaza-based fashionistas post images online and market their own and other brands. A customer in Nermine's shop notes how some students in Gaza follow international fashion trends closely, sometimes taking up new styles even before friends in Europe and the US have heard of them.

This shift poses a challenge to those who favor a more conservative dress code. But fashion marches forward, in Gaza and all of Palestine. Twenty years ago, a woman might be stopped at the gate of Gaza's strictest university for wearing eyeliner or nail polish. Now, many of the old dress codes have been discarded as girls and women have pushed back.

Nermine studied history and architecture at Gaza's Islamic University, and now she is one of a few young designers managing to prosper amid Gaza's highest-ever unemployment rate. Social media is a lifeline that allows her to share her passion and products with others worldwide. In her small factory, Nermine works at her modest sewing machine as orders come in daily from clients across Europe, Canada, and the Arab region—fans of the original fashion designs she displays beautifully on her social media pages.

The biggest hurdle is the blockade imposed on the land where she lives. Despite her ability to see new fashion materials instantly on social media, they often arrive with a delay of one or two years after their global release.

"It's hard to find fabrics and accessories, so we have to be creative and resourceful in order to produce high-quality designs," she says and tells me about her network of friends acting as shipping agents around the world to get materials into Gaza through traveling passengers. "I tend to buy my materials and trimmings for abayas from Dubai, Saudi Arabia, and Turkey, but it takes so long to get it," she says. "If we had open borders, I could bring in so many more materials and design freely."

The blockade also makes international export nearly impossible, but she remains committed to her calling. Her dream is to expand her small factory, located next to one of Gaza's biggest university quarters, and establish Gaza's first fashion school. Her factory also serves as a salon where young women discuss their fashion projects, use their phones to surf the internet, or enjoy a manicure before placing their orders or taking new garments home.

"I fled to Egypt one summer," Nermine tells me with a smile. "But then decided I should come back and add some brightness and color to the misery." She proudly holds up a dazzling dress for a customer's engagement party.

She often meets resistance for modifying the traditional Palestinian dress, considered a vital part of Gazan cultural heritage by traditionalists. "I want to create designs reflecting our cultural identity, but I also want to bring something new to the table," she says. "It's a challenge to strike such a delicate balance."

Despite the many difficulties, she manages to find ways to remain hopeful and overcome obstacles. "Fashion is my passion, and I believe it has the power to bring people together and make a positive impact on society. I want to support our Palestinian economy and send the 'Made in Palestine' label out to the world." She talks with me while she trims the shoulder pieces of a yellow dress that will be delivered to a mother for her daughter's wedding. She needs to finish it before the electricity cuts out again.

I learn from a magazine editor friend about a famous fashion magazine in the Gulf whose distribution is delayed because the designer of its stunning covers cannot connect to electricity. Astonished, I ask which world city has to face such electricity cuts. The magazine editor laughs and explains that the creative genius behind their front covers is a young woman working remotely from Gaza. Turns out, there are many virtual workers and customer service professionals in Gaza, though it's kept a bit quiet so as not to mix business with politics.

Of course, some minds resist change that involves women breaking out of their traditional roles. Stigma around monthly periods, for example, remains a persistent taboo rooted in myths, misconceptions, and cultural images of menstruation as shameful, dirty, or impure. It is heartening when the revered blind Sheikh Hassan Jaber in Rafah publicly takes a brave stand to condemn the stigma. Responding to a man who expressed disgust at menstruation, Sheikh Jaber replied, "Are you objecting to God's judgment, since women are born with this? I expect the congregation to support women and girls during their periods, not to blame them."

When asked how men could support women, the Sheikh answered, "Empathy and understanding are important, but it's not enough to simply mind your own business and remain silent. By staying silent, we allow harmful attitudes and beliefs to persist and continue to harm women and girls."

There is much more work to be done on gender equality. Yet in Gaza, the days when women were relegated to secretarial or administrative jobs and treated as mere accessories to male professionals are gone. In today's Gaza, women are entrepreneurs, CEOs, creators, and business leaders and are proving they can succeed on equal terms with men and sometimes surpass them.

One group of Gazans is enjoying the new fashion trends, like blending sporty brands with locally-made designs and traditional Palestinian clothing. They can be spotted running, jumping, and climbing around and across obstacles of all kinds, practicing the sport of parkour.

The sport appeals to a new generation brought up in a society defined by war and youthfulness, where the majority of people are young adults and children. Gaza is so crowded with refugee camps and bustling neighborhoods, deserted ruins can feel like the only open spaces left. Any kind of obstacles can be 'parkoured,' and Gaza's rubble and debris provide unique environments for exploration and discovery. Parkour transforms the bombed-out chaos around these young women and men into something like the scene of a computer game where they can jump, leap, swing, slide, climb, and flip.

Nineteen-year-old Amira finds in parkour a sense of freedom she has never known before—the same feeling, perhaps, that the surfers talked about. "Starting out, I received a lot of criticism from my family and community, who viewed the sport as too challenging. But I couldn't stop. I couldn't give up the feeling of freedom, excitement, and joy. As time passed, more girls started to join in."

Doing parkour in the ruins of Gaza is an exhilarating experience that fills Amira and others with adrenaline and excitement. She likes the challenge of navigating complex landscapes, leaping over obstacles, scaling walls, and testing her physical strength and skills to their limits. She often brings along her twelve-year-old brother Shady as she explores abandoned areas. For Amira, going on parkour trips with her little brother is a way to challenge gender norms and stereotypes.

"At home, my parents taught me gender shouldn't determine how I'm treated compared to my brother. We were both given equal opportunities and treated with the same level of respect," she says and explains that by physically and mentally pushing her own boundaries, she frees her mind of cultural expectations and demonstrates her own strength, courage, and zeal to succeed and overcome the fear of falling.

Amira wears leggings and a sports blouse with her hair pulled back in a tight ponytail. Her brother Shady takes it easy while she vaults over walls, leaps over gaps, and performs precision jumps to land on small surfaces. Each time she flips, Shady cheers. She seems unstoppable. With drive and focus, she is determined to achieve with her body what she sees in her mind.

This is the new generation in Palestine, a new mentality refusing the culture of being blocked—by checkpoint or roadblocks, by a blockade or a buffer zone, or by cultural expectations—and waiting, waiting, waiting for a future of freedom that never seems to come. This digitally savvy generation is getting out of the house, putting on their smartwatches and Adidas shirts, and refusing to be intimidated by norms and traditions that inhibited many of their grandmothers and mothers from going outside to play sports and achieve their life goals.

Like other parkour adepts, Amira does not let setbacks and failures deter her. "I am capable of shattering obstacles and defying preconceptions about women's abilities," she says as she swings from suspended bars.

When asked what she enjoys most about parkour, she pauses. "The sense of freedom and empowerment in the face of daily life challenges." It is her way to turn the destructive threats of occupation into a creative freedom to risk and dare.

Unafraid to push her limits and embrace the unknown, Amira is a captivating presence, seeming to hover outside the usual societal restrictions. Now and then Amira and Shady come across another parkour athlete out on a thrilling experience in spaces shared by men and women, girls and boys. They nod to each other, sharing a bond of finding this unexpected silver lining in the face of tragedy and mass destruction.

Amira is thrilled that the first-ever parkour gym in Gaza will open soon in Gaza City, fully equipped with props like wooden boxes and padded mats to ensure safe landings. She hopes it will bring together even more young women and girls who share her passion. Already hundreds of athletes, boys and girls, ages six to twenty-six, are on the waiting list.

When I talk with Hassan at his lab in Rafah about Amira and Shady, he says the siblings represent a powerful form of resistance against the blockade—a whole generation that is refusing to be forced into boxes, trembling in fear at home. Hassan acknowledges this was not the case for his generation. Of course, many youths are glued to their phone screens, monitoring their weight and dabbling in health crazes and other passing fads. The beauty of parkour is that takes place outdoors, and there is a reconnection with the physical environment.

"Amira and her brother are shining examples of determination and perseverance. They are the new face of Gaza, refusing to give up on their dreams." He tells me about four schoolgirls who meet in a smashed vehicle box to play guitar and sing despite the miserable living conditions all around them.

"This is not just about gender equality," says Hassan. "It's also about creating a better future for all Palestinians. We need to break free from the cycle of violence and poverty and focus on education and innovation. We need to encourage our young people to dream big and pursue their passions, like Amira and Shady. People who are surfing, skateboarding, and parkouring are not going to blow themselves up for any abstract cause."

He wants to hear about my latest visit to the US, the speaking tour, meeting with US Congress members, and winning a journalism prize. He asks if Americans understand our situation.

I explain that, generally, Americans are kind people but often misled by misinformation, especially about Arabs and Muslims. Hollywood's representation of Arabs significantly influences public opinion, and the mainstream press only makes things worse.

Hassan asks about my experience arriving at the airport. Since Hassan hasn't traveled in his entire life, I add a few details to help him understand. I recount how immigration officers at the international arrivals terminal asked where I lived and struggled to locate the Gaza Strip in their system. After several attempts, one officer suggested registering me as being from Libya instead. Another officer volunteered to search for Gaza and eventually said triumphantly, "I found it! Ghana."

Hassan laughs.

I tell him I felt it was important to meet with members of Congress and advocate for change. But they generally lacked understanding, exemplified by one member's disbelief that there was a severe blockade on Gaza. To illustrate the difficulties faced by Gazans, I purchased a can of powdered milk and requested that he send it to a Gaza family. Two months later, his staffer informed me of the logistical nightmare involved; no shipping company could fulfill our request.

During the speaking tour that followed, organized by the American Friends Service Committee, I learned more about and witnessed their efforts to address various forms of oppression within the US, such as those at the border in San Diego, in Ferguson, MO, and in private prisons in Arizona. These experiences allowed me to draw connections between these struggles and the occupation and oppression in Palestine. Hassan finds this intertwining of issues complex, but I assure him that when it comes to basic rights, nothing should be complicated.

Unfortunately, upon my return home, my luggage was delayed in Paris. I was especially irritated because I had four pairs of new shoes in my luggage, and they were on Israel's list of banned items at the time.

"What did you do?" he asks.

"Reported it to the missing luggage desk," I reply.

"What happened to the luggage?"

"The lady at the missing luggage desk assured me it would arrive on the next flight," I say with a smirk.

"But how would they get it to you in Gaza?" Hassan asks.

"That's another story, my friend," I tell him with a laugh.

"But you got the luggage?" he asks, intrigued.

I confirm that I did, but not like other passengers.

"How?"

The airport attendant instructed me to fill out a form with my address and a description of the missing bag, which I did and handed it to her.

"The luggage will be delivered to your house between 4-6 pm," she tells me and apologizes for the inconvenience.

"Are you sure, madam?" I inquire.

"Yes," she replies confidently.

"To my address in Rafah, Palestine?" I clarify.

"Yes," she confirms.

"How is that possible?" I ask skeptically.

"We will give it to our airline partner that flies from Cairo to Gaza International Airport," she explains.

"But the airport is out of service," I point out.

"Sir, trust me, I see the flight schedule in the system, landing at 1 pm tomorrow," she insists.

"In Gaza?"

"Yes, the Gaza airport," she affirms.

"I'm sorry, but this is not possible. We live not far from the damaged runway, and I promise I would have heard about it if it had been rebuilt in the past two and a half weeks."

"Sir, our tracking system is accurate, and here is a tracking number," she reassures me.

Despite her confidence, I remain unconvinced. The next afternoon, my cellphone rings, and it's the same airport attendant. She expresses regret, admitting the system failed her and there is no flight departing to Gaza. She tells me there's a system mistake that needs updating.

"My colleagues told me it's a nightmare to send luggage there," she admits.

"I told you, but you believed the tracking system," I remark.

"Please send us an address in Egypt," she requests.

"I am already at the Rafah gate."

The luggage remained in her custody for several months at Cairo International Airport until my next trip, when I was able to retrieve it on the way back.

Hassan bursts out laughing. "You could do a whole comedy routine about that. You know, I saw on social media some people in Gaza are starting to do stand-up comedy. Can you believe it? In the midst of all this chaos, we're finding ways to make each other laugh."

As we say our goodbyes, I feel immensely cheered by his words and the spirit of so many of the young people in Gaza.

Chapter 8

Football and Poetry

Seven miles south of Amira and Shady's parkour performances, I walk into Rotana Café in Rafah, an expansive yet cozy space with bright accent lighting. There is a low hum of conversation and a soothing soundtrack of clinking cups. The air is filled with the aroma of freshly brewed coffee and the space is packed with young people—standing room only—eager for an uplifting moment in Palestine's history. More keep arriving by the minute.

All eyes are on the large projector and the two flatscreen TVs mounted on the side walls, right and left. Everyone is wearing the colors of the national football team and many have flags draped over their shoulders. With red shorts and matching red socks, the team, known as Fida'i—meaning "The Redeemer" in Arabic—is about to kick off an exciting Asian Cup match against Malaysia.

This World Cup qualifier match is being played in Jordan because Israel makes it nearly impossible for matches to take place in the occupied Palestinian territories. But its impact is probably felt most keenly in Gaza, where young people are especially fanatical about soccer. Most support Spanish La Liga teams like Real Madrid and Barcelona or teams from the English Premier League like Manchester United or Arsenal. But this means so much more to all of them.

Chants resound as the Palestine national football team takes the field, proudly wearing the iconic red uniform. The jersey features the vibrant colors of the Palestine flag on the upper left chest over the heart of each player.

"Go Fida'i! Go Fida'i!"

The room is charged as spirits are lifted by the sight of the beloved team. The players assemble on the turf, their faces highlighted by bright spotlights and the camera's intimate focus as pundits expound on each player's unique talents and deficiencies. As players take their positions and the referee checks his watch, the anticipation is almost unbearable.

"Go Fida'i! Go Fida'i!"

In Palestine, the simplest of pleasures, like watching a soccer game, requires permission from multiple authorities. For most Gazans, it would require a Messiah-like miracle to see this game in person. But they are grateful they can still savor the thrill of the game on the big screen without missing a single moment.

"Fida'i! Fida'i! Fida'i!"

Young people exchange high fives and fist bumps, their excitement palpable. Others hold hands, united in support for their team. As the match progresses, the room becomes quieter, everyone holding their breath. The only sounds are the commentator's voice and occasional cheers. The young people are deeply engrossed, and I watch their expressions shift from nervous anticipation to elation to disappointment, mirroring the ups and downs of the game.

I take a moment to step outside for fresh air and find an atmosphere reminiscent of a curfew. Rafah is home to around 300,000 people, yet the streets are eerily silent. The shared passion for the game is keeping everyone in Rafah glued to one screen or another. Locals everywhere are gathering and pooling money for fuel to power small generators in cafés and falafel shops. The sky is a dusky purple and the streetlights cast a pale glow.

Back inside the bright, packed café, the atmosphere remains full of camaraderie amid the hum of the generators that make the moment possible. Young people lean forward in their chairs, hanging onto every second of intense action. It's a rare treat. Palestinians in Gaza are used to seeing nothing but bad news on the television.

"Fida'i! Fida'i! Fida'i!"

Pretty soon no one is sitting at the tables anymore. Everyone is standing up.

When the Palestinian team grabs the opening goal, the Rotana Café erupts into a frenzy of cheering and jumping. Some are even crying. Young and old, men and women, all are cheering and chanting as one.

"Fida'i! Fida'i! Fida'i!"

Amjad Hassouna, 19, a student of Public Management at Gaza University, is enjoying every single moment, hanging on to the words screamed by an overexcited commentator.

"It is a rare occasion when we sit, laugh, and chant for a positive reason. This is a moment where I really feel the joy of being a proud Palestinian," Amjad says. "We have our own national team to shout for and be proud of. This seems like a historic moment, watching our national team play. For a few fleeting, precious minutes, I feel like a normal human."

The electric atmosphere becomes ecstatic as the Palestinian teams scores a second goal. The noisy excitement drowns out the commentator's equally enraptured voice.

"Fida'i! Fida'i! Fida'i!"

When a third Palestinian goal hits the back of the net one minute before halftime (Ahmed Abu Nahyeh's second goal of the game), Sharief Al-Nearab, a Gaza-based broadcaster, bursts into tears of joy. Sharief's eyes are usually fixed on Camp Nou, the home stadium of FC Barcelona, or the Bernabéu, the home field of Real Madrid. But this is on a whole other level.

When Palestine grabs its fourth goal, Sharief jumps up and screams "Palestine!" prompting some younger members of the audience burst into their own tears of joy.

One of the Palestinian players, Abdelhadi Al-Buhdari, is from one of the poorest refugee camps in Rafah and lives just a few blocks from the Rotana Café. This makes it all the more special for the Rotana audience, as many have a personal connection with the player, who used to sit with them watching Real Madrid and Barcelona matches.

"It feels great. My next-door neighbor is making us proud out there," says one young fan at a nearby table.

This game is a golden opportunity to remember there is more to life than attacks, bombs, and death, and there are still things to look forward to. Gaza has some of the wildest fans around, but the owner of the café says he has rarely seen such joy from soccer fans—even when Real Madrid or Barcelona is winning. While the café is always full for important matches in Spain or Egypt, the atmosphere feels different today.

"There is deep emotion in the cheering—something coming deep from a national heart that is usually grieving. This is a rare joy," he says as he sits down to watch the second half of the game. "If you ask me, it's not the blockade that will change us, it's our real connection to the world."

After a fifth Palestinian goal, the audience settles down, reassured their team is cruising to victory and will move ahead to the next stage of the Asian Cup.

On social media, Malaysian fans express solidarity with Palestinians despite the pounding their team received. One tweet, read out at the café, asks how Palestinians manage under the strain of the blockade and in conditions of armed conflict.

The crowd laughs at this comment. Sharief says, "We have turned the ruins of our demolished homes into football fields, because we love life. This is the reality, and this is what the world should be seeing." His eyes brim with tears of joy tinged with hope—such a rare commodity in Gaza.

As the final whistle blows, the crowd erupts in a kind of bliss. Cheers and high fives ring out and fans celebrate as if they had just won the World Cup themselves. All tension dissipates; only joy and elation remain. People chat excitedly, reliving the game's highlights. The energy is contagious and the staff join in the celebration, turning the main café area into a makeshift dance floor. The victory of the Fida'i team sets the streets of Gaza ablaze with celebration as Palestinians of all ages come out to dance, sing, and celebrate. For one night, the city can rest easy knowing victory in a soccer match is the most pressing issue of the moment.

Most Palestinians accept that their heroes are not widely known on the international stage. The team is still relatively new and lacks the sustained media exposure they would need to be more widely appreciated. They compete with wealthy teams in neighboring countries where vast sums are spent promoting the national brand and where players have citizenship and basic human rights, can train and travel freely, and aren't subject to regular violence, restrictions, arbitrary imprisonment, and other collective punishment.[13]

Despite it all, the Palestine team reached a significant milestone by merely qualifying for the Asia Cup for the first time in history. After beating Malaysia 6-0, the Palestinian team has its eyes fixed on qualifying for the World Cup. It remains an unlikely feat for such an underfunded team, but Palestinian fans in Rafah are hopeful—and they'll grab onto any hope they can. Soccer provides a brief distraction from the daily reality of

military occupation, the petty oppression of Israel's long blockade, and constant fear of raids and demolitions. The joy of victory in a soccer match is about the closest thing to freedom and
sovereignty that Palestinians can presently experience.

"It just takes a couple of happy hours like this to recharge
my batteries for national hope," says Amjad, the student I spoke
with earlier, as he heads out of the café. He calls his mom and
dad to tell them the Fida'i made it, but they already know—they
were listening to the match on a battery-powered radio.

Later, Malaysia will win against Bahrain 2-1 in their final
group stage match, which feels like further vindication for the
Palestinian team, the underdogs who played with all their might
and emerged victorious.

Matches between local Palestinian teams in Gaza and the
West Bank can be almost as exciting, but they are frequently
disrupted. Travel between the West Bank and Gaza is extremely
difficult as permits to move from one area to another can be
arbitrarily delayed or denied by the Israeli authorities that rule
our lives.

When a Gaza team had an important game scheduled
against Hebron, FIFA had to intervene to pressure Israel into
allowing the match to take place. This tournament is always
watched enthusiastically by Palestinian football fans—another
rare moment of unity and joy, with people from all corners of
the country gathered on the same soccer field celebrating their
shared love for the game. When the Al Ahli team finally entered
Gaza, the first thing they did was visit the destroyed homes of
athletes in Shujaiya, which was a gesture of solidarity appreciated by everyone.

Hebron's Al Ahli team beat Gaza's Shujaiya team on Gaza's
Al Yarmouk soccer field, claiming the 2015 Palestine Cup.

"It's a dream come true for us to see a West Bank sports
club play alongside our friends and fellow Palestinians in Gaza,

representing one nation," says Kifah Al-Shareef, Al Ahli's Club Director.

I know the celebration and chanting will go on all night, and I wonder if Hassan is still awake. He is not the type to stay up late, but I check Facebook and see that he's online. Who can sleep after such good news? So, I give him a buzz to check what he is up to.

Before I can utter "Hello" from the western side of Rafah, I hear the excitement in Hassan's voice as he picks up the phone.

"Did you watch it? They did it, they did it!"

He tells me how lucky he was to catch the game with his family and neighbors during the four hours of electricity in his area. "It was a blast," he says, a rare expression for him to use. He is usually precise and measured in his words, and if he can simply nod or gesture, that is his preferred response. Right now, he's gushing.

"We are a nation that knows how to live it up!" he says with a giddy laugh, unable to contain his excitement. He tells me celebrations are still raging on the streets of every city in the Gaza Strip (and surely in the West Bank, too) and how the win brought the entire community together.

"It's like a beautiful kiss on a wound. And someday the wound will heal, and life will go on. We love life!" he shouts to the heavens.

Interlude: Toys and Books

Life for Malak and Mohammed has been transforming. Malak previously lacked even essential school supplies for preschool and now has a new schoolbag, plenty of stationery, and a full lunchbox every day. A monthly allowance means her father can afford his medications and care for his wife. Malak learns English quickly, which makes it much easier for the family to stay in touch with their new friends in Houston. She loves colorful dresses and is the center of the attention lavished between Houston and Beit Lahia. Mohammed discovers a passion for drawing and uses the school supplies to hone his art as well as his education.

The completion of their home marks a fresh start, one where Naji can proudly call himself a citizen of his village, complete with access to electricity and water. No more relying on neighbors for basic necessities. The family's long-awaited abode stands proudly, all facilities duly licensed.

Malak may not grasp the full scope of her family's luck, but she's always thrilled by the toys arriving with foreign aid workers from her friends in Texas. In the dusk of a hot afternoon, Malak finds herself in possession of a skateboard, a symbol of rebellion against the shackles on young women in this confined land, while her brother receives a bicycle, a fearless emblem of freedom within the boundaries of Gaza.

Malak's father and I share a knowing look, aware of the challenges facing the family in this new chapter of their lives. Naji's discerning gaze now ventures into the realm of private-sector enterprises, exploring new horizons. As they embark on this transformative journey, their story captivates another family, connected by a profound bond that transcends oceans, sharing immeasurable love despite the physical distance that separates them.

Now that they have access to electricity and the internet, Malak is facing a future where she can communicate as a global citizen through a computer screen. Before I leave, I witness the family in Texas patiently teaching Malak and her brother English, and I have faith and hope that the impact of their kindness will resonate for generations to come. Thanks to the American family's support, Malak will discover passions not only for studying English but also for writing and teaching.

Life teems with exhilarating surprises. I savor every one as it unfolds like an opening leaf before my eyes. It took a simple act of kindness to spark this beautiful connection at the far tip of the north of Gaza, and it all started with an image that shocked an American family living seven thousand miles away. Had they not been in transit through an Arab Gulf airport, the fortuitous hands of fate would never have dealt them a complimentary newspaper adorned with the image of Malak's father. And Malak herself might never have had a home, a future, or a skateboard.

The Houston family remains in direct touch with Malak and her family, and I decide to let this connection flourish on its own. I bid farewell to Malak and to the American clan, confident their bond will continue to grow naturally without my help.

I can't help but think how Mahmoud Darwish, Palestine's beloved national poet, would have been thrilled by the Palestinian team's victory. He would have seen it as a powerful symbol of his people's perseverance and spirit, overcoming countless logistical and financial challenges in their day-to-day struggles for freedom and self-determination.

Darwish would have been impressed by the players' skill and dedication, their pride and determination, and how positively they represent Palestine on the world stage. He might also have contemplated the broader meaning of this triumph for both the Palestinian people and the world community. Victories in sporting events hold the potential to motivate other kinds of struggles for justice and equality.

Darwish might have repeated that message of hope and resilience found in his famed poem "Identity Card." This powerful meditation on the experience of Palestinian identity under occupation uses stark, evocative language to describe how Palestinians have to navigate their way through checkpoints, surveillance, and oppression to assert their simple humanity and dignity in the face of dehumanization. His poem's opening lines are:

Record! I am an Arab
And my identity card is number fifty thousand
I have eight children
And the ninth is coming after a summer
Will you be angry?

Darwish was born in the village of Al Birwa in the Galilee of Palestine. He became a refugee at the age of seven when Israel drove 750,000 Palestinians out of their homes and destroyed hundreds of Palestinian villages, including Darwish's. His journey of exile took him to Moscow, Cairo, Beirut, Tunis, Paris, Amman, and Ramallah, where he settled in 1995. One of the most revered poets in the Arab world, he is the author of more than thirty books of poetry and prose, and his works have been translated into thirty-five languages. His many honors include being named a Knight of the Order of Arts and Letters by France in 1993 and being awarded the Lannan Cultural Freedom Prize in the US in 2001, the Prince Claus Award in 2004, and the Cairo Prize for Arabic Poetry in 2007.

Darwish's poetry conveys the power and beauty of the natural world, and he often writes about living in harmony with the earth. One of his best-known poems is "On This Earth." In it, Darwish describes the beauty and fragility of humanity and the natural world seamlessly:

We have on this earth what makes life worth living:
April's hesitation
The aroma of bread at dawn

A woman's thoughts of men
The works of Aeschylus
The inception of love
Grass on a stone
Mothers who live on the sigh of a flute
And the invaders' fear of memories.

We have on this earth what makes life worth living:
The waning of September
A woman leaving forty in the fullness of her splendor
The hour of sunlight in prison
Clouds imitating a host of creatures
The people's cheers for those who face their end
with a smile
And the tyrants' fear of songs.

Though I never had the opportunity to meet Darwish in person, I have been regaled with tales about him from people who did know him. An Armenian-Dutch journalist friend, Heiko Jessayan, once interviewed Darwish for the Dutch newspaper *Het Financieele Dagblad*, and they got on well together. Among other things, they discussed the plight of Armenian Palestinians who also face the challenges living under a regime that views and treats them as "less than" because they are not Jewish.

One amusing anecdote unfolded on a wintry day in Amsterdam in 2004, after Darwish received the Prince Claus Prize in a ceremony at the Royal Palace in Amsterdam, where he was praised for his unique literary achievements and celebrated for his courage in the struggle for the right to freedom of imagination and cultural expression.

Darwish was strolling alongside Queen Beatrix of the Netherlands in his cozy winter coat when he spotted Heiko among a crowd of gathered journalists. The famous poet paused to greet him with a warm smile and a hearty "Hello, my friend!" showing how he valued friendship in a way that transcended even the presence of royalty.

Arabic poetry can be difficult to translate. In Arabic, the seemingly simple word Ard means land, soil, and planet Earth—an all-encompassing term that speaks to land as a living thing, a cosmic home, a provider of life and delight, not merely something to be bought and sold.

Samira Radwan exemplifies Darwish's love of the land. I meet her on ten dunums of leased land located near Israel's buffer zone in the eastern part of Gaza.

Under the scorching sun, Samira tends to her beloved potato field. She gazes at the rows of potato plants with a mixture of pride and responsibility. Her bond with her land runs deep. She feels a profound sense of duty toward it, akin to a mother caring for her child. "There is no greater joy than witnessing the fruits of our labor coming to life on our own land," she states, her face and arms shimmering with sweat. "Our ancestors planted for us so we could eat, and now we plant for the generations to come."

As she tirelessly harvests the potatoes, each one symbolizing hours of dedication and hard work, a feeling of contentment washes over her. "This land is the cornerstone of our existence and our livelihood. It is the core of our being," she declares, gazing across the expanse of her field. "As long as we stand on our land, we are in control." Samira considers herself fortunate to be from one of the few families who were not displaced from their homes in 1948. Having grown up in Gaza, she's only known farming as a family trade.

"This is my home, and I have nowhere else to go," she says as six family members use a donkey cart to spread fertilizer on the soil. When asked about the significance of the land to her at the age of sixty, she responds, "The land is a living, breathing entity that I am fortunate to nurture and care for. There are no words to describe the connection I feel with this land." She speaks to me while she clears harvested potatoes from the ground and her sons and daughters plant zucchini seeds in another section of the plot.

As she moves on to the next row of potatoes, Samira declares with a playful smile, "I'll never let any potato get away from me." Each dig of her shovel unearths more potatoes, filling her with a profound gratitude for the abundance of the land. Gathering all the boys and girls under a farmer-made canopy, she invites them to admire her handiwork, instilling in them a sense of pride and accomplishment. Samira can't help but smile as she gazes at her hands, covered in dirt, cherishing the connection she feels with the earth.

"Having dirt under my nails is a small price to pay for the joy of being one with the land," she reflects before sending her grandchild to fetch lemon sorbet from a nearby mini-market, providing everyone with some momentary relief from the heat.

I have the privilege of meeting Samira on multiple occasions. She shares with me how she continues to view international visitors to Gaza as an opportunity to share her story and the stories of her people. With open arms, she welcomes visitors, eager to showcase the beauty and resilience of Gaza. She sees guests as brave and compassionate individuals who willingly risk their own safety to bring attention to the suffering of the Palestinian people. She has a deep appreciation for their efforts to tell the world that, behind the headlines and statistics, there are real people with real lives.

After the sorbet tasting, Samira leads her latest guests, including two international journalists, on a tour of her land, proudly displaying the fruits of her labor alongside the challenges she faces. The guests are moved by her words and inspired by her determination. Following the tour, Samira warmly invites all of us to share a meal with her family, and we savor a feast of traditional Palestinian dishes. Samira captivates them with stories from her childhood and her life on the land she leases from her uncles. Touched by her hospitality and warmth, the guests depart Gaza with a renewed admiration for the strength and courage of the Palestinian people.

Chapter 9

Weddings and Woofs

As the sun rises over Gaza City, the steamy summer air hums with excitement and anticipation. Ethereal clouds float by and a gentle breeze is scented with carnations and other freshly cut flowers. It sets the scene for hundreds of couples getting married in a mass wedding, perfectly coordinated under a brilliant blue sky.

Gaza's streets are abuzz with guests in their finest embroidered clothes, linen suits, and dresses sparkling in the sunlight like a thousand diamonds. A joyous din mingles with soft strains of music. Crowds of friends and families drift into the massive soccer stadium where the ceremony will take place. There is a touch of traditional beauty in this modern occasion where vows will be exchanged and couples will embark on a journey of loving togetherness.

This mass wedding of approximately four hundred Palestinian men and women was made possible by the support of Arab donors. Such occasions are rare, happening maybe twice per decade when a benevolent donor steps forward to bring hope and happiness to couples facing financial challenges.

These festivals of love not only unite hearts but also exemplify the compassionate spirit that binds communities together in times of need.

Typically, tens of thousands of couples register for mass weddings and wait, hoping a donor will be found. A lucky few are chosen either through a raffle or through what is drolly called Vitamin W, which stands for *wasta*, meaning "connections."

I spoke with political analysts in Gaza about the huge expense of these occasions. Adnan Abu Amer, a dean at Al-Ummah University, said, "It seems Gaza is becoming a place for regional powers to show off, dropping money here and there to influence the political map where people are most desperate. Nonetheless, Palestinians will accept help when it is offered."

Preparing for a Gazan mass wedding typically involves the whole community. Family members, municipal councils, community organizations, neighbors, and local businesses all pitch in. Some provide food and decorations. Others help with setup and cleanup. Gaza's sense of community is unparalleled, and everyone takes pride in these events and the happiness they bring.

Anticipation permeates the stadium as guests take their seats. The air seems charged with love. The music swells, gates swing open, and brides enter grandly in flowing white gowns— visions of beauty and grace. Normally, a newly wedded bride holds a separate, closed-door celebration, but in mass weddings, the celebration is open to the public and every bride brings not only their partner but also a sister, niece, or other relative for the photo opportunity. Proud grooms in their wedding finery part the bustling crowds to locate their brides in the throng.

A student who's skipping her late-afternoon summer school mathematics class tells me she's here to witness a friend get married after a four-year college love story. "Why settle for a mere slice of wedding cake when you can indulge in a whole banquet of love and celebration?" she says, excited to share her friend's joy. Her friend's groom teaches computer skills to children, which doesn't pay enough to save up for a wedding. "I'm so happy they got this opportunity!"

The custom of mass weddings in Gaza dates back to 1977 as a means to help couples who could not afford an expensive traditional wedding ceremony. Since poverty and unemployment are widespread, it's not just weddings that are unaffordable. Expensive household goods like appliances and furniture are also out of reach for many. Some Palestinian companies step in to offer gifts like fridges, cupboards, and washing machines for newly married couples to help ease the financial burdens. (Of course, nothing says "newlywed bliss" in Gaza like spoiled food in a useless fridge during yet another power cut.)

One of the remarkable aspects of Gazan mass weddings is the sense of equality they create among the couples. A fancy wedding ceases to be a privilege reserved for the wealthy few. Couples from all backgrounds and financial situations celebrate their commitment to their partner together in a way that is as meaningful as it is affordable. Though not everyone will be lucky enough to receive free appliances, any couple who needs a washing machine will receive support, even if it means a neighbor will offer to do their laundry for a year or two.

As couples exchange vows, a feeling of elation pervades the festive crowd. Once the brides and grooms unite as one and the ceremony ends, the true celebration begins. People cannot contain their desire to cut loose and dance. Soon the floor is filled with swaying hips and shimmying shoulders, and the dancing continues well into the night.

One couple, Ashraf, 31, and Aisha, 28, have been in love for more than a decade. When they first met, Ashraf would often race through Rafah's crowded streets to reach Al Qadisiya Secondary School for Girls, where Aisha eagerly awaited him.

Ashraf understood the perils of waiting for Aisha outside her school, given Gaza's more conservative social norms. A special unit police force might even detain Ashraf and shave his head as punishment if he was caught. Still, Ashraf was determined to be with Aisha and was willing to take the risk; he was in love and couldn't imagine a life without her. So, he waited for her outside the school every day and kept a low profile. As Aisha came out, he followed her quietly. Anyone passing would think nothing of a random pair of students returning from school, apparently unconnected to one another. She was secretly thrilled but initially a bit shy. Sometimes I would spot him following in Aisha's wake when he passed by Hassan's lab. When they thought no one was looking, they would talk quietly back and forth. Sometimes crowds also gave them cover to chat covertly.

Aisha's father is known for his talent in growing and making green olive pickles. He is a proud man who works tirelessly to ensure his pickles are made from only the freshest, highest-quality ingredients. His home is a destination for people from all parts of Gaza who love the unique taste of his creations. Aisha grew up with the aroma of olive oil and spices all her life. She watched her father carefully select each olive and conjure a perfect blend of flavors. She has learned the value of hard work as well as the weight of honoring and cherishing one's craft.

She inherited his passion for excellence and is determined to make a name for herself in her own right. Through her father's example, Aisha has also learned generosity and hospitality, as her family's home is always open to visitors, and her father's tasty pickles are shared with all. Even so, if her father caught her with Ashraf, he might not be happy at the thought of her being courted by this young man!

Aisha and Ashraf were determined to be together, even if they couldn't afford the cost of marriage. They found small moments of joy in stolen glances and secret meetings. Their bond grew stronger until they shared a deep love for each other, but their dream wedding, plus setting up a new house, proved impossible as the price tag reaches $13,000 for a dowry, a traditional communal feast, transportation expenses for huge extended families, a wedding hall, dresses, make-up, flowers, and furniture and appliances. Even wealthy Gazans can barely afford it.

After eleven long years of knowing and then loving each other, luck was finally on their side when they were among 400 couples selected out of a waiting list of over 12,000 for the latest mass wedding.

When the day arrives, Aisha's happiness shines in her eyes. "This is finally a chance to be recognized as a couple and to share our happiness with our families and friends," she says. "Our love, patience, and commitment have paid off."

"I have not been wasting my time," Ashraf says, looking lovingly at his bride. "I was in love. If you are in love, no time is wasted." He laughs, holding Aisha's hand, and says he wants to walk with her on all the streets where they couldn't walk together before.

Aisha's uncle, a retired public servant, rolls up in a beautifully decorated dark blue Mercedes adorned with bright colorful flowers, red ribbons, and white balloons. Red lightbulbs hang inside. He's built a business repairing and reselling old luxury cars and is an expert on the fifty-year-old Mercedes Benz model that's a common sight in Gaza, often used as shared taxis.

Aisha approaches the car and her uncle greets her with a broad smile. "Welcome to my vintage ride, my dear niece!"

Aisha can't help but laugh and admire the car's unique and charming character. She hops in, ready to take in the sights and sounds of Gaza at its best.

"It's a bumpy ride, but we'll get you there in style," her uncle jokes.

Aisha can't imagine arriving any other way and feels grateful for her uncle's special touch on her wedding day. She and her groom are accompanied in the back of the car by Habiba ("Beloved"), a white Labrador retriever with a red ribbon around her neck. The dog looks content as they all set off toward the wedding ceremony, and Ashraf pets her fondly. They know the dog provides their uncle with a great deal of emotional support and loyalty that he relies on during tough times. As they cruise through the city, people stop to gaze in admiration. Aisha's uncle is as vintage as his car, turned out proudly in a neat 1970s suit jacket and white trousers, looking like he just stepped out of an old black and white Egyptian movie.

Ashraf and Aisha arrive at the venue in their finest attire, ready for the big day. The stadium is brimming with music, dancing, and laughter, which quietens as the ceremony begins. Ashraf and Aisha gaze into each other's eyes and exchange rings, sealing their commitment in front of fellow newlyweds, family, and friends. Like the others, they are soon presented with a gift from the event's sponsors: a brand-new fridge. The apartment where they will start their new life is provided by Aisha's father until they can find their own housing. ।

Ashraf and Aisha look back on their schooldays as some of the happiest of their lives. They plan to tell their children and grandchildren of how they were part of a community celebration and about the sense of equality and solidarity that came from being married this way. They snap a picture of Aisha holding the voucher for the wedding gift, her gossamer wedding gown flowing around her. She looks stunning in an ornate headpiece, her hair and makeup done to perfection.

"The waiting is worth it," she says, her smile shy yet beaming.

"It could not be more perfect," Ashraf agrees. "The rich can get married, and the poor can get married, too."

The whirlwind ceremony is a celebration they will never forget, and when it's over, the couple seems to glide back to Aisha's beautifully decorated marriage car with Aisha's mother carrying the train of the white dress behind her.

Cruising through the bustling streets after the wedding, pedestrians stop to catch a glimpse of the magnificent vintage Merc. People wave and shout their congratulations to the beaming newlyweds in the backseat. Habiba has her head out the window, the wind in her fur, taking in the sights and sounds of the crowded city.

Ashraf pulls his new wife close. "Thank you for being my partner for life. And hey, our wedding was as royal as it gets," Ashraf adds, indicating the thousands of people celebrating with them.

He's right. The wedding exuded a regal aura with its impeccable attention to detail, majestic vintage cars, and grand decorations that could rival a royal celebration. It leaves a trail of excitement and hope for thousands of couples waiting for the turn they deserve. The generosity of all who contribute made these events possible, a manifestation of the spirit of community and generosity in Gaza.

Habiba the Labrador points to yet another change sweeping through Gaza. Palestinians have always kept pets at home—mainly cats, birds, and fish—but tend to see dogs as dirty street creatures instead of beloved family members and constant companions. Only recently have social media and outside influences begun to shift this perspective.

On platforms like Instagram and Facebook, dogs doing funny things are unavoidable, and sharing these images and videos helps normalize dog ownership. Thanks to the culture of photo tagging, people from north to south Gaza are connected by their mutual interest in canines.

The sun glints off the water on a peaceful summer morning on Gaza's Mediterranean coastline. The stillness is broken as dozens of dogs rush to the beach for their morning runaround, kicking up sand in their wake, their coats glistening in the rising sun. Tails wagging and tongues lolling, they dart in and out of the surf chasing each other, digging in the sand, or playing fetch with their human companions. Some dogs jump into the water, paddling energetically through the waves, while others prefer to stay on the shore, rolling crazily in the sand or barking at the waves, their yelps filling the air with excitement and joy.

Hundreds of proud owners look on, laughing and taking pictures of the antics. There's a general din of people shouting, "*Taali, Zara!*" (Come here, Zara!) and otherwise talking and bonding with each other and their four-legged friends.

This scene is a departure from the traditional attitude towards dogs in Muslim communities based on Islamic teaching that dogs are *nijs* (unclean/impure)—*haram* in fact. Some *hadith* (prophetic teachings) say that believers are advised not to keep dogs, and certainly not inside their houses. According to Abu Hurayrah in one *hadith*, the Prophet Muhammad said: "Whoever keeps a dog, except a dog for herding, hunting or farming, one *qiraat* [measure] will be deducted from his reward each day."

But dogs are only mentioned briefly, and positively, in the Quran itself.

I'm sure a range of religious pronouncements will continue to be made on this topic. But all evidence suggests a more relaxed view is spreading in Gaza. Local authorities attempted to ban dogs in public places, but the pro-canine community pushed back, and the authorities have been unwilling or unable to stop the meet-ups on the beach.

I meet Mohammed Abdulkhadir, an agricultural engineer who used to fear dogs due to a close friend's terrifying encounter with military dogs during an Israeli invasion. His views changed after his daughter took a liking to another family's dog. Before they knew it, the family began to care for their own friendly mutt.

"My daughter loves the dog, so I now have another member of the family," he says, grinning. "In fact, we now seem to have adopted seven dogs, and the numbers keep growing." The six black and one brown pup surrounding him wag their tails in affirmation.

"When I first brought the dogs, none of my relatives would come to visit. But now everyone comes," he says. "Walking my dogs along the sunny beach is my favorite hobby now. I suppose it's my way of escaping the daily pressures and the ominous political reality that's beyond our capacity to solve."

In recent years, looking after these pets has become more challenging. "Vaccines for puppies are often blocked at the border crossings," he explains. "When supplies get through, the handover time is long, and the vaccines have usually expired." When unexpired vaccines do get through, they are pricy. Farmers with dogs cannot afford them.

"We keep asking for the vaccinations to be allowed through the crossings. It's a matter of public health. And dogs in Gaza have a tough job—they're more than man's best friend, they're also unofficial stress-relievers, adventure buddies, and cuddle partners. Our new Facebook page is full of information about how to take care of them. But we can't make our own vaccines."

As he sets up his lawn chair and opens a cooler full of drinks, he greets other dog owners with a smile and a nod. Soon the group starts chatting and laughing, sharing stories about their furry friends. Mohammed listens intently as someone shares training tips for a particularly stubborn pup and another describes his most recent experience at a dog show in Juhor ad-Dik, south of Gaza City. He shares a story about how his dog protected him during a scary encounter with street dogs on a walk, and the group nods in appreciation.

The dogs continue to run free on the shore, bounding into the waves, chasing each other and splashing water everywhere, their tails wagging furiously. Mohammed notices one dog nearby, a small terrier that seems afraid to join in the fun. Using online courses, he has taught himself a great deal about training dogs and dealing with various disorders. Dog trainers are now in high demand in Gaza, including those who train dogs for security and safety purposes for homes and businesses.

He approaches the dog's owner, a woman named Mariam, and asks if her dog is shy around other dogs. Mariam nods sadly and explains that the dog was rescued from an abusive situation and is still learning to trust other dogs and humans.

He listens patiently and suggests some exercises to help build the dog's confidence. He offers to introduce the terrier to a friend's dogs known for their gentle and friendly demeanor. Mariam and her dog slowly approached Maher Jaber's dogs Ramos and Stella, who greet them with a wag of their tails. The three dogs sniff each other cautiously and are soon playing together, with the new dog friends gently nudging the smaller dog into the waves.

A 28-year-old barbershop owner named Ahmed strokes his German Shepherd affectionately. "With all the chaos going on, having a dog is like having a furry little therapist who never judges and always listens," he says. Ahmed has a dream to design a public platform to advocate for animal rights in general.

There is a special bond, an unconditional love, between a good master and their trusting, loyal dog—a bond that can last a lifetime. You can tell a lot about a person, says Ahmed, from how they treat their pets.

Omaima, age ten, arrives late in the afternoon with her dad and her twin golden retrievers, a breed not often found in Gaza. She had to wait for her father's work day to end so he could give her a ride.

"This is a perfect day for me," she says. A Palestinian woman in an orange hijab passes by with her children who stop to play with Omaima's two dogs. "Who needs toys when you've got sand, water, and a bunch of doggy friends to play with?"

A child says with a grin, "Looks like the dogs are having more fun than the humans."

Omaima jokes, "Hey, dogs, forget these boring humans, let's go fetch some treats and have our own party." She grabs the leash and leads the two furry blonde dogs toward the beach with a carefree laugh.

Omaima is fortunate to have delightful dogs and a caring father who diligently ensures her constant amusement after his working hours. It is an undeniable blessing for a child to be unburdened by responsibilities, exempt from the arduous task of commencing labor at the tender age of six or eight or ten to sustain family members, like many disadvantaged children at quail's nets on the shore, or selling popcorn, juices, and lollies.

The question of which Gaza families can afford the expense of one, two, or even more dogs becomes intriguing. The crowds on the beach appear to have enough income to afford caring for dogs, but they are not among the elite of the tunnel economy. It's possible some are going into debt or going without food themselves to support their canine habit.

Maher Jaber established the Facebook page called "Gaza German dogs" that attracted all these dog enthusiasts and led to this meet-up. He's surprised by the massive response, both online and in person. "We've become the first youth gathering to take care of dogs in Gaza," he says with a broad smile as he lets his two dogs off the leash for a run on the beach with their many dog friends. "Just in Gaza, we have about 60 percent of all global breeds." He explains how Israel's blockade restricts dog ownership. High shipping prices mean the cost is around $500–$1000 to bring a dog into Gaza.

"Despite difficulties, I am delighted to have helped bring twenty-one new dogs from abroad to families here through my Facebook page," says Jaber. Not everyone can afford the special foods and vaccinations that dogs require; most of these dog owners have regular employment. For him, it costs more than $100 per month to cover the costs of each dog's food and vaccinations. But he says it's worth it. His dogs calm him down, teach him patience, bring him joy, and help him focus on the simple pleasures in life instead of politics and wars.

"My dogs' parents are Kisel from Germany and Wenny from Israel." He grins from ear to ear, showing the birth certificates of his dogs to his two children. "Now we have relatives in Germany and in Israel. Remembering this always makes me smile."

After he created his Facebook page, Gazan merchants started to express greater willingness to import canine food and supplies, sensing the growing demand. This meet-up is a way to build community and support among dog owners and to show they are here to stay.

Omaima's mother has brought a basket of fresh Sheikh Ijlin grapes and a chilled bottle of lemonade. The family sits together, chatting and watching as the sun dips toward the horizon and paints the sky in shades of pink, orange, and purple.

As darkness descends, people reluctantly call their furry friends to their side and gather their things, getting ready for snuggles and a good night's sleep. The sound of waves on the shore is replaced by the hum of car engines. Omaima falls asleep in the car, a smile on her face, thinking of the next time she will play with her dogs on the beach. When they arrive home, the dogs jump out of the car, tails wagging. Omaima runs inside to get them treats while her dad takes a moment on the terrace to savor the beauty of the evening sky.

On the same beaches, but at the other end of the economic spectrum, Gaza's fishermen gather to pull what sustenance they can from the sea. I join Ayman Alamodi, a father of four who began his fishing career three decades ago, for a day's journey on the water following a ceasefire after weeks of relentless Israeli air strikes and naval shelling along Gaza's coast.

His boat, stagnant in the water for so long, bears the wear and tear of neglect, with faded paint and parts of the deck showing signs of rot. The meticulously woven fishing nets, crafted by Ayman's weathered hands, hang limp and lifeless, burdened by silt and debris. Nevertheless, he races to catch whatever fish he can before sunset or a breach of the ceasefire.

Sharing a boat with nine other relatives, including his 34-year-old nephew Mouneer, poses a challenge as they collectively sustain seventy family members. All eyes are fixed on them, hoping they will return with enough food.

But after a few hours at sea, the fish we caught hardly cover the cost of the fuel used to run the boat's motor. Ayman and Mouneer clear the fishing nets of crabs and proceed with the small sardines. On his way back to Al Shati refugee camp, Ayman avoids passing in front of the gas station, knowing he can't settle his fuel debt this time. However, he remains hopeful tomorrow will be better.

Palestinian fishermen suffered severe losses when Israeli F-16s repeatedly struck sheds storing fishing equipment.

Amjad Shrafi, deputy head of the Gaza Fishermen's Syndicate, tells me that in one month of bombardment, Israeli shelling cost the fishing industry about $3 million in damage to fishing gear alone. The Israeli navy also regularly confiscates fishing boats on the thinnest of pretenses.

Sadly, the loss does not end with money and equipment. It's common for Israeli navy ships to fire on Gaza fishermen without provocation, or for approaching the arbitrary three-nautical-mile limit imposed by Israel. Occasionally, Israel "generously" grants access to six nautical miles. Under the Oslo Accords, Palestinians should be granted access to twenty nautical miles off the Gaza coast, but this almost never happens in practice. Ayman knows all the names of his fellow fishermen who have been arrested, injured, or killed while fishing. The list is long, and some are his own relatives.

As a result of Israel's theft, violence, destruction, and restrictions, about 95% of Gaza's fishermen live in poverty.[14]

"It's honestly a waste of time," Ayman says. "There are no fish within three miles now. Further out, beyond six miles, there are natural stones where we can find a variety of delicious and nourishing fish." His hands, roughened by the elements, expertly moor his fishing boat to the harbor with twists and turns of the rope. As the sun prepares to set, I don't envy the plight of the seventy souls dependent on this boat for their lives. Another day will dawn promising nothing more than bread and tea. Even securing them all a morsel of fish to eat is not assured in such a limited, fished-out zone.

A few years later I talk to him again and ask if there's been anything new in his fishing career. He grins before letting go of a rope and jumping sideways onto the jetty.

"After the Arab Spring, I was able to go beyond twelve nautical miles and catch all types of Mediterranean fish."

"Ah, those were golden days," Mouneer chimes in. "We saw fish in shapes and sizes I had never seen before."

"We kept at it for weeks, every single day," Ayman says, relishing the memory. "We were under the watchful eyes of gunships from both sides, but it was such joy when our boats mingled with Egyptian fishing boats."

"That was a lot of fun," Mouneer agrees.

They were able to motor into Egyptian waters after the widely hated Mubarak regime was overthrown. The Israeli army didn't want to chase Gaza fishermen into Egyptian waters, and the "new Egypt" had no interest in chasing them back toward dangerous Israeli war ships.

Eventually the "new Egypt" reverted to a new dictatorship, and the "party" was over. This new dictatorship, like Mubarak's, is complicit in maintaining Israel's occupation and blockade of Gaza, punishing an entire nation in exchange for economic and security incentives, mostly from the US.

Ayman goes on, describing the days when they pulled into Gaza seaport with their boat weighed down by a colorful array of shimmering fish—silver-sided mackerel, iridescent sardines, diplodus sargus, sea bream, sea bass and majestic tuna. He tells me how they gleamed in the sunlight as they were hauled ashore. Being a coastal area, Gaza's culinary tradition naturally includes many fish and other seafood dishes. But the low availability and high price of fish has rendered it a rare luxury.

If Israel would allow Gaza to sustain itself—to fish its waters and trade with the West Bank and Jordan—Gaza's fishermen could freely harvest, enjoy, and share the treasures of their sea and fill Palestine, once again, with all kinds of fish.

Chapter 10

After the Last Sky

In my school days, long before I had any notion of mass weddings or pampered pups or an "Arab Spring," I'm strutting down the road on my way to school. In the nascent hours of a parched and brisk spring day in my tenth year, I wave and greet familiar faces with a smile and pause to pet a friendly, grubby street dog and admire colorful flowers in a neighbor's garden.

Unlike some of my classmates, I don't have a lunch pail with my favorite cartoon characters on it (Teenage Mutant Ninja Turtles). Instead, I transport my bread and *zaatar* sandwich (always topped with strong red *shatta*, a Palestinian chili sauce) in a simple plastic bag. At my UN-run school, I get bored in my math class but perk up when we begin exploring art and folklore. Even better, a visiting artist teaches us how to perform magic tricks with colors on paper.

Walking home again, my head is buzzing from the long day of discovering new knowledge and delving into fresh ideas. Home is a long way off, almost an hour's walk, but I'm used to it and enjoy the fresh air and adventure, at least when the weather's good. I look down at my hands, marked by the lingering cruelty of winter's harsh grasp, with crevices and fissures etched upon my skin. If there's one thing that bothers me as a child, it's this skin rash. I'm so glad those cold days are over, for now.

Today it's beautiful, and I'm looking forward to dishing the juicy details of my day to my mother and siblings. I walk with a spring in my step, humming the national anthem, which has been stuck in my mind all day. It has the same name as our national football team: *Fida'i.*

Along the way I come to the cement wall, almost ten miles long, that divides Palestine from Egypt. Two older women in white head scarves are leaning against the wall, each wearing a beautiful traditional black *thawb.* One has her ear pressed to the wall, straining to hear any sound from the other side.

I hesitantly approach, not wanting to intrude but unwilling to pass by without acknowledging them. As I get closer, the lady with her ear pressed against the wall glances up at me and nods her head in greeting. Her eyes are large and dark, set beneath heavy brows. There is a sense of seriousness but also kindness in her round and weathered face. Her full lips turn slightly down at the corners.

I return the gesture and sit beside them on a wooden plank by the sandy pathway between the wall and nearby homes, watching curiously.

The woman smiles. "My name is Rayah. This is my sister, Hind. You remind me of one of my grandsons," she says affectionately. Hind doesn't say a word, but her sympathetic and supportive gestures speak volumes. From the dust on their feet, I can tell they've come a long way on sandy roads, passing the sycamore tree to get here. The tree is famous in the area, thriving naturally for decades and offering a snack of juicy, zesty sycamore berries to anyone passing by.

"For years now I've come here," she explains, seeming to enjoy an unexpected audience, "ever since this wall separated me from my cousins and my eldest daughter, Samaher. She's married now." Rayah looked longingly toward the wall, as if willing herself to look through it. When the border was imposed, it cut the town of Rafah in half—an Egyptian side and a Palestinian side. It cut many families in half, too.

As I listen, basking in the warming sun and gentle breeze, Rayah hears a familiar voice so distant it sounds like little more than a whisper. She shushes me and gestured for me to listen. I tune in and just barely make out a voice calling out. The streets are deserted—it's siesta time—and Rayah's excitement grows as she tries to discern the words.

"What is she saying?" she eagerly asks me.

"She says she's been waiting under a tree for an hour, and are you there?"

Rayah shakes her head and laments, "I can't make out anything she's saying." Her frustration is palpable.

"I can hear her," I pipe up.

With newfound hope, Rayah asks me to respond, "Oh my love, I am so sorry, we are here, but I can't hear you."

I take a deep breath and give it my all, straining my vocal cords to the limit.

To our joy and amazement, we hear a response. It's Samaher saying, "Mom, I miss you! Who is there with you?"

"I miss you, too, *habibti*, and your Aunt Hind is here with me!" I shout back.

Samaher responds eagerly, asking about her siblings and Aunt Hind.

"We are all doing fine, love. Tell me about your wellbeing?" I call out to her.

Samaher answers that she is doing well and her mother-in-law treats her kindly. Rayah asks about her son-in-law, Fouad, and Samaher responds that he is doing well, too.

Rayah suddenly takes my face in her hands and thanks me, pressing her lips gently to my cheek, a simple gesture that conveys warm appreciation. I can feel that despite the physical barriers separating her from her daughter, their bond transcends all boundaries.

Hind holds Rayah's hand tightly while I strain to hear more. The wind is capricious, sometimes carrying her words over with ease, at other times snatching them away so they are lost in the distance.

In a moment of stillness, the faint voice conveys exciting news: "Mom, I am pregnant and we are expecting our fourth child!"

"*Mabrook*, my love! How long have you known?" Rayah asks me to call out.

"Four months, Mama," Samaher replies.

Overwhelmed with emotion, Rayah sits on a cornerstone and sheds tears of joy.

My curiosity is piqued about what Samaher looks like and what life is like on the other side of the wall. After a few moments of searching, I spot a small crevice in the wall just wide enough for my foot. Ignoring warnings to desist, I wedge my foot into the crevice and begin to climb, gripping the rough surface with my fingers and pulling myself up one handhold at a time.

"Oh, my Lord, be careful," Rayah warns.

As I climb higher, the world around me is transformed. Silence gives way to the rushing wind and my own heart pounding in my ears. I feel exhilaration but also fear. When I reach the top of the wall, my arms and legs trembling with the effort, I peer over the edge and see the world beyond the border, a place of mystery and wonder that I have only ever dreamed of. I feel a sense of freedom and possibility that I never felt before. Looking down the steep drop behind me, I tell Rayah that I see her daughter and a child with her. I look into the distance and wave hello to Samaher for her mother.

"Who do you have with you?" Rayah asks me to call out to her daughter.

"Mansour is my youngest. He's four years old." I describe the scene as Samaher and little Mansour wave. They are standing in the sun on the side of the road. Behind them is a border police officer next to a tree, observing. Beyond them I see an expanse of empty asphalt, then yellowish Egyptian houses.

I don't dare stay too long, as I might be spotted from an Israeli watchtower. As I climb down, my heart is filled with a mix of excitement and reluctance to head away from what looks like a world of adventure just beyond the border.

"Mom, are you okay?" asks Samaher.

Rayah's voice breaks through my thoughts. "I'm fine. A little overwhelmed." My voice shakes with emotion too.

"How's everything on your side?" Samaher's voice asks.

"We're all doing okay, waiting for your father's exit permit so he can visit you."

"I just want you all to be safe." Samaher's voice trembles.

"Your sister, Sherine, is pregnant with her third baby," I say on behalf of Rayah, who's changed the subject.

"*Alf alf mabrook*! How's her son doing, the one born with a cleft palate?" Samaher asks eagerly.

"He's doing well, he's in preschool now," Rayah replies.

"Mom, what about my brothers? How are they?" Samaher's voice is loaded with longing.

"Walid is finishing up his last year of school and wants to go to teacher college in Khan Younis," Rayah answers.

"I remember holding Walid as a baby." Samaher's voice breaks with nostalgia.

"Yes, and you got married in Egypt, my dear," Rayah reminds her. "Everyone sends their love. Your Uncle Jamal asks about you often."

"I miss him so much. How is he doing?"

"Last week he turned 65 and is a happy grandfather," Rayah answers.

As they continue to talk, the mother relaxes and settles into the moment, basking in the warmth and love they share. She closes her eyes and smiles, savoring the simple joy of this connection with her child. These moments remind them how deep-rooted the love of family is that shapes their lives. The daughter eagerly shares updates on her husband's physiotherapy after he slipped at work, while Rayah talks about her third daughter's wedding plans and other anecdotes from their daily life. Hind sits and nods.

Samaher confides that she had irregular spotting during early pregnancy. Her mother offers words of encouragement and support, drawing on her own life experiences to offer guidance and advice to her daughter. She explains possible reasons for the bleeding, which Samaher mistakenly perceived as a delayed period.

"Darling, always say *alhamdulillah*, for the bad news and for the good news," Rayah tells her daughter. "What is meant to be is meant to be, okay, love?"

"Yes, Mama, *Alhamdulillah*," Samaher replies.

It seems they forget sometimes that a ten-year-old boy is acting as their telephone. The conversation is teaching me lessons beyond my years.

The mother reminisces about happy times from their past and shares her dreams that Walid will attend college and become a teacher. "My sweet love, stay strong—you are not alone. Even if you feel alone, we are with you," says Rayah. Hind listens intently. This is a long goodbye as neither mother nor daughter wants to depart.

"Mama, I worry about you," the daughter says.

The mother laughs. "We should be worried about you, darling. I may be old, but I'm tougher than a camel's toenails."

Their banter makes me smile, too, reminding me that we can almost always find humor in life's difficulties.

Finally, the daughter prepares to leave, saying she needs to catch the last public bus to town. "I love you, Mom, love you, Aunt Hind—*salamat* to all," she says and briskly departs with her small son.

Rayah turns to me and asks, "She is all right, isn't she?"

I assure her that her daughter is doing great.

"Did she put on weight?"

"Do you think she might be storing up for the next winter?" I ask.

Rayah chuckles. "No, you... Hm, I do not know your name."

"I am Mohammed, and my house is over there. You can always come to me and I can shout out for you after school."

Rayah digs into her chest pocket and pulls out her wallet. She sifts through it for a moment before pulling out a coin and extending it toward me. "You've been calling out all afternoon. Go get yourself an ice cream. It'll do your throat good."

I take the coin, touched by her kindness. Even in tough times, there's still so much good in the world. I tell her I don't know who should pay whom, as I learned so much from this exchange between a mother and her daughter. Hand in hand, Rayah and Hind wander off toward their homes, going over the latest family updates from the daughter who feels a little closer now, yet still much too far away.

Decades later, the border beckons me to embark again on the familiar path I once took accompanied by Rayah and Hind. The stark transformation strikes me deeply. The houses have been ravaged and the landscape bears the scars of hardship. My favorite cactus plants are gone.

I'm guiding a group of friends from *Vice*, offering them a firsthand encounter with the harsh reality of life in Gaza as part of a poignant film series. Walking along the border between the Palestinian and Egyptian sides of Rafah is a wild and zany adventure. The towering cement wall and the military patrols add to the feeling you're on a top-secret mission.

At the same time, there's a familiarity and sense of community in this border area. On either side of the wall, homes and mini-markets bustle with family activity, as if the wall is just another part of our daily routine. I can hear children playing, vendors peddling their goods, and families chattering away on both sides of the divide. On a quiet evening, I hear a neighbor on the Egyptian side yelling at her husband to pick up toilet paper on the way home. I hear a son whining about how there's no salt in his salad. On a particularly silent night, I hear a mother sing a lullaby to her baby.

Living on the border brings home the ingenuity and resilience of people in Palestine and Egypt, who find ways to carry on with humor and positivity despite facing many challenges. At any moment you can stumble on a hidden gem like a street vendor who sells the best falafel in town, decorated with sesame seeds in the unique Palestinian way, or a carob juice cart that springs up out of nowhere offering ice-cold cups of exotic sweetness that sing through the body on a hot day.

I make my way west, planning to walk the twelve kilometers to the beach, and am struck by the multitudes of people shouting to their loved ones on the other side, a cacophony of voices. This divide has had a profound impact on two or three generations already. The Barhoum family, for instance, is divided almost equally between the two sides. One half has proper documentation, citizenship, and human rights, and the other does not. The powers that be cannot seem to grasp the importance of familial bonds.

I meet another woman, Layla El-Masry, sitting amid the trees on top of a hill overlooking her grandmother's home in Egypt. Layla's name has a romantic, poetic feel to it, as it means 'night' and is featured in the famous Arabian love story of Layla and Majnun. But this story is about Layla and Maisoon, her mother. Layla has been allowed to see her mother only twice in the past twenty years.

"The sole distinction between us is simple—my mom holds Egyptian citizenship, while I am a Palestinian with no citizenship anywhere," Layla says.

Born in 1986 to an Egyptian mother and a Palestinian father, Layla came into the world four years after the wall dividing Gaza and Egypt was built. At the time of her birth, Layla's mother happened to be on the Egyptian side of Rafah visiting her parents and was unable to return to Gaza and reunite with her husband after Layla was born. A border policy was imposed by the Israeli military administration deciding who was allowed to enter and who was not. As an Egyptian, Israel considered her a foreigner and refused to grant her Palestinian papers.

"It wasn't until I was five years old that I finally made it back to Gaza," she tells me. "I visited my father to meet his sick mother, my grandmother. And I never got a permit from Israel to leave Gaza again."

Israel still controls the Gaza population registry, which includes family reunification requests. Without the permission of Israeli authorities, her mother cannot enter Gaza legally.

Her next opportunity to visit her mother came in 2005, when Israel removed illegal settlers from the area. Layla was nineteen years old, and the reunion with her mother was poignant and emotional, almost overwhelming. For so many long years she had only known her mother through photos and distant interactions behind a heavily guarded divide. She was able to visit many other relatives, too.

"But our joy was short-lived. I had to leave a few days later, before the border closed."

Layla often wonders if her life would have been easier if she was just one or the other. At least, she jokes, she is not half Klingon. That would really complicate things. On the bright side, she can always choose which half of her body gets to experience the electricity shortage and which half gets to experience water shortages.

She points to the spot in the distance. "That's where my mom's home once stood."

Egyptian authorities have been destroying homes on the other side of the wall to curtail tunnel smuggling. Most Gazans know the tunnels as a lifeline in the face of Israel's relentless blockade, which imposes severe restrictions and micromanages everything that gets into Gaza, from chocolate and pasta to insulin and sanitary products. Dov Weisglass, an adviser to Israeli Prime Minister Ehud Olmert, said, "The idea is to put the Palestinians on a diet, but not to make them die of hunger."[15]

It's meant to pressure the people of Gaza to overthrow a regime the American CIA failed to overthrow in 2007, when it attempted a coup against the democratically elected government using Fatah operatives as proxies.[16] The blockade is collective punishment—a war crime—to try to force Gazans to fix the mess the US and Israel created (which ordinary Gazans have very little power to do).

The tunnels are dangerous and illegal but are seen as a necessary means of survival, as crucial food and medicines come through along with cars and motorcycles and appliances. People have managed to bring in more exotic items such as camels, cows, and horses. Nearly all the animals at Gaza's South Forest Zoo, including the hyenas, wolves, ostriches, chimpanzees, and the prize lion came though the tunnels.[17] Some wealthy people even managed to smuggle full-sized billiard tables and Jacuzzis.

One wily entrepreneur brought KFC deliveries into the Gaza Strip, making a neat $6 profit per meal, delivered room temperature after several hours of transit time.[18] The Egyptian government cracks down on the tunnels by flooding them and building underground walls to block them, but the tunnels reappear elsewhere.

In Rafah alone, a local bank manager told me, six hundred people have earned at least one million US dollars from the tunnel economy in just a few years. Many got started with a $20,000 capital cost for digging a tunnel, a dangerous job that often ends the lives of young workers, who are desperate due to the catastrophic poverty and unemployment enforced by the siege.

As the internet gradually makes its way into people's homes and phones, only people who inherited a tradition of visiting the border divide continue to do so; others talk on the phone. But of course, there is nothing like personal contact with loved ones.

Layla feels fortunate to have seen her mother again in 2008, when frustrated Palestinians broke through a section of the Gaza-Egypt wall. "I had the good fortune to spend five consecutive nights with my mother in Egypt that time, and also met a man at the border whom I fell in love with. Thankfully Firas is from the Palestinian side! But, of course, he also has relatives in Egypt that he can't see."

Since Layla met Firas during a daring tunnel run, they have been inseparable. When they decided to get married, they arranged a Facetime call with the couple on one side and both of their mothers on the other. She missed physically embracing her mother on her wedding day, but she is happy that, months later, her mother was brave enough to travel through a tunnel to Gaza after giving up on waiting for her paperwork to come through. It was the only way she was able to meet her son-in-law.

She still hasn't met Layla and Firas' child, and their child is missing out on countless grandparents, aunties, and cousins. She finds comfort in the dream she shares with Firas to travel and reunite with them one day.

Layla finished her studies in Gaza and is a respected member of the visual artist community. Her artistic approach intertwines surrealism with traditional Arab artifacts. A fellow artist describes her work as "hauntingly beautiful and deeply emotional, with a profound sense of connection to her art." She is a spirited young woman but rarely mingles with her own community. She confides in me that she feels a bit of a stranger in her own town, as her heart aches for her mother just a few miles away in Egypt.

The sand dunes around us shift and reshape continuously, a reminder of how nature always finds a way to create something beautiful. Over the hilltop a bird soars with ease, chirping melodies to the land, winging on the breeze. Layla reflects on the bird's love for the sea, the sunset, and their cause of freedom, as birds fly freely between her mother's home and her own.

"Oh, how I wish I could traverse these borders just like this bird," she whispers wistfully as the red glow of sunset reflects in her eyes.

I'm reminded of a line from another Mahmoud Darwish poem:

Where should we go after the last frontiers?
Where should the birds fly after the last sky?

Layla paints a future where the borders fade and freedom reigns. She believes there will one day be no more walls, no more hateful divide, only peace and love, which will abide.

Layla surveys the empty row of houses in the five-hundred-meter buffer zone as the sun disappears below the horizon over a dark blue and pink Mediterranean. Several of her aunts lived there until Egyptian troops destroyed the homes in their determination to end the smuggling.

When I speak to Layla a couple years later, she says there are no more tunnels to transport her to her family. They have finally been closed, perhaps for good, after Israel and Egypt began working more intensively to destroy tunnels and widen the buffer zones.

Resilience and hope remain on both sides of the border, despite all of it. As one local put it: "We are like trees. We bend, but we do not break."

Chapter 11

Living History

One of Gaza's most affluent and daring dreamers, Jawdat Khoudary is a Gaza native with a passion for antiquities and a family history dating back over two centuries. Upon stepping into his small, eclectic, fantastical museum at Al Mathaf Hotel, visitors marvel not only at the treasure trove of ancient artifacts but also at the awe-inspiring array of cactus plants that festoon the building's interior. He has been cultivating and nurturing these spiny plants for years, finding solace in their resilience and adaptability.

They set the stage for an astonishing display of Gaza's rich and intricate history as a center of trade and travel by land and sea dating back to at least the Bronze Age. I bring visiting ministers and friends to his collection whenever I can. As Jawdat proudly leads distinguished visitors through his exhibition, he shares insights into the captivating history and culture of this coastal enclave.

In the Madaba Map, a sixth-century mosaic of the Holy Land, Gaza City is mentioned as the seventh oldest city in the world. The name "Gaza" likely came from a Canaanite word meaning "strength," and it fits well, considering the city's turbulent history of destruction and reconstruction by the various civilizations that have swept through it.

From its apparent origins as a Canaanite settlement, it came under the sway of Egyptians (both ancient and modern), Philistines, Assyrians, Greeks (including Alexander the Great), Bedouins, Romans, Jews, Christians, Muslims, Crusaders, Ottomans, and the British. Then in 1948 it was crowded with refugees driven from their towns and villages in what became Israel. Refugees now make up 70% of Gaza's population. Following Israel's conquest of the territory in 1967, it became an island of stateless people under military occupation.

Locals have tried to document and conserve the artifacts that embody the vibrant cultural heritage of Gaza, given the dearth of national museums. We don't have the resources of institutions like the Louvre, the Smithsonian, or the Met, but we have something unique to offer: unyielding passion and dedication. Afficionados like Jawdat exhibit an ardent commitment to sharing their treasures with the world, giving rise to this Aladdin's cave of wonders.

"We were once connected to the entire known world through our seaport, trading with Cyprus, Alexandria, and China," he says on a fine Saturday morning, indulging in his favorite pastime of expounding on Gaza's opulent past while seated on a bench in his hotel's garden facing the calm sea. "We've been a civilized city, a thriving hub of trade, exploration, and spirituality for thousands of years. A beating heart of this region. We have coins from Gaza from the fifth century BC. The coins have a special Gazan logo just like other Mediterranean cities did," he says proudly.

His plethora of meticulously arranged ancient objects is ensconced in a long, narrow chamber of stone adjacent to the reception desk of the hotel. Jawdat offers free admission to all, allowing anyone to experience the rich history and culture of

Gaza. His artifacts cover the full range of Gaza's long history, from jars and glassware to coins and columns, and from traditional costumes to historical manuscripts. He loans some of his eight hundred artifacts to museums in six locations worldwide.

"I can't allow anything to leave permanently," he assures me. "This is the history of Palestine, and it should be passed on to our future generations."

Jawdat's admiration for cacti, an emblem of persistence in adverse conditions, rivals his penchant for preserving history. His collection comprises several species and sizes, with some growing so prodigiously they have breached the greenhouse's roof like fairytale beanstalks. As I stroll through the garden with Jawdat, he explains the significance of the Arabic word for cactus, *sabr*, a word that also means patience.

"What we need in Gaza is patience," he says. "Cacti can teach us patience because they grow very slowly. But they don't stop."

Another prolific collector is nineteen-year-old Bara Al-Susi from Gaza City. He has already amassed over 4,000 items from various eras, including old fishing equipment, spoons, needles, metal and bronze pans, and writings carved in rock that he cannot decipher but he suspects may be from the Canaanite or Pharaonic eras. He also has a collection of modern postage stamps from several Arab countries and from Russia and Germany.

Bara shows me his coin collection in the small room he has filled with his finds. He explains how he searches for items when people dig or excavate for various reasons, usually to build foundations for homes for the booming population. "I immediately rush to find or buy whatever is unearthed," he says. "I use all of my pocket money for this."

Bara also searches for items in archaeological sites like Tell Umm Amer, Anthedon (the ancient port of Gaza), Tell el-Ajjul, Tell es-Sakan, and the Ancient City of Gaza. Sometimes objects appear on the beach after rough storms. He does his best with little knowledge of coins, searching websites that focus on ancient history and comparing his objects with what he sees online.

"I most often find Byzantine, Greek, and Roman coins. Many still have clear images on them so that it's easy to identify them using the websites," he says. "Some coins need delicate cleaning with chemicals to take away the rust without ruining the images and writing on the metal or stone."

Bara is disappointed with the lack of expertise and patronage for Palestinian artifacts. "Over time, my hope is to establish a museum that explores the depths of the artifacts I have amassed, to educate Palestinians about the rich history of their homeland," he says with fervor.

A few days after I meet Bara, I sit down to tea with Dr. Jamal Abu-Reda, the deputy head of the Palestinian Ministry of Tourism in Gaza. He says local collectors are not seen as a threat to Palestine's history or its ancient artifacts.

"We are aware of the people collecting them, and we thank them for taking care of valuable artifacts during these difficult years," says Dr. Abu-Reda. "Private collectors may be the safest way to preserve at least some of our artifacts given the dire limitations and instability due to the Israeli siege."

While Bara pursues his studies in business administration, he hopes Al Basha Palace will temporarily house and exhibit some of his treasures for the public to behold. Known in Arabic as Qasr al-Basha, and also known as Radwan Castle and Napoleon's Fort, it is a historical palace in the Old City of Gaza. The first floor was built by Mamluk sultan Zahir Baybars in the mid-13th century. The façade bears the mark of Baybars: a relief sculpture of two lions facing each other. The geometrical patterns and domes, fan and cross vaults are typical Mamluk architecture. It later served as the official governor's residence when Gaza came under Ottoman rule and as a police station under the British Mandate. It now houses a girls' school and a small museum that contains an assortment of ancient manuscripts, artifacts, and relics. It also serves as a venue for contemporary cultural discourse.

Local legend has it that in the 13th century CE, when future Egyptian Mamluk sultan Baybars was still a general fighting the Crusaders and Mongols throughout the Levant, he passed through Gaza on several occasions. During one of his visits, he married a local woman and built a grand mansion for his Gazan wife and children. It is said that Qasr al-Basha is what remains of this home. Visitors step into the rooms and are transported back in time. It is incredible to think how this palace has stood the test of time, standing tall after so many centuries.

Throughout Gaza, magnificent artifacts continue to be unearthed, including a rare bronze statue of the Greek god Apollo weighing 450 kilograms and approximately 2,500 years old. A man was fishing from a cliff near the Gaza town of Deir Al-Balah in the summer of 2013 when he noticed something peculiar in the sea below. Investigating further, he found a partially buried figure. Astonished but unable to lift the heavy statue alone, he sought assistance and proudly presented the find to his mother—who insisted on covering its male parts when she saw it inside their home. Word spread quickly, and relatives came to witness the extraordinary guest.

When one of them suggested involving the authorities, the fisherman hesitated but eventually let them take the statue for safekeeping. The remarkable artwork's value could reach up to

$340 million, and he was promised a reward of 10-20 percent of its value. However, he has not heard from them since, and the statue's whereabouts remain unknown. It briefly appeared on eBay for sale at a fraction of its estimated value, and police are investigating who tried to sell it. The statue has since vanished from public view, and experts worry this treasure might be lost or damaged forever.[19]

According to Marc-André Haldimann, an expert on Mediterranean archaeology at the University of Bern in Switzerland, Gaza has seventeen major archaeological sites that are largely unknown to the outside world.

The Byzantine Tell Umm Amer site, in Nuseirat in the middle of Gaza, is one such fascinating site. Archaeologists believe it could be the oldest monastery in the Middle East, and it's awaiting approval as a UNESCO World Heritage Site. Historians of the Byzantine era believe St. Hilarion (291-371 AD) was born in Gaza and founded the Tell Umm Amer monastery on a hill overlooking the Mediterranean after he converted to Christianity during his travels to Egypt. St. Hilarion is believed to be the founder of monasticism in Palestine. The site also contains incredible mosaics, an ancient church, a hotel, and public baths for merchants and pilgrims passing through.

Ten miles away is Barquq Castle in Khan Younis. Constructed during the reign of Sultan Barquq in 1387 CE, it is a beautifully preserved architectural gem that takes visitors straight back to the fourteenth century. Born in Circassia (which is now part of the Black Sea region of southern Russia), Barquq was the first sultan of the Burji dynasty of Egypt's Mamluk era, which ruled until the era of the Ottomans. The castle now serves as a local destination where children flock to play the timeless game of hide-and-seek.[20]

Less than a minute away, I come across a magnificent staircase leading down to a cellar beneath the home of Marwan Shewan. One can see the big walls of the castle from his doorstep. Descending the staircase, I'm engulfed by a feeling of a journey through time. The air carries a smell of dust mingled with history.

An eclectic assortment of historical treasures and artifacts greets us below, crammed together in harmonious chaos. A soft yellow light from above casts shadows on the walls, and the sensation is like stepping into an Indiana Jones film. I have to navigate with care to avoid inadvertently toppling a priceless relic as I maneuver past fellow visitors in the narrow corridors. The abundance of sights and tactile wonders enthralls the senses: there are helmets and swords that date back to the early Islamic era, intricately carved stones and metal coins of the Byzantine and Roman epochs, and even the poignant memento of a train track from a railway station, its surface etched with the unmistakable signature of Ottoman Sultan Abdulhamid II.

Visitors also discover more contemporary articles, such as old-fashioned wireless sets and vessels crafted from iron and copper from not so long ago. Within the depth of this subterranean sanctuary, time dissolves, and past and present blend in an ethereal mix.

Marwan, 47, is a master craftsman and architect by trade. He finds solace in his archaeological pursuits, searching for treasures in moments of respite from work. Marwan deems it his duty to accord them the reverence and delicate care they deserve. As he gently polishes one of his regional heirlooms with a soft cloth, his gaze moving upward to the light. "These relics, my friends, demand the tender care we bestow upon our own infants," he says.

All these peculiar, exquisite, and utilitarian objects give him an intoxicating sense of being in touch with the remnants of a multicultural tapestry woven by all the peoples who have traversed and settled in Palestine.

"I acknowledge my limitations as an amateur," confesses Marwan. Yet he remains unyielding in his resolve, and for nearly half a century he has followed in his father's footsteps, diligently amassing and safeguarding these relics. Any artifact that sheds light on Palestine's history, however humble, sparks insatiable curiosity within Marwan about their uses and meaning. The most seemingly inconsequential object might unexpectedly turn out to be a rare and priceless historical gem. He knows that not all objects have the same historical or pecuniary value, but whether it is an agricultural implement or a coin, each object for him has the same potential to unveil the reality of bygone epochs.

"In the late eighties, I grew increasingly engrossed in the task of safeguarding artifacts, concerned by the lavish offers Israeli military generals extend to Palestinians in exchange for their discovered treasures," Marwan explains.

The issue of Israelis buying up antiquities, trying to strengthen their claim to the land, raises important questions about national identity, historical narratives, politics, ethics, and cultural heritage. The Ramallah-based Ministry of Tourism and Antiquities has documented endless Israeli violations of archaeological sites in Palestine, including theft and destruction of historical sites as well as imposing full control over most of them and preventing any Palestinian attempts to restore, rehabilitate, and renovate them. Many Muslim and Christian shrines and other holy places have been "Judaized," seeking to erase centuries of history that undermine the Zionist narrative and delegitimize the agenda of exclusive Jewish rule over the land.

Marwan tenderly cradles ancient coins encrusted with weathered stones. "These I unearthed from a diminutive pot," he continues, showing me the coins' irregular shapes and diverse sizes. The badly damaged coins are invaluable to Marwan. He says the pot may be related to tales of a queen who purportedly amassed her tears within the vessel. His sense of belief is contagious, as is his relentless dedication, love, and reverence for all these objects, large and small, banal and precious, bequeathed by the ancestors.

He tells me the genesis of metal coins can be traced back to the Lydian kingdom of western Asia Minor, when they were forged from electrum, an alloy of silver and gold. Coins of bronze, other alloys, and even stone have also been discovered, and each carries its own tale. Some of the coins in his collection clearly bear the visage of an Emperor accompanied by Latin or Greek inscriptions. The reverse sides feature diverse images that may represent various imperial regions.

Beyond the invaluable service rendered to humanity through the preservation of fragmentary glimpses into lost cultures, Marwan's subterranean realm is a source of personal tranquility. When the weight of work and societal pressures bears down on him, he retreats to his quiet cellar and immerses himself in the waves of civilization that have shaped his homeland.

Marwan shows me a photograph of the visit of China's Minister of Industry and Information Technology to his makeshift museum. As long as Gaza remains under a stifling blockade, only a few global experts will arrive to see Marwan's subterranean sanctuary and scrutinize, date, and document his trove of antiquities. He looks forward to the day when experts from all over the world can visit and appreciate the wonders of Gaza freely.

The only disquiet that gnaws at Marwan is the bickering among political leaders, which could compromise his lofty ideals. Cherishing and preserving Palestinian heritage seems to languish at the periphery of political priorities.

Moving on to the twentieth century, the Gaza War Cemetery lies slightly north and west of Gaza City, where the Salah El-Din main road traverses the Strip. It is the final resting place of over 3,000 Commonwealth soldiers who served in the First World War. The cemetery, under the administration of the Commonwealth War Graves Commission, resides in a serene area adorned with jacaranda trees. Local residents seek solace in this peaceful and historical space away from the dust and trauma of recent conflicts. School buses often bring students to this landmark of Gaza history, where they learn about the site and the battles for Gaza in the spring of 1917.

The cemetery contains graves for 3,691 dead, nearly all from WWI, including 3,082 British, 263 Australians, 184 Turkish (Ottoman), 50 Indians, 36 Poles, 23 Canadians and 23 New Zealanders as well as smaller numbers who were South African, Greek, Egyptian, German, French, or Yugoslavian.[21] Hundreds remain unidentified, and these words are etched upon their tombstones: "Soldier of the Great War, known unto God."

This cemetery is largely unknown to the international community. But Ibrahim Jeradeh, residing in a modest house near the cemetery, has devoted himself to the care and maintenance of the burial sites that he inherited from his father. His son Essam is poised to carry on this responsibility in his turn.

"Whatever you do, make sure you remain sincere in your job," Jeradeh says to me as he moves with deliberate precision from one grave to the next, ensuring each receives the necessary amount of water to revive the surrounding grass.

Jeradeh receives many British families who come to visit the graves of their relatives in Palestine. He was awarded an MBE in "grateful recognition of outstanding contribution to the Commonwealth War Graves Commission." (MBE stands for

Member of the Most Excellent Order of the British Empire, a civilian honor also held by famous singers and soccer players like Adele and Harry Kane.) The accompanying certificate was signed by the Duke of Kent.

However, as Gaza remains under Israeli blockade, most families find it impossible to obtain permits from the Israeli authorities so they can enter Gaza to visit the cemetery. The cemetery was also struck by Israeli missiles in two assaults. 350 headstones were damaged by Israeli fire on Christmas Day in 2008, and the cemetery was struck again on New Year's Day. Israel paid £90,000 in compensation to the CGWC for the damage to the sacred burial site.

Whether soldiers were Christian, Jewish, Muslim, or from another religious tradition, Jeradeh gives equal respect and care to all. As he comes close again, carefully watering the thirsty grass, each blade seems to come alive, standing tall and green again. Cool water droplets cling like diamonds in the morning light.

"I take care of this place—it is part of my life," Jeradeh tells me. "I started at the age of eighteen and will ensure that my grandchildren care for it too. The cemetery is a place of comfort for me; it has become part of the family soul and will remain so." As he ventures deeper into the cemetery, the gentle sound of water meeting the earth gradually fades and is replaced by the melodic chirping of birds and gentle rustling of leaves. A serene breeze caresses the grounds, carrying the sweet fragrance of freshly watered flowers and imbuing a sense of tranquility and peace. For a moment, I can feel what he feels about this place.

World War I had far-reaching repercussions, not least in the Middle East, where the Ottoman Empire was cast off and the age of European imperialism began. Britain occupied Palestine, Iraq, and other regions while France held sway in Lebanon and Syria.

Unfortunately, Palestine bore the worst of it due to Britain's support of an ideology known as Zionism, which aimed to establish a new country on the land of Palestine that privileged Jews above the many other religions and ethnicities of the region.

Many Jewish people immigrated to Palestine to escape European antisemitism, and of course Palestinian Jews already lived in Palestine among their Christian, Muslim, and other neighbors. Some of them were opposed to Zionism. But in 1917, the British government announced its support for a "national home for the Jewish people" in Palestine, even though Jews comprised roughly 10% of the population, many of them fairly recent immigrants. This raised alarm bells that Britain was prepared to give Palestine over to permanent foreign colonial rule, which they feared would result in carving up the region, expelling the native inhabitants, and severing access to many major holy sites.

Palestinians tried to free themselves from British rule in the 1930s but were defeated, leaving them largely disarmed and leaderless. Zionist militias turned to terrorism and sabotage to drive the British out, then they committed massacres and terror campaigns against the native Palestinian inhabitants, expelling 750,000 people from their homes and land and conquering 78% of historic Palestine by force of arms in 1948-49. At least four hundred Palestinian towns and villages were destroyed and 15,000 Palestinians were killed. Some are still abandoned today while others were given Hebrew names and repopulated with Jewish immigrants.

Khalil Al-Jamal's story is one of countless Palestinian stories of displacement and survival. I met him in the Brazil camp area of Rafah. He owns a mini-market selling goods to his neighbors.

A short man with a mustache and silver hair, Khalil's weathered face bears deep lines, and his tired eyes hold a wisdom that transcends time. He navigates his small shop with a graceful shuffle. Despite the nightmares he endured, his movements retain a quiet strength and subtle elegance.

As I gently asked about the origins of the name of his community, he couldn't help but talk about where he originally came from: Yibna, known as Jabneh or Jabneel in Biblical times, Jamnia during the Roman era, and Ibelin by the Crusaders.

Accounts from the tenth century describe Yibna as an ancient city perched on a hill. Arab geographer Al-Muqaddasi (c. 945–991), author of *The Best Divisions in the Knowledge of the Regions*, praised the beauty of Yibna's mosque and mentioned the exceptional quality of Damascene figs originating from this area. Greek Muslim scholar Yaqut added intriguing details about a tomb believed to belong to Abu Hurairah, a companion (*sahaba*) of the Prophet.

Yibna also happens to be where my grandparents were born and raised. They met at the village water well and were eventually married. The village harbored a population of 5,420 before it was seized by Zionist forces on June 4, 1948. Khalil and his family, like mine, were expelled by Zionist militias when Khalil was only seven years old.

Seeking refuge near Rafah in the southern Gaza Strip, they named their new camp 'Yibna' to preserve the memory of their cherished birthplace. In 1974, the Israelis dismantled part of this refugee camp to build a highway that they considered strategically necessary to maintain their military occupation. Many families were forcibly removed again, this time to an area designated by Israel as Dekel B.

"We refused to take a Hebrew name that the Israeli occupation imposed on us. Because Brazilian UN troops had their camp nearby, we started to call the camp Brazil," Khalil tells me, his grandchildren huddled around him. "It was more honorable to name our camp after peacekeeping Brazilian troops."

It's an example of the complex tapestry of Gaza's history embedded in its place names, such as the Swedish Village, the Canada Camp, the Austrian neighborhood, and the Saudi neighborhood.

Khalil assumed the role of the oldest senior in the Brazil camp, which once housed 10,000 inhabitants. It stands as a distinctive enclave, boasting wider roads than some other refugee camps. Unfortunately, it, too, was largely destroyed by Israeli forces when Israel decided to expand the buffer zone near the border with Egypt. Khalil lives in what is left of Brazil camp with his wife, four children, and twenty-four grandchildren.

"Seventy-five percent of residential homes here have been demolished by Israeli bulldozers since the second Intifada." The area used to be renowned for tunnels that served as lifelines for Gaza's population, enabling survival amidst the continuous blockade. As I walk alongside Khalil through the camp, the tough life for residents becomes apparent.

"Brazil has become a home for people from all over the region. Many who lost their ancestral homes came to settle here, hoping one day to return home."

In recent years, I was able to visit the real Yibna. The ruins are located immediately southeast of the modern Israeli city of Yavne. I had my grandmother on the phone as I walked into what remained of the town. She guided me step-by-step how to navigate and search for landmarks such as the well where she met my grandfather, the stone chair, and the fig tree. This was the moment I learned the story of their meeting.

The remains of a damaged mosque, a minaret, and the well still stand in Yibna today. The mausoleum of Abu Hurairah has been transformed into a synagogue. Israeli authorities claim it is the tomb of a historic Jewish figure. Yibna's figs are still grown; they are now sold by the Mizrahi Jews who inhabit Yavne.

Khalil firmly believes the day will come when he returns to the land he was forced to flee as a child. "There is growing hope of returning to our original homes in the real Yibna," he asserts. "Brazil is only temporary, but Yibna is sufficient to accommodate all its people again. They like to say, 'The old will die, and the young will forget.' But we have not forgotten. I still have the key to my house, which still stands. If not me or my children, perhaps my grandchildren will finally be able to return home."

Chapter 12

Melodies of Cultural Revival

As the "Arab Spring" unfolds in Tunisia, Egypt, and other Arab countries, Palestinians are heartened by this wave of change that seems to herald a shift in the region's political landscape. In Gaza, there is a palpable sense of optimism and anticipation as its residents dare to believe something positive lies on the horizon, such as a unity deal between estranged Palestinian political parties in hopes that Israel will allow new elections to take place.

Palestinians have hope that a new Egyptian regime will open the Rafah border crossing and Israel will free a thousand Palestinians held in Israel's brutal military prison system, many without any due process, in exchange for an Israeli soldier captured in a military operation.

Add to that, a series of Freedom Flotillas are attempting to sail to Gaza. After the 2007 coup attempt—which the US and Israel provoked and then lost—Israel and Egypt imposed a blockade on Gaza, preventing most goods and nearly all people from going in and out. Collective punishment is a war crime, yet governments around the world failed to take steps to compel Israel to follow international law. The flotillas were collections of boats full of activists, humanitarians, and politicians from around the world uniting to break the brutal siege of Gaza with grassroots action.

Sadly, the previous flotilla had been raided in the dead of night by Israeli soldiers in international waters. Ten people were killed, including a Turkish American teenager named Furkan Doğan. Israel faced international criticism for the brutal raid and subsequently eased the blockade in some ways.

Another Flotilla is reportedly on the way, and all eyes are on the horizon, searching for the miracle of a friendly ship heading toward our shores, even as Israel continues to employ all diplomatic, economic, and other channels to block its progress. We hear reports that some of the ships were tampered with, possibly sabotaged, before they could sail.

Mahmoud Al Abbasi, a 23-year-old falafel sandwich seller, says the vital aid supplies are not the main thing. The most important aspect is their chance to be our guest in our homeland and convey our greetings and our message to the world.

Yasmine Hayek, a 16-year-old passing by the harbor, expresses the hope that Israel will allow the flotilla in this time and that the world will really see how it is in Gaza under land, sea, and air blockade.

Shaymaa Miqdad, a young writer from Gaza, knows it is not likely to end the blockade and its vast and devastating impact or create enduring pathways for trade and human movement. But she celebrates the flotilla as a powerful symbol of international solidarity with her homeland.

Sixteen-year-old Abdullah Hamdan's dream is that the flotilla will come laden with books. He has been trying to get hold of all the Harry Potter books since he was first hooked by the fantasy of Hogwarts. This longing for escape is shared by many other young Gazans. But even if a kid from Gaza orders a Harry

Potter book from Italy or the UK, there's almost no chance it will arrive due to the poor mail services. (I once ordered three pairs of shoes and finally gave up when they didn't arrive after ten years.) Online reading is difficult, too, due to limited access to libraries and electricity cuts. Abdullah dreams of owning a Kindle.

Books are windows into the world beyond Gaza. They are gateways to knowledge, empowerment, contemplation, reflection, and inner peace. The director of Gaza's Municipal Library, Hassan Abu Attaya, recognizes their importance in knowing the past, understanding the present, and creating a better future. He does his best to maintain a collection of the latest books despite the challenges posed by the blockade. Four thousand books donated by Arab states in North Africa provided a much-needed boost to Gaza's libraries.

Through it all, Gaza's appreciation for literature remains steadfast, and our central literary hub is a beloved community bookshop and publishing house called Samir Mansour's Bookshop. Samir worked tirelessly for years to build a collection of tens of thousands of books and provide a beautiful gathering space. Students and readers of all ages spend many happy hours browsing the shelves, curling up with a novel, or chatting quietly over tea and coffee.[22]

Mansour's small publishing house plays a vital role in producing locally printed books (including my own book, *Shell-Shocked*), serving dozens of local authors. He also navigates the challenges of shipping books into the region or searching out travelers to transport books into Gaza from Cairo. The bookshops and cafes of Gaza also create spaces for literary discussions and reading groups. A scarcity of books in Gaza has led to common practices like copying pages from existing texts, particularly in educational institutions. When students in Gaza have the rare opportunity to travel outside, they often prioritize bringing back books.

The actors in Gaza's theater community also see their art as a form of resistance and empowerment for Palestinians. The Said Al Mishal Cultural Center[23] is packed for the opening of a play called "The Photographer." The events of the play take place after a young man named Aatallah is killed by an airstrike on a refugee camp. His mother Suma goes to the camp's photographer, Darwish, to ask for a picture of herself with her son that he had taken six years ago but she never picked up.

Darwish tells her the picture is still available and goes to the studio to search for it. His journey through old photos summons memory after memory, and Darwish begins recounting stories, starting from life as a refugee and passing through uprisings and wars, recalling those who were killed and imprisoned, life in the camp, and relationships with neighbors. The stories lead him to discover something about himself for the first time.

"Darwish is like Gaza: everyone lets him down, but despite this, he lives, breathes, dreams, and rebels," says Dr. Atef Abu Saif, the playwright and Palestine's Culture Minister. He studied English Literature at Bir Zeit University, inspired by his grandmother Aiysha, who was never allowed to return to Jaffa but loved telling stories of her hometown. He earned his MA in Bradford, UK and a PhD in political science in Florence, Italy, and he has written several novels and other works.[24]

Darwish carries the burdens of the entire nation on his shoulders as he documents the life of Palestinians longing to return to their own villages and cities. He bears this weight and captures the essence of the camp and every corner within it, the joy and beauty, the pain and suffering. The mother, Suma, endured sixteen years of fertility struggles before she finally had her son. She watched him grow before her eyes only to be killed just after enrolling in college. Her yearning for the photo takes us into the real Gaza.

Darwish does not find the photo he was searching for, but on the stage, he tells the story of the refugee camp and its people, leaving the audience feeling hopeful and reminding them of their history.

Months later, Israeli warplanes fire three missiles, completely demolishing the five-story building where "The Photographer" was performed, injuring twenty-four people and damaging several nearby houses.

But that does not stop Palestinian theater. The musicians scheduled to perform a concert at the Al Mishal Center still do so, in the ruins of the building.[25]

Still, it's a devastating blow to the artistic community, with performance spaces, a library, offices and spaces for dance troupes and musicians, costumes, equipment for collaborating with artists outside Gaza, and countless fond memories obliterated in the blink of an eye.

In the same month of the airstrike, Israel's Arabic Twitter channel announces, "Arab-Israeli[26] singer Dalal Abu Amneh will perform at a concert tomorrow, Thursday, at the Egyptian Opera House, sponsored by the Ministry of Culture. Abu Amneh is a talented and famous artist in Israel and both Arab and Jewish circles. She is distinguished for her ability to sing Umm Kulthum's songs. We hope to see more such cultural cooperation in the future."

Abu Amneh herself responds on Twitter: "We came to Cairo as Palestinians who are steadfast with regard to our land, carrying Palestinian concerns and raising the Palestinian voice loudly. This is our identity and this is our cause, which we will never abandon. Whether they like it or not."

Shaymaa Badran, a young English literature student, finds comfort in the company of her good friends Maria and Rania in the quiet interlude before their final Victorian Age class at Al Azhar University. Like countless young souls in Gaza, they share the same longing to immerse themselves in the world's literary trends and take part in current intellectual debates. All were born as refugees, and Maria still speaks about the fleeting years spent in Kuwait where her father, a dedicated teacher, fostered their hopes for higher education. Fate dealt a different hand, and her father's visa expired, forcing them to return to the place they now call home. Maria and her mother, father, and sister had to reweave the fabric of their lives.

Maria now yearns to get hold of the novels of Egyptian writer Nabil Farouq. She envisions herself enraptured by the tales of *The Man of the Impossible* and *The War of the Spies*. Her dream remains confined by the blockade, imprisoned, her sails forever caught in the stillness of the dry dock of Gaza. Shaymaa invites her friends to head to the university cafeteria for mouth-watering falafel and hummus sandwiches with tangy pickles. With each crispy bite, the flavors seem to mingle with their dreams, satiating hunger and adding to their yearning for more plays to attend and books to read. They share stories, jokes, and ironic banter about power cuts.

Rania regales the group with a tale of her cousin's pet parrot, a mimic of such proficiency, it once fooled the entire family into thinking their grandmother was calling them. The anecdote elicits uncontrollable laughter, prompting the girls to emulate the parrot's voice, which redoubles the laughter, now mixed with the playful cadence of their impersonations of the parrot's impersonation.

Maria, ever surprising, unveils a hidden talent—beatboxing. With rhythmic pulses from her mouth accompanied by claps and table taps, she gives an impromptu performance. Applause and cheers resound from other students in the cafeteria as the circle of the moment's joy expands. They seem to know that, despite Israel's constant destruction of their cultural spaces, taking a new stage is only a matter of time.

The time comes quickly as an unparalleled opportunity arises to reach the world stage via the TEDx platform. One early afternoon, I find myself in the company of an ardent collective of Palestinian youths, the oldest of whom is just twenty-five, who wish to unfurl their narratives before the eyes of the world.

"Our endeavor was driven by an earnest desire to create something solely for us, by us—purely Palestinian," says Heba Madi, the lead architect of TEDx Shujaiya.[27] "We deserve an elevated platform, a podium from which we may address the world."

The event is orchestrated solely through the efforts of Gaza-based volunteers. She and her comrades manage to acquire official authorization from the TED organization. TED does not get directly involved with these breakout events but provides indispensable guidelines for speakers and bestows a license to use the TEDx logo.

"We have always been perceived as residents of a war-ravaged region, but now we want to showcase another facet—lives filled with hope and ideas—on the TEDx stage," asserts Asem Alnabeh, who helps with social media for the event.

Heba hopes eventually to get permission to host an event known as TEDx Gaza, but for now the guardians of TED would not agree to this. The name 'Shujaiya' was selected, referring to an eastern neighborhood of Gaza City that bore the brunt of Israel's deadliest and most destructive attacks in the three successive wars. Within the hearts of Gazans, Shujaiya is emblematic of their collective experience.

In a mix of English and Arabic, twelve speakers captivate an audience of over a hundred people at a Gaza hotel.

The hallowed event includes the testimony Mazen Elsayed, an expert in software development and project management. He shares how the lessons he has gleaned from playing chess—patience, self-assurance, and confidence— can be applied to the lives of all Palestinians. The reverse is also true—his chess game was inspired by his experience as a Palestinian in Gaza.

"If someone were to assert what your worth is equivalent to this chess piece I hold in my hand," he poses, raising a pawn, "how would you feel?" Al-Sayed expounds upon the indispensability of each chess piece on the board, emphasizing that without the collective contribution of everyone, the game cannot flourish. "Each and every person in this room possesses inherent value."

Hashem Ghazal, who is deaf, uses sign language (and an interpreter) to tell his story. He has worked at the Atfaluna Society for Deaf Children[28] since 1994 and is in charge of the Carpentry Section and Adult Deaf Affairs. He traveled to several countries representing the deaf of the Gaza Strip and is now known as the Godfather of the Deaf in the Gaza Strip.

He talks about how leading a successful life, defying stereotypes, and overcoming disability is a metaphor for Gaza. Despite the siege, aggression, internal division, and many hardships, Gaza shows that hope, growth, and kindness can still be nurtured, even in the darkest of times and places.

Professor Refaat Alareer speaks on the importance of keeping the stories of our parents and grandparents alive. He explains the necessity of owning our narrative, with examples from Africa and Canada. The people's narrative does not need to be marginalized by internal or external politics, nor should it be determined by the local or global elites.[29]

Perhaps the most poignant presentation is that of Ahmed Alfaleet, who was held captive in an Israeli prison cell for twenty years until his emancipation was granted through a prisoner exchange deal in 2011.

"We were so happy to get an apple inside the prison cell," he tells a rapt audience. "We would keep it as long as possible, then eat it only before it became rotten. We took turns holding it in our hands before we slept as evidence of the natural world outside the prison walls."

He spoke about the profound erosion of his personal identity. His name was stripped away and supplanted by a number—1044036—a designation he had to utter three time every day. As he says 1044036 mechanically on the TEDx stage, a crescendo of thunderous applause erupts. "We have not yet succumbed to the crushing burden of adversity," he proclaims resolutely. "Against all odds, I have obtained my bachelor's degree in International Relations and my master's degree in Public Management while I was in prison." He also mastered Hebrew and volunteered to teach the language to his fellow prisoners. He read over 3000 books, enlightening his mind and heart, and once back in Gaza, he worked as a Hebrew-language trainer and then opened his own center for Hebrew and Israeli studies.

Alfaleet astounds the audience with his revelation of a coping mechanism he uses since his release. "When queried about my age, I solemnly proclaim myself to be four years old," says the forty-five-year-old. "The day I emerged from the shackles of my Israeli imprisonment, I experienced a rebirth—a renewal of self." He believes life is too beautiful to dwell on hardships and says that spending twenty years of one's youth in prison taught him to find what makes him smile and feel thankful for life.

Alfaleet's message resonates deeply within the hearts of the youth. These talks humanize and contextualize the multifaceted conflict that engulfs Gaza, which is all too often reduced to a one-dimensional portrayal of little more than "victims and terrorists" in the media, devoid of all humanity. Gazans can see the way they are dehumanized and know this puts them in more danger, as the world is more likely to forget about them or even justify the brutal abuse Israel has imposed on them for so many years. The youth of Gaza clamor for their voices to be amplified in the hope of reshaping global perspectives on Gaza. They aspire for Gaza to be recognized not solely as a besieged and war-ravaged enclave but as a place inhabited by over two million real human beings—many of them young, intelligent, proactive, and brimming with hope for a better and more peaceful future for Palestine.

"We yearn for the world to perceive us as a nation that cherishes life," a young participant shares with me after the event, among an audience that swelled to hundreds of attendees. The event ends with a soul-stirring musical performance by twins Ghada Shoman, a 19-year-old student, and her brother Mohammed Shoman, a 16-year-old student, as they sing a heartfelt anthem for Palestine.

The videos and social media posts reach millions worldwide with a new and humanizing vision uniquely crafted in Palestine.

After the 2006 Palestinian election, Israel unveiled its ban on a long list of materials into Gaza, both for "dual use" concerns (with security as the convenient smokescreen) and for "economic warfare" to collectively punish Palestinians. The list comprised an absurd array of banned items, including lentils, pasta, A4 paper, ginger, chocolate, hatcheries, wheelchairs, books, shoes, crayons, and even toilet paper.

Feeling the weight of the population on my shoulders, I ventured forth into Western diplomatic channels and journalists' dens to champion the noble cause of allowing women's menstrual products into the Gaza Strip. The gallant knights of Western diplomatic and political circles offered to rescue Gaza from this quagmire with their heroic diplomatic car deliveries—a feat they managed multiple times to bring in shoes that never fit my feet. Of course, these were mere tiny plasters on a gaping wound.

Eventually, enough diplomatic pressure was brought to bear that feminine hygiene products were removed from the list of banned items. But the blockade continued, putting all of Gaza "on a diet" of severely restricted food, fuel, construction and agricultural materials, and household goods for the next sixteen years—and then it got much worse.

Amid all the joy and hope that Gazans can scrape together and try to share with the world, the fact remains that due to the blockade and military occupation, unemployment hovers around a catastrophic fifty percent, the highest in the world, according to the World Bank. Youth unemployment is even worse. Among the 32,000 students who graduate from Palestinian universities each year, the majority are forced into unemployment or underemployment. According to the Palestinian Statistics Bureau, the highest unemployment rate is among male graduates, reaching 75 percent.

All too many men with fine minds and engineering degrees have nothing to do but sit around in their mother's parlor and drink tea, dying inside as their youth—and their hope of starting a family—slips away. All too many women who dream of creative and fulfilling careers have no option but to marry young and stay home with kids. For these young people facing an uncertain future, the stories shared at the TEDx event about resilience, determination, and optimism offer a valuable addition to their repertoire of coping mechanisms. But everyone knows Gaza's GDP could double if not quadruple if only we had freedom of movement, education, and trade. Assaults and access restrictions have relegated Gaza to a shell of its potential. Millions of human beings are basically warehoused in Gaza, largely dependent on remittances and aid.

And they feel powerless to change anything, especially since Israel and the US effectively overturned their democracy and the international community said and did nothing. Since then, Israeli authorities have consistently sabotaged possibilities for calm and unity. For example, in late 2012, Hamas leader Ahmed Jabari was in talks with an Israeli intermediary about a long-term truce agreement. Hours after he received a draft of the agreement, which he was expected to accept, the Israeli army assassinated him and his bodyguard with an air strike on his car.[30]

People have no choice but to find what joy they can in their impossible situation, discovering hobbies and building businesses against enormous odds, always with the specter of annihilation hanging over them. The horrible and depressing situation makes it all the more remarkable how many find joy in nature, friends, and family and find ways to connect to the outside world despite it all.

Unfortunately, it seems people avoid discussing awkward topics such as internal corruption in public spaces like TEDx. These are extremely sensitive issues, as they imply problems with the rule of law and cast blame on the people involved. My standpoint remains clear: corruption undermines current and future prospects for human development and diverts valuable resources away from boosting the Palestinian economy.

Palestine's current anti-corruption efforts lack a comprehensive approach that should encompass several key elements: strengthening anti-corruption institutions and court systems, promoting transparency, accountability, and the rule of law, and fostering collective action. Unfortunately, this journey often becomes a solitary one, as people hesitate to join, including my photographer who refuses to participate in an investigation concerning possible corruption in development cooperation assistance.

In the theater, too, most conversations revolve around blaming the occupying power or inter-Palestinian divisions or focusing on societal issues like divorce, online bullying, early marriage, depression, and social cohesion. Often, people with differing ideologies neglect to speak to each other about how to cope with a foreign military occupation, giving rise to division between Palestinian parties instead of articulating and debating disagreements.

An even bigger failure lies in addressing the abuse of national resources, including the Gaza Marine gas field, located approximately thirty kilometers off the coast of the Gaza Strip in the Eastern Mediterranean Sea. It is believed to hold significant natural gas reserves, which could provide a valuable source of energy and revenue for the Palestinian territories.

Unfortunately, Israel has so far blocked any Palestinian progress on developing the gas field. Israeli authorities have also floated the idea of the so-called Ben Gurion Canal from Eilat on the Gulf of Aqaba to the Mediterranean as an alternative to the Suez Canal controlled by Egypt. Passing the canal through Wadi Gaza, a valley that bisects the Gaza Strip, would significantly shorten the route, saving significant time and cost. Given that 12% of global trade currently passes through the Suez Canal, it would have profound geopolitical implications. Removing or further disempowering the population of Gaza would thus be doubly tempting, on top of the usual right-wing ambition to establish an exclusively Jewish state on all of historic Palestine.

Regrettably, I encounter individuals in Gaza who defend corruption and misuse of funds, even using the Arabic term *shataara*, loosely meaning "cleverness" or "ingenuity," to justify such actions.

For example, I often come across information about historical artifacts being smuggled and sold outside Gaza by private merchants. The Palestinian antiquities ministry has not been able to protect the antiquities from brokers and excavators who smuggle Palestinian artifacts out of Palestine on the directives of the Israeli occupation authorities. These are then often presented as Jewish historical and cultural heritage in Israeli, European, and American museums.

I am also perplexed by the fact that despite arbitrary restrictions on numerous food items and basic goods after 2007 (including sage, cumin, ginger, vinegar, and chocolate), fresh bananas seem to arrive in Gaza every single working day. Curiosity drives me to the Israeli-controlled Kerem Shalom (Karm Abu Salem) crossing, where a back-to-back truck driver is transporting bananas.

"Why bananas?" I ask him.

"We are just simple employees trying to survive."

I'm not surprised by his answer, especially considering the security cameras overhead.

Later, I spot the same truck driver handing over his orange safety vest at the gate before heading home. I take the opportunity to inquire, "Are you not puzzled by the abundance of bananas when other essential items like toilet paper are banned?"

"Don't ask me, ask them."

"Who are 'them'?"

He looks me straight in the eyes. "The bananas come from farms owned by an Israeli military commander." He appears to have limited knowledge about the motivations behind those demanding banana supplies, marketing them as the only fruit available besides the grapefruit and pomegranates smuggled through tunnels from Egypt, or what they might be gaining in return. Few others are willing to talk at all due to fears of retaliation. Almost everyone providing information wishes to remain anonymous, which hinders the story's credibility.

On a calm evening while I am drafting a feature story for the next day's newspaper, I receive a threatening phone call. An unknown voice snarls, "If you dare to keep digging into this, I will utterly destroy you." When I ask for clarification, he says, "You know well what I am talking about," and abruptly ends the call.

I report the incident to the Gaza authorities. They ask me to visit the closest police station first thing the next morning to document the event and so they can examine cell phone antenna activity to try to determine where the threatening call originated and continue the investigation from there.

Chapter 13

The Author is Rudely Taken

On a cold and sunless morning shrouded by wintry melancholy, I set out on a long day of errands. The plan is to begin with a brief stop at the local police station to give them my report about last night's threatening phone call, then visit my favorite bakery to collect fresh sesame bread complemented by the indulgent combination of falafel and fiery red chili. I'll take it to Hassan's lab in Rafah, where we plan to enjoy breakfast together accompanied by his signature *zaatar* (thyme) tea.

I never make it to the police station. I've driven barely 150 meters from my home in west Gaza City when I notice a man huddled in the middle of the road, his hand raised to signal for help. A broken-down white Hyundai is parked on the left side of the road. Curiosity gets the better of me, and I pull up to him and roll down my window.

"What can I do for you?"

He scans the buildings surrounding us before giving a hesitant nod. I meet his gaze quizzically, taking in his dark complexion and guessing he is slightly older than me. Dressed in a black jacket with a military emblem on the shoulder and sporting an untrimmed beard, he exudes a rough and intimidating aura.

He stands, tall and serious, and carefully surveys the area for a second time. As our eyes lock, a chill runs down my spine. He unlocks my car door with a swift poke of his finger and gestures for me to step out. I stay frozen in place, confused. Two men emerge from the white car that I had thought was broken, also dressed in black winter jackets, and forcefully drag me out of my vehicle. One grips the back of my neck while another holds my arms from behind.

"Who are you?" I ask with alarm. "What do you want?"

The man with the untrimmed beard reveals a Glock weapon, silencing my questions.

"We are the security apparatus of this land," one of his henchmen replies.

It's just after 8am. The streets are quiet. Children are already in school, industrious morning workers are busy at their jobs, and everyone else is sheltering from the miserable weather. Everything feels wrong. I have fallen into a trap, unknowingly lured into the clutches of… whom?

The men drag me to their car, throw me in the back seat, and bind my hands behind me with heavy metal cuffs. I struggle, I protest, but it's futile. One of the men says, "It's an automatic transmission." I realize he is talking about my car, which is being driven away.

I ask again where we are going. They ignore me. I'm sandwiched in between two heavy guys. I try to push against them, but the weight of the man with the untrimmed beard confines me, pressing against my core.

A prayer rug is thrown over my head and they tell me to duck. I don't comply, but I lose any sense of which street we are on. A phone rings with an incongruously religious *nasheed* in a capella: "*Ya taiba, ya taiba.*"

The man seated on my left ends the call quickly. "Tell your man we got him and we're on the way," is all he says.

My patience is running thin. Not today. I really can't today.

"What is going on?" I shout again.

The figure to my left pivots towards me. "Shut up if you want to survive." His voice drips with malevolence and disdain, sounding almost like a vengeful former lover.

Feeling even more disturbed and baffled, I set my mind adrift, desperately trying to unravel the twisted strands of fate that have woven me into this dire predicament, abducted and spoken to in this way with absolutely no warning and for reasons I can't begin to fathom. The car hurtles on through nameless avenues, its speed matching the rapid thumping of my heart. Foreboding settles within me. How capricious life can be, astounding us at every turn.

After half an hour or so, the car stops and my body is yanked out of the vehicle, the prayer rug still veiling my sight. They remove the rug and replace it with a brown cloth bag forced over my head. One of my captors guides me, my hands shackled behind my back. Unlike the others, he seems reluctant to carry out these "duties." His hushed voice counts each step as we descend into the depths, his words a lifeline in the abyss: "Four more steps to go."

Like a captive marionette, I follow obediently down into the unknown, my pulse racing. I vow to resist the encircling gloom that threatens to engulf me. I refuse to panic or succumb to desolation. I will endure and find a way out.

Untrimmed Beard seems to be the leader of this little operation, and he approaches me. I can't see his eyes, but I can feel his gaze piercing through me, searching for any signs of resistance, defiance, or fear. I remain still, masking my fear behind a calm façade. I refuse to grant them the satisfaction of witnessing my spirit sagging and shattered. The others in the room remain silent. It seems they are a tightly-knit group, united by a common purpose.

My metal handcuffs, still securing my wrists tightly together, are hooked to the ceiling. It dawns on me that I might never lay eyes on my loved ones again. Bidding them farewell before I die and expressing the depth of my love to them may now be out of reach.

Untrimmed Beard begins to speak. "You may be wondering why you're here. Let's just say you've stumbled into something much bigger than yourself." His demeanor is vulgar and heartless. He doesn't seem to know anything in life but hatred and violence.

My legs are placed on a chair, and Untrimmed Beard picks up a stick and begins beating the bottoms of my feet—a common form of torture. Bolts of intense pain shoot through my legs from the point of impact. I try to distract myself by counting the blows. I play with the hope that the number will be ten or twenty or thirty and then will stop. But I lose count as blow after blow shatters my senses until I forget there is anything in the world but pain.

Finally he finishes, breathless with exertion, and leaves without a word. I take a moment to catch my breath and wonder what is the point of this excruciating ordeal. My feet throb with pain. I remember waking up and planning a very ordinary day only an hour or two earlier. I close my eyes, willing myself back to that cozier timeline.

Another figure barges in, probing me about my professional contacts and activities. I remain steadfast, refusing to divulge anything that might jeopardize others. I can sense the anger emanating from Untrimmed Beard. I hear his breath quicken. It is as if his entire being is contorted with rage, becoming more menacing with each moment.

A second round of assault on my feet begins. The strikes are even more forceful than before. The room echoes with the sound. Each blow feels like an eternity. My suffering consumes me. Despite the agony, I remain silent, determined not to give my captors the satisfaction of hearing my pain.

Then once again, just as suddenly, he leaves.

Hours pass and time becomes a blur as I am subjected to endless questioning and physical and psychological torment. I'm not very cooperative, and they end up doing more beating than questioning.

I have no idea how much longer I can endure this agonizing torment. In a futile attempt to find solace, I silently whisper a request that the assault will cease. Untrimmed Beard and his accomplices remain unyielding, devoid of any empathy for my pain or exhaustion. I'm also thirsty and starving. It's been many hours since I set off toward my friendly neighborhood bakery to seek the comfort of breakfast. Time seems to stretch endlessly while I remain trapped in the clutches of the never-ending nightmare of the present moment—now, now, now.

Yet, with this continual uncertainty and fear, I feel sparks of strength within me. I may be confined physically, but my spirit remains free. I hold onto one flame of hope: whether I end up dead or escape with my life, this horror show will eventually come to an end. I gather every ounce of my remaining determination and vow to find a way to climb out of this abyss. I listen to their every move keenly, dissecting the patterns of their comings and goings and possible vulnerabilities, desperately searching for an opportunity to break free.

Someone approaches and begins to untangle me from the ceiling. I am asked to stand on a freezing cold floor. I can barely stand on my aching, cramping feet. Abruptly, the door slams, accompanied by a piercing scream that sends a shiver up my back. It is UB's way of announcing he is back and in control.

I freeze on the floor, unsure if the man's outburst is directed at me.

Summoning my courage, I ask, "Are you talking to me?"

A stinging slap lands across my face. Instinctively, I move to protect myself, but the metal handcuffs dig into my wrists, restraining me. Untrimmed Beard orders me to pivot toward him. Disoriented, overwhelmed, and still blindfolded, I grapple to comply, my body betraying my inner disarray. He seizes me and flips me over forcefully, unleashing a tirade of insults as he plunders my pockets like a relentless scavenger, snatching any items of value. My jacket, shoes, and even my belt are stripped away, leaving me exposed to biting cold. He meticulously counts the coins confiscated from my pockets, relaying the total sum before vanishing once again. It is a fleeting solace to hear him count my coins so carefully. It might mean he will give them back sometime. I desperately cling to this small, absurd hope in this valley of desperation.

A veil of silence is pierced with the crackle of distant gunfire and the low, mournful howl of the wind, which keeps me on edge and amplifies my mounting sense of anxiety. Pressed against the cold, unyielding wall, I shudder as frigid damp mercilessly infiltrates my bare feet, a haunting echo of my childhood experience of lacking proper shoes in the cold of winter.

I am lost in a state of shock. My mind spins with possibilities, feverishly pondering potential destinations within half an hour's drive of where I was kidnapped. No discernible sounds betray my location. I don't even know whether I am confined above or below ground, within Gaza or beyond its borders. I have an inkling we are below ground, as it cooled markedly as we descended. I suddenly notice a sickening odor and realize the mask on my face carries the residue of another's blood. Nausea and desolation descend upon me along with the beginnings of despair.

I strain to relegate the revolting odor of the mask to the recesses of my mind and focus on crafting a plan. How can I negotiate with these men? How can I unearth their motives?

Which of them will deign to engage with me? They feel like pawns in a nefarious game of chess, foot-soldiers who whisked me away from the streets like it was just another mundane task. It feels as if all this horror is of absolutely no consequence.

Suddenly, the door slams once more and another bone-chilling scream pierces through the sound of gunfire. A surge of adrenaline courses through my veins. Untrimmed Beard orders one of the men to twist my handcuffed arms and reconnect me to the ceiling with my feet on a plastic chair. He ruthlessly strikes my bare feet with a new weapon, a hard, elastic stick.

This time the pain is unbearable. I scream, demanding to know the reason for my torment and who is responsible. A second man joins the assault on my feet. "Those who want you are on the way," he says between blows.

It dawns on me that this is just the beginning of what may be an agonizing trial by torture. Their objective is to break me down before someone else arrives. I should have been prepared for this persistent beating. As I attempt to reposition my hurting wrists, my feet slip off the chair, resulting in even more pain as my body weight yanks on my wrists and I'm left dangling from the ceiling, my arms stretched behind me. The agony is indescribable. I resolve to stay alert by holding my breath for as long as I can, so I can endure. My only goal is survival.

A heavy silence descends upon the room. I can't hear any breaths. It seems I am alone, and a wave of apprehension runs through my body.

The door slams again and someone demands my touch iPhone ID.

"Is there any sensitive information on your phone?" he demands.

I reply through clenched teeth, "Yes, everything."

He unhooks me from the ceiling, holds the phone out, and insists I place my finger on the home button to unlock my phone. It fails to recognize the fingerprint, prompting a request for a passcode. Fumbling with my cuffed and trembling hands, I struggle to enter the correct numbers.

He exits, and I am alone once more. The acrid odor of the mask overwhelms and sickens me. I find comfort in the realization the previous wearer might have survived. If they didn't, there would be reports of a missing person or a discovered body, which I would likely have known about.

The door slams once more. The presence of Untrimmed Beard is unmistakable. I feel his malevolence emanating from every pore as he revels in the sadistic act of striking my restrained legs again, and occasionally my face, in a display of sheer cruelty. He seems to be one of the most abhorrent people I have ever encountered.

Amid the agony, my longing to be back home, lying down, replenishing my body, and breathing fresh air intensifies. I am determined to preserve my own dignity and strive to project a sense of strength, inhaling deeply and exhaling steadily with each blow he inflicts upon my feet.

He pauses, perhaps exhausted from the relentless assault. When he starts in again, my body surrenders to numbness. The stick's impacts no longer register as pain. My feet are gripped by an icy cold sensation and my shoulders ache from the strain of being suspended, but hope flickers within me. I continue assuring myself: I will reclaim my freedom, and this torment will become part of my past.

With a mix of trepidation and desperation, I ask, "Do you have children?"

He continues his assault. Undeterred, I ask again. He screams a demand for my silence.

Despite the pain gnawing at my chest, I strive to heed his command and remain silent. Eventually, he notices my diminishing reactions to the strikes, realizing that pain is confined to my chest and the unforgiving metal handcuffs digging into my flesh as I hang helplessly from the ceiling. I ask him again, "Don't you have children?"

He pauses again. "Yes. I have two children."

"Nice. How old are they?"

"Six and eight years old."

"Mine is only a few months old."

"So, you should help us, so you can get you back to your child."

"How?"

"The people who want you are on the way. But if it were up to me, you wouldn't deserve to live."

"Why?"

"They are coming, they will tell you."

He abruptly shifts his focus back to mercilessly striking my feet with the hard stick. Then he grabs hold of my feet and forcefully pulls me, causing my body to stretch downwards. The pain is so intense, reality blurs into undifferentiated agony. I hear the unsettling sound of my ribs cracking under the pressure. I am no longer certain if what I'm seeing and feeling is real or not.

The door slams shut as he takes another break from the hard work of torturing me. His absence brings a wave of relief. I strain my ears, hoping to catch any sign of life or movement around me, but I am met with only haunting silence. I had hoped my linguistic skills would enable me to decipher the identity of my captors, drawing on my university classes with Noam Chomsky and his behaviorist view of language acquisition. I count myself fortunate, at least, for possessing fluency in Arabic, a privilege not bestowed upon all hostages. My mind races, replaying his words and voice in my head, analyzing every sentence, every breath, every intonation, trying to decipher any clue that might reveal my location. His accent offers a hint, indicating that he hails from either Beit Lahia or Beit Hanoun in the north.

The door slams again. This door does nothing but open and slam, it seems.

"Here it is," says the guy who forced me to unlock my iPhone.

"Show me," Untrimmed Beard demands. They seem to be scrolling through my phone's call and chat history. "*Mashallah*, all your contacts are infidels," Untrimmed Beard says and smacks me across the face with breathtaking force. The most painful hits are the ones you don't see coming.

"Take my mask off so I can see what you're referring to," I request.

Another smack lands on my face.

"He's trying to be smart," says the other man. "Tell us, do you have GPS in your car?"

"Not that I know of, but sometimes my car's Bluetooth syncs directly with my phone, I don't know how…"

"What?!" Untrimmed Beard screams. The door slams again. Everyone seems to be running away, slamming the door behind them. "Switch off the phone and take the car out," I hear him command. I'm left wondering what prompted such a lightning-fast reaction. Even Untrimmed Beard seems momentarily out of control. This change of mood brings me some relief.

I am again left with only the howling wind and the intermittent gunfire, sealed off from the world in this mysterious metallic tomb. I yearn for someone to tell me what time it is. It feels I've been here an eternity, and the very concept of time—of a world where time moves at the normal rate—feels comforting. I ponder if they have simply abandoned me here, and if so, how I will manage to free myself from the ceiling. I'm willing to endure the ripping of my skin to escape these handcuffs, but my bones remain trapped. I wonder how much force it would take to break the bones…

The door slams again. "Prepare yourself for the orange jumpsuit," a new voice declares. It's neither Untrimmed Beard nor the one who took my cellphone. This voice is even more sinister. I say nothing, uncertain if he is addressing me directly and trying to make sense of his intentions. He erupts with anger, bellowing, "You… Get ready. They're bringing you an orange jumpsuit!"

Perplexed, I inquire about the meaning behind the orange jumpsuit.

"It has already been decided. The orange jumpsuit is on its way." His voice is laced with cruel satisfaction.

"Remove the mask and let me see you," I say.

Someone slaps me on the back of my neck. "Behave when you talk to Emir Abu Bakr!"

"Emirs don't kidnap and beat people."

Another slap.

The so-called Emir tells him to take it easy and offers me two choices: I can meet the fate of the Jordanian pilot or the Japanese journalist.

Muath Al Kasasbeh's F-16 fighter jet crashed during a mission against the IS group in Syria, and he was brutally burned alive on camera. The Japanese journalist, Kenji Goto, was beheaded. At the same time I am processing the gruesome threat, my curiosity is piqued about who Emir Abu Bakr might be. Another forceful blow lands on my head, leaving me disoriented.

"Abu Bakr is the Emir of the Islamic State in Gaza," another voice interjects, "and together we will bring an end to Hamas. Will you help us?"

"Take off my mask." Another strike finds its mark, punishing my audacity. The ground trembles with the entry of someone else.

"Unless you cooperate, we will summon Abu Dujana!" a voice shouts. "He may decide to end your life by slitting your throat with his knife." I suspect he has revealed the name of my tormentor, Untrimmed Beard. They press me to declare allegiance to the Emir, saying they will record my pledge on film.

"I will not serve your interests or anyone else's. My only allegiance is to humankind."

Anger simmers among them. I hear the sound of a gun being loaded. "Step back," one man says to another, apparently signaling his intent to shoot me. I brace myself. I am ready for it. Do it.

"Do you harbor any last wishes before your demise?" I'm asked by a voice tinged with morbid inquisitiveness.

"Yes." I keep my voice steady. "I request some water and the use of the toilet."

In the deafening silence, I catch the faint sound of cautious footsteps growing nearer.

"I'll unlock the ceiling handcuff. You have two minutes to drink water," a voice says, offering a sliver of respite. He unhooks me from the ceiling and changes the handcuffs from behind my back to in front of me.

Summoning my dwindling strength, I rise, my feet numb and unsteady. The frigid floor sends icy fingers through my bare feet. The numbness engulfs me. Faltering and kneeling as instructed by the Emir's nameless henchman, my face meets the freezing cold wall. I stay there for a moment, because my feet cannot hold me.

Trembling, I fumble with the sight-obscuring mask, revealing a glimpse of the desolate, dimly-lit room. A glimmer of hope flickers within me as I spot a half-empty plastic bottle. I bring it to my parched lips, the water in it tainted with the faint taste of green apple soda. The bottle slips from my shackled arms, clattering against the floor.

"Can anyone help me?" I plead into the empty void. No response. "Is anyone here?" The echoes of my voice are swallowed by oppressive silence. I crawl on the cold floor, the handcuffs restricting my movements. My hands guide me toward the decrepit toilet on my left, its stagnant stench filling the air. Bloodstains mark the wall. I dare to remove the mask, and a small window is revealed. But all I can see is a barren expanse, a distant dune or sandy hill devoid of any sign of human presence. My legs tremble with pain and bitter cold as I survey the rest of my surroundings. I'm in a prefab metal shipping container. In its center stands a gray plastic table adorned with the remnants of a meal. Chicken bones are scattered about. A worn brown blanket barely conceals a threadbare mattress. I lean against the cold container wall, burdened by the weight of the shackles and the torment of swollen feet. I feel sick.

A fleeting ironic thought crosses my mind: I've been saved by a toilet. It's a hollow attempt to find peace in the absurdity of my situation. The laughter dies as swiftly as it emerges. I have a cut on the inside of my lower lip, but I think my right foot is where the most damage has been done. With a heavy sigh, I resign myself to an agonizing wait.

Footfalls resonate from outside, echoing through the metal chamber, and the door slams open once more in this prison of despair. With an air of authority, Emir Abu Bakr asks why I am seated on the floor. "Have him seated on the chair," he commands the group.

Someone lifts me to my unsteady feet and unlocks the handcuffs. A brief moment of relief ends quickly as he moves my hands behind me and cuffs me once again. Then I'm pushed into a seated position on a plastic chair.

Abu Bakr's piercing gaze falls upon me, and he asks if I am missing something.

"My freedom," I respond, my voice infused with defiance.

"You are free after you pledge allegiance to us."

"What if I tell you I don't want to do that?"

"You will."

"No. Under no circumstances will I work for you."

He cuts me off dismissively. "Abu Dujana, take care of him."

Blows begin to rain down on my face.

"I'm holding an orange jumpsuit. It will be your new uniform!" he screams, sounding deranged. He demands that I speak, but I remain silent, which further enrages him. They take turns sitting on my head and chest, pinning me to the bone-chilling floor. Abu Dujana, fueled by rage, grabs a knife and threatens to slit my throat.

"Do it," I say. "Go ahead."

Bracing myself for the worst, I have a vision of life and death as interconnected entities, forever entwined like two sides of an endless spiral. I realize the line separating life from death is far more delicate than I had ever conceived—one is just a single breath away from the other. As I stare death in the face, I realize it holds no more mysteries for me, being a mere step away from life, separated from what I am now by the thinnest of margins.

One thing remains certain—I refuse to be remembered after my death as a pawn in the hands of these vile goons. My legacy will be defined by the actions I take, not the demands they sought to impose upon me. It is a surprisingly easy decision, and I feel a sense of peace to find that my integrity matters more to me than my life.

But the death blow still doesn't come. Emir Abu Bakr attempts once again to coax cooperation from me, offering to remove Abu Dujana if I comply.

"If the price is to die for rejecting your office, then do it. Because I would rather face death than collaborate with creatures of the night. I am a servant of the sun, destined to toil under its warm rays."

Abu Dujana slams me once more across the face. "There's no room for poetry here." He grips a machine gun tightly and begins to count: "One, two, th—"

"Don't count, just shoot!"

The counting ceases. I wait for the bullet. Instead, a blow lands on the back of my head that causes a surge of pain more intense than any bullet could have inflicted.

"A video shoot has been arranged outside. Align yourself with the Emir of the Islamic State or prepare to meet your grisly fate."

A voice unfamiliar to me sneers, "You're just another one of the losers."

Emir Abu Bakr reenters the room and instructs Abu Dujana to remain silent as he interrogates me. He asks why I chose to attend Columbia University in the United States rather than the Islamic State-affiliated universities in Syria or Iraq.

"ISIS universities?"

"Yes, of course. You never knew?"

"No, I didn't."

"We have the best universities offering quality education for our brothers and sisters."

"I am not interested in your education."

"You instead went to a *kufur* university in the oppressing States." He practically spits the word for 'infidel.'

No matter how diligently I attempt to elucidate the merits of development cooperation, they remain unconvinced. I can hear Abu Dujana's predatory growls as he circles me. The cold floor trembles beneath me with each menacing stride. My hands remain bound behind my back. I sit on the plastic chair, my face still concealed by the hood.

The so-called Emir implores me to assist his brethren in uploading videos online, claiming it's something I must have mastered during my time at Columbia. "We offer good money for the service."

"Money does not buy genuine values."

He asks me to aid them in their quest to reclaim Gaza from its current rulers. I refuse.

He wants to know why European nations provide development assistance and aid to Gaza, questioning my associations with the last three ministers who visited the region. "What do they want?"

"Your universities must be teaching human development 101," I say, trying to keep the sarcasm out of my voice. But I am denied the chance to expound on my theories about addressing the root causes of instability, radicalization, poverty, and violent extremism. Each time I attempt to speak, Abu Dujana interrupts with an unsettling hum. The Emir dismisses me as nothing more than a mouthpiece for Western propaganda. They clearly have no interest in entertaining ideas that might challenge their entrenched beliefs.

Abu Dujana again brandishes his gun, but the Emir instructs him to stand down, assuring him I will demonstrate allegiance to the Islamic State in due time.

Left alone again, the silence stretches into an interminable void. It feels as though an eternity has passed when someone enters with a message: "The Emir has grown impatient with you."

Evidently, he has some requests in mind that will guide me from what he perceives as my state of "darkness" into the "light" he claims to see. I can't help but ponder how these guys define light and darkness, right and wrong, justice and injustice. Every action they have taken since my capture has been unequivocally wrong. It's as if they are drawn to the allure of darkness like moths to a flame, unable to resist its seductive pull. By now I have lost any curiosity regarding their intentions. I ignore the man until he leaves.

The call to prayer reverberates again, signaling it is the third, late afternoon prayer. The familiarity of the *adhan* and the way it anchors me in time is comforting, like a message from a better world.

Suddenly the self-proclaimed Emir bursts back into the room. He and Abu Dujana continue their futile quest to extract an avowal of loyalty from me. The Emir promises to spare me from the "long nights" of beatings being planned by Abu Dujana and his cohorts if I comply. He is aware of my role as advisor to ministries in the Netherlands and Norway, specializing in development cooperation—my position is a matter of public record—and he seeks to exploit my knowledge. He makes two specific requests: First, he asks for my assistance in facilitating a Schengen visa for one of his associates. Second, he inquires whether I can arrange an armored vehicle akin to those used by European diplomats capable of traversing a dead-end road. They seem to have a specific place they want the car to be driven through, perhaps to target diplomats.

He pauses, awaiting my responses, while Abu Dujana emits guttural sounds to assert his loathsome presence. Abu Bakr insists they seek an armored vehicle merely for transportation needs.

"I am not interested in working with you," I say again.

To my surprise, he does not press the matter further but simply leaves.

Abu Dujana informs me, "Your impending slaughter, captured by the film crew, will be broadcast live. I am breathless."

I am tired and restless and afraid, but I am not so stupid as to believe any media outlets will do a live broadcast of my shooting, immolation, or beheading. I maintain my silence, and he prods me to speak. Finally, I say with a tone of resignation, "Do as you wish."

The door slams shut once again, plunging me into another stifling silence. This feeling of having no control over what comes next is as exhausting as anything. I'm starting to wish they had shot me at the beginning and been done with it. The men seem to revel in their own twisted rituals. My feet are numb and my body wracked with uncontrollable tremors. I only wonder whether I will be allowed to utter my final words before the camera. I contemplate the message I wish to convey, should fate allow me this privilege.

Out of nowhere, a new voice shatters the stillness.

"Stand up!"

I have no idea who is helping me up and guiding me as I struggle to bear weight on my throbbing feet. He warns of steps and obstacles along our path until we pass through a doorway and emerge into the open air. I implore him to give me my jacket, seeking some respite from the biting cold, but he says there's no time. He orders me to lower my head and settle into a seat. In an instant I realize I am in a car. It is my car. My fingertips brush against the upholstery, which evokes a sense of familiarity.

"First, I go. Then you follow," he instructs someone in another vehicle and pushes my head down in the back seat, near the transmission gear. Silence hangs heavy in the car. My hands are still cuffed. The captor is apologizing for using my cologne, which feels out of place. Why is he seeking forgiveness for this trivial transgression while ignoring what has been happening to me? I fear there is more to this situation, something he is not revealing.

My hands are still shackled, and I attempt to remove the mask. Frustration sets in as I struggle with limited mobility and with my head pushed down. I attempt to steal glances out the window, trying to gain any sense of where we are, but it's in vain. The surroundings are alien to me, devoid of recognizable landmarks. My captor's occasional mention of the cologne intensifies the knot in my stomach. Is he trying to confuse me?

The car finally comes to a stop and I hear the sound of a gate rolling open. My captor exits the vehicle. I take a moment to gather my thoughts, my heart pounding in my chest. I feel a glimmer of hope that this unexpected turn of events might lead to my escape. Then he gets back in and the engine accelerates.

"Where are we? Can you at least tell me that?"

Silence.

"Can you tell me where we are going?"

Silence.

"I deserve some answers. What do they want from me?"

"I can't say anything. Just trust me for now."

"Trust you? Why should I trust anyone?"

"I understand your apprehension, but there's more at stake here."

"More at stake? What could be more important than my life?"

"I can't explain it now, but you'll understand soon enough."

I give up, the captor's vague responses only fueling my frustration and confusion. Questions swirl in my mind, unanswered and unresolved.

Without warning, the car comes to a halt, jolting me back to the present moment. My captor commands me to sit up straight with my arms extended forward. One click and the handcuffs are released. My hands are finally free. I remove the mask and revel in the rush of fresh air in my lungs.

"Get out of the car, jump in the driver's seat, start the car, and drive away," he says, as if he is granting me a generous favor.

I'm too stunned to move. I observe him closely as he heads toward the white car that must have been tailing us. He is dressed in a black jacket, black trousers, and polished black military boots and carries himself with a military air. Some kind of embroidered logo adorns his shoulder. He has a nice face. Not good-looking, but nice features.

I am too weak to do as he says. My legs tremble. Pain radiates through my entire body. It is unbearable to consider pressing the accelerator. My instincts tell me to do something else. I turn off the engine, get out, lock the car, and take off running in the opposite direction. The last thing I want is to remain trapped in that car, which may be booby-trapped. The surroundings vaguely trigger a sense of familiarity. My mind races. I dart into the nearest mini-market and urgently ask to use the phone.

The shopkeeper eyes me warily. "Are you alright?" he asks.

"I'm okay," I manage to utter before hastily departing. I can tell he will ask too many questions, as I probably look like a madman with no jacket, no phone, no ID, low-hanging trousers, and bare feet, and I want to put more distance between myself and my captors.

I'm freezing and can no longer feel my legs at all. My injured feet pound against the rocky road as I sprint through Sheikh Radwan, a neighborhood in northwestern Gaza City. Recognition slowly dawns on me and then hits like a jolt of electricity. I am near Al Shati refugee camp, close to Al Shifa hospital. With a renewed sense of purpose, I push my weary body forward until I pull myself into the emergency room.

"What happened?" the attending doctor inquires, concern etched across his face.

"I was kidnapped by a group of militants," I manage to reply, my breath coming in ragged gasps.

Without hesitation, the ER doctor guides me to a bed and calls for additional medical assistance. A police officer arrives from the adjoining police room, requesting an account of my harrowing ordeal.

"I was taken by a group of militants who say they are IS."

"There is no IS," he replies sternly. "We are the only power here."

The staff nurse interrupts. "He is not the first person to be abducted in this manner. Earlier this morning, we received a physician colleague who'd been seized and released in a similar condition."

Apparently, no one knows who is responsible for these abductions or their motives. The policeman takes notes as the doctors complete their examinations. The worst pain is in my chest and arms from being tied to the shipping container ceiling. My legs feel devoid of sensation, chilled to the bone. The doctors administer intravenous fluids with pain relievers and order X-rays of my chest and legs. I have no cellphone, wallet, shoes, or any of my belongings. How do I prove who I am to a hospital? I can't, and anyway, I just want go home.

Fortunately, a doctor concluding his shift offers to drive me home, which is on his way. He could not be more sympathetic and concerned. Fifteen minutes later, we pull up to my house. I am free but uncertain what lies ahead or how to reconnect with family, friends, and contacts I have lost touch with. But I feel grateful for the kindness of the doctor who escorted me home, and I tell him so.

I step through the threshold of my house and a wave of relief washes over me. I am finally home and safe, consoling my anxious family, even as the memory of the kidnapping haunts me. I collapse into bed, exhausted beyond imagination. But sleep eludes me. I face a long night replaying the events of the day in my head, followed by nightmares. Then an early morning. Because this is not over.

Chapter 14

Searching for Answers

News of my capture is leaked to a national newspaper moments before it hits the presses, and the next morning I find myself surrounded by well-meaning visitors. Journalist friends tell my family how they tried to contact me without success. I obtain a new cellphone and SIM card with the help of a family member. My new phone number spreads rapidly, and major news outlets such as *The New York Times*, *Newsweek*, CNN, and *Al Jazeera* reach out to me.

I appreciate their interest and care, but it only adds to my inner turmoil. The last thing I need is to tell the story hundreds of times. All I really want is to rest my weary body and make sense of the ordeal.

As a career journalist, I have always been captivated by people who choose to remain silent in the face of life-altering events. I understand now. Sometimes we must seek a full understanding of what happened before we can articulate our experiences to others.

A security officer contacts me on the new number, cautioning against any public statements that can "compromise further police investigation." This attempt at a gag order is preposterous, and I let it be known that my silence is not a result of external demands and certainly not because of death threats. My silence is driven by a desire to fathom the depths of my ordeal and its significance.

Despite the anguish and weariness pervading my chest, each breath brings me back to a sense of hope.

In the early hours of the next morning, an exceptional visitor pays me a call. Abu Salman Al Moghani is the Head of the Supreme Commission for Tribal Affairs and Reform in Gaza, and he arrives dressed all in white. He is disturbed by what he has heard of my ordeal, and after collecting my personal testimony, he departs from my home to confer with Gaza's leaders and the heads of various political parties, conveying a resounding message: "Do you wish for all families to forsake Gaza? We endured when our homes were ravaged, but we shall depart when inner tranquility eludes us."

He informs the chief of police he met with me, witnessed my bruised limbs, and heard a harrowing tale that was a stain on the splendor of Gaza. Four hours pass and Abu Salman receives the first official police reaction. He returns to my home to share his news: The police suspect my kidnapping is a fabrication orchestrated to bolster my case for a humanitarian visa so I can seek asylum in Europe.

I present him with my Dutch passport, rendering him speechless. The police officers are visibly embarrassed, as my passport shatters their feeble excuse for neglecting to investigate my abduction. Abu Salman is not pleased at being misled. He gives the policemen a very sharp look and vows to keep pushing until he finds the truth.

Gingerly, I navigate my way downstairs, limping to the street where the white car lay in wait for me that morning. Venturing into the supermarket, I grab tubs of hummus and yogurt and proceed toward the cashier, who eyes me warily. As he scans the items, I request access to yesterday's front-door camera footage.

"I don't have them. Armed men came and took them."

I believe him.

There's one more possible clue. According to a UN field security office, a young woman standing on a balcony on the fourth floor of a residential tower bore witness to my kidnapping and reported it to the radio room of the International Red Cross Committee, where her uncle happens to serve.

Still, no one can locate the white car or find my captors.

Another day passes and I'm feeling a bit defeated. As the evening draws to a close, I remain largely cut off from communications with friends and connections. Some arrive after fruitless attempts at calling my confiscated cellphone. I wish I had better news to share with them.

A few minutes past midnight, there's a reverberating knock on my door. I carefully peer through the window. Two men are standing beside a parked civilian car. They apologize for the late hour but insist on an immediate visit. I grant them entry.

In the light, I can see they are two high-ranking officials from the police unit. My family serves them coffee. The officers sit on the living room sofa, one in plain clothes. The chief asks me to sit on the other sofa facing them. They introduce themselves, but I am not really concentrating. As they sip their coffee, I once again recount the events of two days before. The chief says they heard it before from the hospital police report and Abu Salman. They need more clues. I mention the security cameras. The deputy tells me they are investigating the other police departments who confiscated them.

The deputy fidgets on the sofa, moving his legs from side to side. "Are you alright?" he asks me. He mentions my slurred speech due to the cut on my lip but fails to notice the scalding water bottle on my right foot, searing my skin while it continues to freeze.

"I was knocked down by so-called Abu Dujana."

"We saw the Shifa hospital medical reports and emergency room cameras," he says.

"I got hit on the face while I was grinning with my teeth tight together."

The deputy's red pen scrapes across the yellow notepaper. The scratching of his pen and the pounding of my neck vein echo in my ears.

"Tell us about any distinctive traits in your captors' voices or speech, or any other observations that might help."

"I was mostly covered with a mask."

"Any piece of information, no matter how small, could be crucial in unraveling this mystery," the chief says.

I shrugged. "So-called Emir Abu Bakr kept circling me and asking me to perform tasks for him after I refused to pledge allegiance to him."

"Emir Abu Bakr in Gaza?" the chief asks.

"Yes, and someone else they referred to as Abu Dujana."

"Tell us more about this Emir Abu Bakr," the police chief urges sternly.

"A man with deep and distorted voice," I say.

"Like how does he sound?" the deputy asks.

"He spoke with an air of authority, as if he believed he was above the law," I say.

"Dr. Mohammed, please focus. I need specific details."

"He thought he knew me because he read some of my work."

"Parents want to believe they know their children, wives know their husbands, and friends know their friends," he says, nodding.

"I don't recall hearing any voice like his before in my life," I say. I wrack my brains and try to bring to mind the atmosphere around Emir Abu Bakr. "The mask smelled of blood, but when he moved around, I could smell a strong smell like the copy oil version of Sculpture cologne."

"The copy oil version of Sculpture?"

"Yes."

Both of them look at each other, put down their small coffee cups, stand up from the sofa, and march toward the staircase and down to their car.

Some minutes later, the deputy knocks at the door again.

"I think you should not stay here until we get to the bottom of this," he says.

I tell him there is nowhere else for me to go at this late hour. My car is still parked on that street in Sheikh Radwan.

"I really think you should not be here tonight," he repeats and tells me how IS in Gaza remains a puzzle. Not a very intelligent one. He says they are often misguided people who've been exploited by extremist groups seeking power and control in Gaza. No one knows the entire plan, and no one really understands what is supposed to happen next. Even recruiters don't necessarily know what comes next after they receive their $2000 per person for joining IS. But they soon find out. Their actions bring immense suffering to innocent people and tarnish the reputation of an entire religion.

The cops are aware I am determined to unravel the truth and won't remain silent for long. The deputy assures me he won't be able to sleep tonight until they uncover the whole truth. He insists I rest and refrain from exerting myself.

"We have our police investigation unit heading to inspect your car right now for potential threats," he assures me. It has been parked in the same spot for the third night running.

I ask a relative to drive me to my parents' home in the south, with a police car following us halfway to ensure we're not being tracked. I'm amazed the police are undertaking these responsibilities, considering the scarcity of fuel for their vehicles due to the blockade.

Early the next morning, the police declare my car was not tampered with. Even if my legs recover enough for me to drive, I now lack an identity card, driver's license, any proof of insurance, and all other documents that might help me prove my identity. It was fortunate I left my Dutch passport at home that day. Thankfully, the Deputy Chief of Police and Abu Salman are miracle workers, bestowing upon me the necessary papers as if they possess the power to create a new being.

On the fifth day after my release, the police assure me they have uncovered the truth behind the incident, promising it will never occur again. I have no idea what they mean or whether to believe them, but I have little choice.

"You should freshen up, shave, eat well, and take it easy. My beard is not too popular with my wife and daughters," the deputy jokes. "Your case has occupied the Police Directorate phone lines for the past few days. It is heavy on our heart that this happens under our control."

I know my quest for the truth has kept them on their toes, and I appreciate the sentiment.

Another officer confides, "When the community mobilizes, it means our job is at stake because we have failed to protect the people."

I am still in shock and struggling to comprehend the identities of my captors.

"What if this Emir Abu Bakr and Abu Dujana show up again?" I ask.

"They will not," he says, his voice filled with conviction. "We have dealt with the issue swiftly and thoroughly. The case was broken open when you said someone smelled like the fake version of Sculpture cologne. It brought together all the missing pieces."

It sounds like something out of an Agatha Christie novel.

Another senior police investigator shares a crucial detail with me: I was held captive in a shipping container intended for donation to families made homeless from the latest Israeli assault. But it was either sold to or seized by militants as a place of torture and confinement.

When he tells me the exact location, I am stunned. The proximity of this place to my childhood playground in the north haunts me. It lies just a short distance from where I spent happy days with my grandparents, sliding downhill on an empty water tank. If I had screamed, my grandmother's house would have been within earshot, where I once delighted in her delectable okra stew and steaming rice. The familiarity of the location cuts deep, and the pain is overwhelming.

The vehicle that abducted me matches the description of the one caught on camera planting an explosive device that caused slight damage to the French Cultural Center in Gaza City in 2014, thankfully without any casualties.

Women's beauty centers have also been harassed and intimidated by these guys. A leaflet circulated among the public, purportedly from the Islamic State, issued threats to women in Gaza and instructed them to dress modestly, avoid "tight, transparent, or eye-catching attire" and refrain from using adornments or perfume. Another leaflet targeted eighteen Palestinian intellectuals, journalists, writers, and poets. Most of the individuals on the list fled Gaza. A prominent lawyer was captured and subjected to assault by three armed assailants, with no resolution to the case. I discovered through my own investigations that more individuals had experienced similar ordeals and had been coerced into silence under threats of harm to themselves or their families if they reported it to the police or to the media.

In 2011, a similar IS-like group kidnapped Italian journalist and activist Vittorio Arrigoni, a fervent advocate for Palestinian rights whose grandfather had fought against the fascist regime in Italy. Vittorio was strangled to death by his captors, a pointless and gratuitous murder that sickened Palestinians who only wanted to welcome this kind and committed person.

In March 2007—just before the US-Israeli-Fatah coup that attempted to overthrow the democratic elections in Palestine—BBC journalist Alan Johnston was kidnapped by another mysterious clan. He was the only Western journalist working full-time in Gaza at the time. He was released only after the coup failed and Hamas officials put immense pressure on the group to release him.

In 2003, three American private security specialists were killed and one diplomat wounded by a remote-controlled bomb that exploded beneath one of the armored cars in a diplomatic convoy. They were on their way to Gaza City for interviews with Palestinian Fulbright scholar candidates aiming to pursue graduate studies in the United States. All Palestinian political factions disavowed the bombing, and no one claimed credit. Not only did it serve to alienate Americans from Palestinians, it was also an indirect assault on all young Palestinians who aspire to broaden their lives. The Israeli government immediately called for all Americans to leave Gaza "for their own safety," which left Palestinians more exposed to indiscriminate Israeli violence, with fewer potential advocates or witnesses and less hope for the future.

It makes one wonder, who has so much interest in keeping Palestinians away from education? Who has an interest in driving away sympathetic humanitarians and journalists? There are still no definitive answers, and there may never be.

What I can say is that it has been an effective way to keep Gaza more isolated, fractured, intimidated, and silenced.

Whoever was ultimately behind it, we must remain vigilant against outside interests playing these and other games with our lives.

In the Dutch Parliament, a select group of MPs go above and beyond after learning of my ordeal, pushing the Israeli government to facilitate my exit out of Gaza for medical treatment. Their support, even as it disconcerted some Dutch diplomats, is invaluable. Hans van Baalen, a staunch advocate of classical liberalism, emerges once again as a figure of great significance in my life, offering his sincere support in a gesture stemming from his core beliefs. Times like these show people's true faces.

During my period of medical rehabilitation in the Netherlands, I spend a day in the company of an affable Norwegian friend traversing Amsterdam's idyllic canals, flitting from one cafe to the next. Even during hot summer days, my right foot constantly remains freezing cold. Despite the lingering pain, such a beautiful and carefree day helps me regain some hope and peace within myself.

In light of my experience, I make the decision to forge ahead with the launch of my book, *Shell-Shocked*, an on-the-ground report of Israel's so-called Operation Protective Edge, launched in July 2014. It was the third major Israeli assault on the Gaza Strip in six years. At the time, it was the deadliest. In seven weeks, Israel killed 2,200 Gazans, around 70% women and children. More than 10,000 people were injured, including one thousand children left permanently disabled. 7,000 homes were razed, rendering 10,000 families homeless, with 89,000 more homes damaged.[31]

My book aims to capture the untold narratives of war that are often overlooked by mainstream media—the shocking horrors as well as the way the community comes together even in the worst of circumstances.

When I launch an online campaign to promote the book's release, the response from readers worldwide is overwhelming. Messages pour in from Australia, Brazil, the United States, China, South Africa, Spain, New Zealand, Sweden, Argentina, Norway, Jordan, and Panama, among others.

The one disappointment is that the book remains unavailable in Gaza itself. This prompts me to collaborate with OR Books in New York and Haymarket Books in Chicago to design a Gaza-specific print edition of the book, ensuring it reaches the people who experienced the impact of the onslaught firsthand. Creating the Gaza print version is an arduous task, rife with challenges, but eventually we succeed with the help of Samir Mansour's bookshop.

Several organizations bestow their sponsorship upon the launch, including the UN, Palestine's Union of Cultural Centers, and many Palestinian universities. Abu Salman, the Head of the Supreme Commission for Tribal Affairs and Reform, surpasses all expectations, leaving no stone unturned to ensure the event is successful. He extends his personal invitation to all the mukhtars and organizes a local bus company to ferry a multitude from every corner of the Gaza Strip.

On launch day, the event hall at the Roots Hotel, overlooking the sea, teems with an exuberant throng: Academics, ministers, diplomats, UN officials, mukhtars, journalists, members of the police force, and other influential figures converge. The four-hundred-seat chamber is filled to capacity and extended to the beachfront hall. Seven more buses arrive full of mukhtars and heads of police from Al-Nuseirat, Al-Mughraqa, Wadi Gaza, Bureij, Deir Al-Balah, and Maghazi, which drags the book signing on for four hours instead of two. Thankfully the hotel owner can accommodate everyone. (When I go to thank her later, she says, "I should thank you! I wish our own opening day had been like this.")

Abu Salman extends warm salutations to the attending ministers and governors from every corner of the blockaded Gaza Strip. People from all backgrounds and walks of life— Muslims, Christians, and non-believers alike—converge in solidarity, channeling their collective energies toward peace, freedom, and Palestinian unity. The profuse displays of support and affection from both new and familiar faces leave me humbled. As I warmly embrace each person and receive their affectionate gestures of greeting, the power of unified action impresses itself on all my senses.

Someone remarks to Abu Salman about the intimidating number of mukhtars. He replies, "That's precisely the intention. Today we are sending a message of rejection to whoever is behind the kidnapping and destruction of our social fabric. It's also restitution to someone who is dear to our hearts."

As I witness the serpentine queues winding through the book ceremony, each person patiently awaiting my signature, a tide of hope surges within me. This occasion is a proclamation, a clarion call echoing through the halls. It is a collective gesture, a testament to resilience and defiance. Each signature I bestow becomes a symbol of resistance against the specters of so-called Abu Dujana and Emir Abu Bakr. Their doctrines of violence and extremism are repudiated with every stroke of the pen.

In addition to the awe-inspiring outpouring of national support and encouragement, there are also messages from across the globe, including handwritten missives from the Foreign Ministers of the Netherlands and Norway. It re-instills my faith that compassion and benevolence can exist even in a world seemingly plagued by the forces of hatred and intolerance.

I express my profound gratitude to figures within the Dutch and EU Parliaments whose dedication to monitoring the circumstances surrounding my kidnapping have been a source of encouragement, even if they never came to any firm conclusions that I'm aware of.

This is beyond a mere book launch. It metamorphoses into a symbol of the combined exertions propelling transformative change in Gaza. After all, Palestine is not represented by one or two factions. Palestine is my mother, grandmother, sister, and aunt. It cannot be defiled, marginalized, manipulated, or hijacked by any group. Palestine will be liberated because it is a just cause, not by aligning itself with this ideology or that. Palestine transcends ideology. It embodies all colors; it is our diversity and resilience that make us strong. We also reject the war crime of collective punishment when a few individuals decide to take actions that affect all of us.

I'm inspired today more than anything by the people of Gaza and their resolute refusal to succumb to violent extremism, their courage, and their solid commitment to fostering meaningful discussion about the realities of war.

I gleaned several lessons from these experiences. First, in the grip of hardship, one needs quiet support and understanding, not advice, and certainly not criticism and probing questions.

Second, I chose to maintain silence at the time, refraining from imposing presumptions or biases on what happened. I declined numerous interview requests from journalists. How could I narrate to others a tale that I myself had yet to fully comprehend? However, silence is not an appropriate response when faced with injustice. Without accountability, history only repeats itself.

Third, while no one should endure a traumatic abduction for responding to an apparently stranded person, and I acknowledge the harsh reality of how I was deceived, it will not deter me in future from offering help to someone in a similar position.

Fourth, the searing cold that tormented my feet during the long assault evoked vivid memories of my own impoverished childhood, when I often walked in improper footwear in winter. When that biting chill permeates the soles of a person's feet, the pain with each step is unbearable. When children's feet are exposed to freezing temperatures, each outdoor step becomes a grueling ordeal, sapping warmth from the body and rendering children susceptible to frostbite and other cold-related injuries. This is a reality for many children around the world. Gaza is blessed with a reasonably mild climate, but temperatures in winter can still approach or even reach freezing. There is no heating in houses or schools, exacerbating the cold. Children's feet can further be covered in cuts, bruises, and abrasions from sharp objects and rough terrain.

The excruciating pain of walking barefoot on an ice-cold floor during my ordeal fueled my determination to secure warm footwear for every child in Gaza who cannot afford a decent pair of shoes.

That leads to my fifth lesson. My kidnapping experience compelled me to delve deeper into what drives radicalism and violent extremism.

In our current world, great powers often decide what happens in less powerful countries with little or no input from the rest of the international community and scant regard for international law or human rights. It is my belief that this increases violent extremism in the world of the type that ensnared me in my own homeland. The ravages of manmade disasters like those in Somalia, Libya, Sahel, Yemen, Syria, and Ukraine and human-caused climate emergencies in Vanuatu, Haiti, and the Philippines worsen the problem.

A Japanese diplomat in Amman shared profound insights gained by his country's lawmakers in their pursuit of addressing violent extremism after the case of the Japanese journalist kidnapped and killed by IS. This is one of the very few occasions where I sat in front of someone and was unable to say a single word.

He told me the beheading of Japanese journalist Kenji Goto by IS in Syria shocked everyone in Japan. It prompted them to reconsider prioritizing the human development agenda. Addressing the root causes of violent extremism is now their number one priority in development cooperation.

The time has come to adopt a more comprehensive and well-rounded approach with a strong emphasis on taking preventive measures by addressing root causes. It should be obvious that no single country can address violent extremism alone. It is clear to me that a collective effort is needed to address these challenges and reform the system to be more multilateral in approach.

An agile and responsive UN system is imperative to help prevent and resolve conflicts. Violent extremism often thrives in regions plagued by instability, grievances, unemployment, and unresolved disputes.

Whether in the realm of development, humanitarian efforts, or peacekeeping, the UN has a very weighty mandate. If we neglect to invest in the UN, what alternative are we left with? Narrow nationalistic approaches only perpetuate divides as the rich grow richer and more powerful, and the poor become poorer and more desperate.

Hassan, like many Palestinians, expressed his doubts about the UN, which has so far been unable to do anything about the decades of occupation and now the blockade, merely making it easier for Israel to warehouse the population of Gaza without taking responsibility for it. I implored him to recognize that the UN is not an alien entity—it encompasses all of us, representing the collective spirit of humanity. It is in fact the nearest there is to an embodiment of "all of us," the people of the world.

As individuals and communities, we have the power to mobilize our parliaments and communities, fostering support for a more robust UN system. Together, we should be able to amplify our voices and advocate for a UN that can address global challenges effectively and promote international cooperation.

One powerful symbolic gesture would be to appoint a woman as UN Secretary General. It is shameful that since its establishment in 1945, this position has been occupied exclusively by men. I recognize that it's entirely possible to select a woman who would be no different, or even less interested in multilateral reforms, than her male predecessors. But it would be one step toward showing our true colors around gender equality, sending a powerful message of hope to women and girls globally.

By embracing diversity and cooperation, I firmly believe we can diminish the appeal of extremism.

A few weeks before my kidnapping, I arranged for a Dutch expert to visit Gaza and share the latest knowledge in the world of chocolate-making. The expert willingly left his wife and grandchildren to share this knowledge, as he had already done in forty-four other countries, in a gesture that carried great meaning for the people of Gaza.

The expert taught managers at two Gaza factories how to properly roast cocoa beans, blend different kinds of beans to achieve desired flavors, and temper the resulting chocolate for a smoother texture. Al Awda Factory was thus able to reduce electricity consumption, reinforce professional hygiene standards, and cut added sugar in chocolate bars by 40 percent.

He also advocated for addressing the gender pay gap, creating fair conditions for women and men doing the same or similar work. He established Sara, the double amputee working as an accountant at ice cream companies, as a precedent in the private sector and food industry in Gaza, effectively addressing the income gap among people with disabilities. Her case has been instrumental in advocating for fair pay for all women with disabilities, whether victims of war or domestic violence or disabled from birth.

Once export permits were obtained from the powers that control our borders, the same Dutch man helped Gazan chocolate compete in national and regional markets. Other experts have similar lessons to teach about coffee beans, tourism and hospitality, and the dairy sector.

Emir Abu Bakr and his henchmen failed to recognize the connection between chocolate, resilience, and economic growth. They thought these influences were *kufur* and refused to engage with them. They envisioned Gaza as isolated, hopeless, and devoid of pleasures and joyous moments.

So, I decided to write this book to prove to him and his associates that they are wrong. Gaza persists in its desire to live, prosper, and grow. After so many decades of living under military occupation, our people deserve to make connections with the world. Our people deserve the finest of international knowledge, cultural exchange, and expertise to build on. Our people deserve the long-denied but inalienable rights to life, liberty, and the unhindered pursuit of happiness.

Chapter 15

Beginning Again

Nearly twenty years have passed since that sticky afternoon when Leena's husband arrived on his motorcycle, anxious and defensive.[32] Hassan sits at his desk in his dimly lit laboratory, as usual, surrounded by stacks of files and test results. He still willingly carries the burden of unraveling the mysteries of conception. By now he has saved countless women from being blamed for fertility struggles. Hassan's lab always has this air of purpose, an atmosphere in which hope thrives.

He has seen so many changes since his first son Bilal was born. His dream was for Bilal to be a medical doctor, but Bilal found his passion in technology, creating a hub of like-minded engineers and serving clients in Europe and the Gulf working with large-scale data systems and cloud computing technologies. Hassan is just as proud of his six other children and three grandchildren, with another expected soon. For him, every baby is an additional blessing.

We are enjoying his famous *zaatar* tea, talking about nothing in particular, when the glass door creaks open and a familiar face appears. It is Leena, the woman who endured ten years without a single pregnancy. The lines of wisdom now etch her face, but I see in her eyes the same shimmering determination that brought her to Hassan's lab every month all those years ago. In her hand she holds a small, colorful box of candy, a token of celebration.

Hassan's smile radiates warmth and he beckons her to take a seat. His heart flutters, wondering if she has come to tell him the long-awaited news of her pregnancy after all this time.

The woman settles into a chair. Her eyes well up with tears. "Hassan, I cannot thank you enough for what you have done for us. Our lives have been transformed."

Hassan humbly inclines his head, acknowledging her gratitude. "I merely facilitated the journey. The true power lies within you and your husband," he replies with gentle reassurance. She nods, her tears flowing freely, releasing the burden of years of doubt and self-blame.

"You were right, Hassan. It wasn't my fault. It takes two to create a baby, and with patience and the right medication, we were able to conceive."

Joy courses through Hassan's veins. His heart swells that the woman's burden is finally lifted. "I'm glad you found the answers you were seeking," he says, his voice filled with genuine care. "But tell me, is it a boy or a girl?"

A smile of maternal pride illuminates the woman's face. "I am a mother of five children—my oldest is sixteen now and excelling in her studies. She recently aced her Tawjihi. I couldn't be prouder."

In Palestinian cities, the Tawjihi is like the SAT on steroids. Students study for years, and when results are released, masses of joyful people celebrate the achievements of the youth with boisterous block parties, food, and fireworks.

Hassan is visibly moved and so am I at this poignant evidence of the lives he has touched. I think of Hassan as a quiet champion of dreams, and I am humbled once again by the magnitude of the human spirit, the profound impact one person can have on those around him.

The woman hands Hassan the box of candy, a small gesture that holds great significance. "I wanted to share this with you, Hassan," she says. "To express my gratitude and to honor the remarkable work you do."

As she rises to leave, her eyes sweep across the laboratory, taking in the rows of test tubes and microscopes. "Hassan," she begins hesitantly, her voice tinged with concern. "Do you ever grow weary of this fight? Protecting women's rights can't be an easy path."

Hassan stretches back in his chair with his hands behind his head, as he always does when he wants to engage deeply with someone. This is when you know you're getting the real Hassan. He shifts his gaze to a photograph of his late mother, an emblem of strength and inspiration.

"There are moments in life when doubt and weariness creep in. But when I think of the lives that have been touched by kindness from others, the dreams that have been reignited, and the barriers that have been shattered, that's what keeps me going."

He pauses for a moment, and for the first time I hear him tell a personal story to a patient. As the middle of nine brothers and one sister, Hassan's life took an unexpected turn when his father, Ahmad, was reported dead in an accident in Egypt, four hundred miles away, during a trip for medical treatment. He explains how the family set up a mourning tent, accepting the loss of their beloved patriarch despite being unable to lay him to rest. Six years passed, and the family lived with the lingering misery of never having bade their father's body a final farewell.

One sweltering summer afternoon, a knock at the door interrupted the siesta hour. Hassan's mom and siblings were taken aback. They were not expecting anyone. They opened the door to find a man in a wheelchair with tears streaming down his face.

"It was Ahmad, my father," Hassan recounts, still amazed by his own story.

No one could believe their eyes. The room was filled with cries of disbelief and joy as Ahmad began to tell the story of his near-fatal traffic accident, his years in a coma, and his arduous rehabilitation. He'd tried to send messages home through nurses and medical staff, but the messages never reached his family, blocked by borders and other circumstances beyond his control. Ahmad touched his children's faces one by one, speechless as he beheld how much his small kids had grown. The entire neighborhood soon gathered to witness the miraculous return of a man they all believed lost forever.

"That experience taught me not to grow weary," he says. "Whatever good one does in the world, it will always be reciprocated."

His story describes the powerful pull of family and the profound blessings that can arise after the hardest moments—pleasures clutched from adversity's depths. In the tapestry of Gaza, their miraculous story is woven into the fabric of the Palestinian narrative.

The woman nods. "You are a source of hope, Hassan," she whispers. "A guiding light in the darkness. I hope your journey continues to be filled with victories."

She walks out, leaving Hassan curious at the mention of her daughter's exceptional academic performance. He seeks out that day's newspaper. Amid all the names, printed in tiny font, he finds her daughter's name, Tala. Next to it, a remarkable achievement: 98.3 percent, the second-highest grade ever achieved in a town of over 350,000 inhabitants. Tala has set her sights on medicine, aspiring to become the city's first female pathologist.

Hassan can't stop smiling. He takes the newspaper back home to share Tala's remarkable accomplishment with his own wife and children.

Final Interlude: Connection and Hope

When I first met Malak, after months of searching for her father, she was a shy four-year-old. Since then, she has undergone a remarkable unfolding and blossoming. Nurtured by her parents and supported by American benefactors who became dear friends, she has become a confident, passionate, and determined young woman and mother, admirably clear on what she wishes to achieve in her job as a teacher. She imparts her energy to her students and becomes their beacon of hope in tumultuous times. She shapes young minds to see their own future.

For me, Malak's journey from timid child to unstoppable force embodies the transformative power of education, courage, determination, and the best of the human spirit. Malak has flourished into a spirited young woman and an unwavering advocate for change. She and her peers form a fervent movement, armed not with weaponry but with the potency of words and the flames of conviction.

Malak jostles for position at the breakfast table, folding a letter she wrote to her second family in Houston, which someone traveling to the US will drop in the mail once they arrive. She puts the letter away and retreats to her room to prepare for another school day, adorning herself in clothes that suit her exquisitely, as always, and packing her things for school, her cell phone charger hanging out of her bag.

"Thank you, habibi [darling] Papa, for such delectable hummus this morning," Malak says before rushing to the taxi that will take her to school.

Amid the ebb and flow of life's interludes, she has evolved into a prime illustration of endurance and resolve. From her dad's scarred past, she has developed into an irrepressible and vibrant woman, an embodiment of hope amid the uncertainties that surround her, steadfast in her mission to make a difference. Witnessing the artistry of her brother, she has come to recognize the profound power of creative expression. Like a brush on a canvas, she endeavors to paint dreams of freedom, transcendence, and resilience for her own children, nurturing them with love and guiding them toward a promising future for her people and land. With patience and understanding, she encourages them to speak their truth, and she listens and offers solace and guidance if they seek it. She assures each of them that their voice and experience matter.

Malak once believed poverty would forever define her reality. She has since learned that human connection wields a power greater than any weaponry—more potent than Apache helicopters, tanks, bulldozers, F16s, or the automated gun machines that restricted her childhood movement. Though she'll never forget those days, she has chosen to forge ahead, constructing a bridge from her war-torn homeland to the rest of the world. These connections continue to ignite within her a desire to hone her new language and foster ever more meaningful bonds. Her heart brims with gratitude for the books gifted to her during her early childhood years, carried by a visiting American surgeon, bestowing upon her a solid educational foundation and unlocking the doors to a realm of boundless possibilities.

Human hearts and minds are capable of hatred, violence, and fear. They are also capable of connecting and fostering mutual growth, joy, and hope. Malak's story illustrates the powerful forces that can be unleashed when we dare to nurture the better angels of our nature, with faith in our fellow humans.

Marriages, power cuts, and baby booms have become the new normal in Gaza, with the vibrant streets more crowded than ever before. Amid the whirlwind of joyful Tawjihi celebrations,

I encounter an old schoolmate, Bassam, outside the lab. To my astonishment, I learn that he has become a father to eight children before reaching the age of forty. I ask how he manages to maintain and raise such a large family.

Bassam's answer intrigues me. He speaks of the sense of unity and interdependence in his household, where each family member takes care of the others and everyone shares tasks. They feel responsible for one another, he explains. It's how he raised his kids. It is all a question of mindset.

He assures me with a smile, "Gaza will endure, strengthened by these bonds of familial love and support."

As a teacher in a national school, he finds immense pleasures in the bustling chaos of parenthood and enjoys being with children before, during, and after school. He recalls how during the 2022 World Cup in Doha, he sat with his kids huddled around a handheld cell phone, hopeful about the positive vibes as Saudi Arabia, Morocco, Tunisia, and Qatar all made it to the world stage. This memory brings him a profound sense of pleasure and unity, knowing his kids were celebrating not just their favorite teams but also the collective spirit of the Arab nations.

The Abu Holi and Al Matahen checkpoints are relics of the distant past, and instead of taking hours, people can now travel from the north to the south of the Gaza Strip on upgraded highways in just 25 minutes. Despite the ongoing horror of the blockade and the absence of basic freedoms, citizenship, or political rights, coupled with the constant threat of Israeli assault, there remains a sense of optimism that these circumstances will not endure forever. The world is evolving, and Gaza is gradually connecting and integrating with it. We hope and trust that the international community will not forsake us to Israel's mercy forever.

Perhaps one day, in the not-too-distant future, we will be as free as anyone else to fish our waters, cross our borders, visit our holy sites in Jerusalem, Bethlehem and Hebron, purchase vaccines for our dogs, procure fabric for our fashion designs, attend university wherever we choose in Palestine, and compete freely in sports.

We aspire to a future characterized by dignity, justice, and self-determination. We seek to reclaim our cultural heritage and identity, embracing our history while striving for a future free from oppression and occupation. We have endured more than enough. We yearn for the right to return to our ancestral lands, to live in peace and harmony alongside our neighbors of all faiths and ethnic backgrounds, and to build a society founded on principles of equality and mutual respect. We envision a future where our voices are heard and our aspirations realized, where we can forge our own destiny on our own terms. We seek not only political freedom but also intellectual and cultural liberation, recognizing the importance of narrative and representation in shaping our collective identity and future. We shall always hold fast to the belief that our dreams of freedom and sovereignty will one day be fulfilled.

In a small strip of land on the eastern Mediterranean, Maher the quail hunter strolls along the beach, his steps mirroring the rhythm of the waves. Italian chefs Domenico and Maria create a symphony of flavors with skillful hands, merging the essence of two cultures on their culinary canvas. Mohammed Qraiqae, the young Picasso of Palestine, paints vivid strokes, his brush breathing life into the very essence of Gaza. Banksy's street art dances on walls and doors, blending seamlessly with the interactions between the American "Doc" Paskowitz and the surfers, their shared laughter like music in the air. Kamal, a Christian Gazan and pillar of strength, guides his blind companion Hatem through the maze of streets, their mutual devotion a forceful expression of their faiths.

Visionary fashion designer Nermine weaves threads of entrepreneurship while Amira and Shady, their hearts ablaze with youth, embrace the exhilaration of movement, their parkour escapades a physical manifestation of their love of freedom. The Fida'i soccer team lifts the hearts of devoted fans. Aisha and Ashraf find solace in each other's arms after long years of waiting. Aisha's wise and eccentric uncle and his loyal canine companion, Habiba, are part of a new trend along with Omaima and others connecting with fellow dog owners on the beach, their love for their furry companions fostering a new sense of community.

Families find ways to connect despite borders dividing them. Dalal Abu Amneh's melodic voice resonates through the air, singing songs of freedom that echo in hearts hungry for true liberation. Jawadat's Al Mathaf museum and Marwan's cave of wonders offer glimpses into the rich saga of Gaza's past, preserving history and inspiring generations. Stories shared at TEDx Shujaiya ignite new ideas and hopes, and the symbolism of Prisoner 1044036 brings an inspiring example of resilience and determination to the collective consciousness.

In the shadows, Abu Salman Al Moghani engages in candid conversations, unraveling fragments of truth and justice, paving the way for a better future. Tunisian president Marzouki sails with the flotilla in a vessel carrying a message of hope and solidarity from the world to Gaza's shores. In the sanctuary of the university campus cafeteria, Maria, Rania, and Shayma, three young women passionate about theater and literature, share national and diaspora experiences, laughter, and knowledge in a bond forged through intellectual curiosity, shared experiences, and inexhaustible loyalty as they navigate life's winding paths, their journeys intertwined.

The lives of all the brave people you have met in these pages are a clarion call urging us all to question the status quo and to challenge oppressive systems wherever we find them so that more of this humanity can shine forth. These incredible people challenge us to confront our own complacency, to dismantle walls of ignorance, and forge paths towards greater truth, justice, freedom, and empathy. Within their stories and voices lies the power to break chains of oppression so that hope and courage can triumph over despair.

All these lives interweave to create the resplendent tapestry that is Gaza today. Of all the pleasures of Gaza, the greatest is the steadfast courage of its people who, faced with insurmountable odds, find pleasures, show strength, and keep a sense of humor even in the most trying of circumstances.

And now dear reader, I must leave you, as tomorrow I leave Gaza for an exciting opportunity as a research scholar at Harvard University. I must get up very early in the morning so I can see my grandmother for breakfast before I catch the three-hundred-mile ride through the Sinai Desert—that is, if I am granted permission to leave the coastal enclave I call home. I hope to bring my new knowledge and connections back to a Gaza Strip that is more vibrant, and closer to freedom, than ever.

Epilogue

Israel has been dispossessing and oppressing the Palestinian people for more than three-quarters of a century, from the Nakba of 1948 to the occupation of the West Bank and Gaza since 1967 to the siege that turned the Gaza Strip into an open-air prison for sixteen years.[33]

But nothing has ever been quite like this, as far as the sheer scale of the killing and the obliteration of entire major cities. The onslaught that began in October 2023 uproots everything in its path. Nowhere is safe. The rare pleasures Gaza once boasted have been drowned out by mass killing, starvation, and destruction.

Israeli leaders' calls for mass atrocities have not been subtle. Israeli President Isaac Herzog said early on at a press conference, "It is an entire nation out there that is responsible. It is not true this rhetoric about civilians not being aware, not involved. It's absolutely not true. They could have risen up, they could have fought against that evil regime which took over Gaza in a *coup d'état*." He seemed to imply that all Gazans were legitimate targets.[34]

Defense Minister Yoav Gallant ordered a "complete siege" of the Gaza Strip. "There will be no electricity, no food, no fuel, everything is closed," he said. "We are fighting human animals and we are acting accordingly." Such collective punishment is a grave war crime.

Israeli Prime Minister Benjamin Netanyahu himself said to the Israeli people and military: "You must remember what Amalek has done to you, says our Holy Bible," invoking a Biblical passage that calls for the complete annihilation of a people, including their women, children, infants, and animals.[35] These and other public statements have been deemed genocidal by people who have studied other genocides.[36]

In a prima facie admission of war crimes, IDF spokesperson R Adm Daniel Hagari said that "hundreds of tons of bombs" were dropped on the Gaza Strip, and "the emphasis is on damage and not on accuracy."[37]

The results have spoken for themselves. It has not been a military campaign so much as a campaign to punish every single Gazan and practically erase Gaza from the map.

Hospitals bombed, schools bombed, markets bombed, homes bombed, factories bombed, mosques bombed, churches bombed, farms bombed, bridges bombed, shelters bombed, roads bombed, water supplies bombed, solar plants bombed, playgrounds bombed, libraries bombed, cultural centers bombed, animal shelters bombed, museums bombed. Nothing is sacred. Nothing is safe. No one is protected. Nearly everyone in Gaza has been made homeless. Thousands of dead civilians remain trapped under rubble, unable to be counted. In areas we can't reach, our people's flesh is consumed by stray dogs until only skeletons remain.

A shocking percentage of Gazans have been killed, injured, kidnapped, and/or orphaned. An accurate count is not possible due to the systematic destruction of the means of retrieving, identifying, counting, and properly burying bodies and the extreme danger of trying to reach large areas where attacks are particularly severe. Israel forbids foreign journalists from entering Gaza to take a look for themselves.

The official toll is nearly 50,000 killed and more than 100,000 wounded, but the real toll is undoubtedly much greater. Many have died due to deliberate starvation, especially children, and hundreds of thousands more are at risk due to growing man-made famine. Roughly 70% of the casualties are women and children, which mirrors the population at large, evidence of the indiscriminate nature of Israel's killings. Every day, there is another series of massacres.[38]

A doctor returning from Gaza reported that "A handful of children, all about ages 5 to 8, were carried to the emergency room by their parents. All had single sniper shots to the head. These families were returning to their homes in Khan Yunis, about 2.5 miles away from the hospital, after Israeli tanks had withdrawn. But the snipers apparently stayed behind. None of these children survived."[39]

After many months of relentless violence, Israel has killed more hostages than it has rescued, and Hamas is nowhere close to being "eliminated." Yet the killing and destruction continue. Even if Hamas ceased to exist, nothing fundamental would change. They are not the root cause of this conflict.[40]

April 2023: Once the tranquil abode of 250,000 souls, our beloved Rafah bears the burden of accommodating over 1.6 million humans, thrust upon them by Israel's ethnic cleansing and destruction of most of Gaza from the north to the south.

Rafah is pushed to the brink, unable to bear the burden of so many displaced and desperate people. The city strains under the mass of humanity, struggling to provide even the most basic necessities to men, women, and children who lost everything in the blink of an eye. Our city can't accommodate such a flood of humans, but it has no choice, as Israel's military ordered people to evacuate south. Yet even in Rafah, crowded to the brim, there are Israeli bombings and carnage every day.

My dear friend Hassan is caught in the madness along with his family, including his wife Rania and children Bilal (29), Aseel (21), Ali (18), Hala (13), and two other married daughters and their young children.

I catch up with Hassan after he flees his house following a one-ton missile that hits his neighborhood north of Rafah—an area Israel officially declared as "safe" for evacuating civilians.

The neighborhood lies in ruins. Hassan counts himself fortunate to have survived, though the same cannot be said for over 80 of his neighbors who are injured, killed, or missing. With his windows and doors shattered, uncertain whether the missile was a harbinger of more destruction yet to unfold—missiles often strike when people dare to return home or gather at bombed-out sites in search of their loved ones—Hassan has no choice but to seek refuge at his brother's house in a nearby neighborhood.

A nephew with cancer is injured, and Hassan goes to Al Najjar Hospital in Rafah to visit him. The hospital is overrun with displaced, dead, and injured, its corridors choked with bodies. A man enters, bearing two bags resembling flour sacks. The shattered remnants of a family are gathered within. People directly hit by massive bombs don't arrive on stretchers.

At the hospital's entrance, Hassan encounters Sabrine and Hanine, a mother and her adult daughter, weary and shoeless. They fled the north after an airstrike, and their predicament adds to Hassan's burdened heart. Without hesitation, he brings them to his brother's house, sharing what little food they can find and cook on wood collected from ruins of demolished homes.

Both women are Egyptian. Hanine was drawn to Gaza by a handsome poet she met online who kept her awake most nights sharing new lyrical verses. Her mother Sabrine entered Gaza a few months earlier to visit her daughter and new son-in-law. I often wonder how both managed to enter Gaza in the first place. At Rafah Crossing, it's usually the rustle of banknotes that smooths the path through the gates.

They had only a precious window into the pleasure of Gaza before the apocalyptic violence began. Hanine's husband went missing in the chaos, leaving them with only a photo of the charming young poet. Hassan's son Bilal recognizes him, saying he used to run into him at the barber shop.

They stay with Hassan's family for nearly two weeks, sheltering in an abandoned mini-market next door.

Hassan tells me how Sabrine and Hanine keep trying to catch the attention of an Egyptian soldier in a nearby watchtower—from the same dunes where Layla used to stand hoping to hear from her mother Maisoon—without much success.

"Exiting Gaza will cost $7000 for each person," says Hassan, "and the mother and her daughter don't have any money."

"They shouldn't have to pay to go home," I say.

"Pull a few strings with your influential friends," he asks.

When I present their Egyptian passports to a high-ranking Egyptian official, he issues a directive instructing border police to unlock the gate.

Before they can make it out, another devastating airstrike hits near Hassan's brother's home. Everyone flees who is able, and when they stop and take stock, Sabrine and Hanine have sustained cuts and bruises, Hassan has head and leg injuries, Hassan's wife Rania has a nasty cut on her head the requires stitches, and Aseel and Ali are missing along with some of Hassan's nephews.

When they reach the hospital, their injuries seem insignificant in the face of children with limbs ripped off. Some of Hassan's nephews are among the dead. A group of four emerges from the smoke, carried on stretchers in the very last ambulance that arrives. Their dusty faces become clear only when the stretcher-bearers draw right up next to them.

"Ali," says Hassan, immensely relieved. "Aseel!"

They are dazed and injured by shrapnel, but on Gaza terms, not seriously, thank God. Aseel, a medical student still not aware that her university has been destroyed, is placed on the ground;

her stretcher is needed for more serious cases. She can walk but with a limp. Hassan looks sadly at her thin, gaunt face. His own injuries seem serious but he keeps downplaying them. Rania is still bleeding. She seeks medical help but is turned away. There are too many people who need help far more urgently. Hassan worries because the bleeding is significant, and there is a serious danger of infection.

In the US, they would all be rushed to the emergency room with their injuries. In Gaza, they are not even counted in the statistics of injured people.

Sabrine and Hanine decide to try to make it to the Rafah Crossing before nightfall. Hassan hopes for a passing donkey cart to carry them at least halfway. Otherwise, the walk from Al Najjar Hospital to Rafah Crossing takes about an hour.

"Is it safe for them to exit?" Hassan asks me.

"Nowhere is safe, Hassan," I say. "Let's face it. Gaza is bleeding, untreated like your wife."

"Hold onto this," Hassan says, pulling Hala's only white shirt from his backpack and placing it in Sabrine's hand. The backpack also contains the children's certificates and 300+ medical lab results yet to be handed to his clients. His lab is now non-functional, inaccessible, and covered in rubble due to nearby bombings.

"Keep waving it this way; the troops will know you are not a military target," Hassan demands.

I don't want to disappoint Hassan, but the Israeli army killed its own hostages while they were shirtless and waving white flags.[41] When the Israeli military declares an area a "military zone" (also known as a "kill zone" or "elimination zone," usually without any announcement), they give themselves permission to kill anything that moves.[42]

Luck is on their side, and Sabrine and Hanine make it to Egypt. Sabrine texts me, thanking me and saying she is home after a long ride through the Sinai with her heartbroken Hanine.

Hassan is relieved but still trapped with his family in the chaos.

"Papa, I am scared we'll get bombed again," Hala says. Just thirteen years old, she should be thinking about music and friends, not bombs and starvation.

"Airstrikes are nothing to worry about," Hassan assures her. "They just slam once. There is nothing scary about them if one dies immediately."

"But where can we go?" asks Bilal. "There's nothing left of your brother's house. Our house is bombed out, too."

Hassan looks around at the people gathered in a makeshift encampment around the hospital. "We can stay here."

"Why don't we go to UN classrooms?" Bilal asks.

"They've been bombed, too," Hassan says.

"We'll stay here?" Hala asks doubtfully.

"We will get some plastic sheets and create something for the night behind the morgue," Hassan says. That's as far ahead as he can think.

The morning of April 3 arrives with a briskness that evokes the zest of freshly squeezed lemon. Hassan and his family settle behind the hospital morgue, seeking refuge amid trauma and horror that never seem to end. He sees more families, more familiar faces from his neighborhood, who have been forced to flee again and again. For some, it's the sixth time. With each ominous rumble of approaching strikes, people scramble to find shelter in new locations only to have their hopes shattered by renewed waves of airstrikes that seem to pursue them relentlessly.

Hassan no longer has to travel to the hospital to see dead and injured loved ones—he has no other place but this spot behind the hospital's morgue to stay for now. Smoke from explosions mingles with the exhalations of passersby, shimmering filaments in the chilly air.

Hassan tells me how his life is now: The family splits up, spending daylight in queues for bread, water, and to charge phone batteries and hand-held lights.

"The kids are losing weight, growing weak from lack of vitamins and minerals," he tells me. "And my nephew's health is getting worse. There is no chemotherapy, and cancer is eating his body."

"Where is he?" I ask.

"Here with us behind the morgue," Hassan says.

"How is your wife doing?"

"The bleeding stopped, but she is still in pain."

Bilal had planned to get married in summer, but the winter and spring are stinking with blood and displacement. The family lost all they had saved, and the woman Bilal had his eye on escaped with her dog and parents after paying $21,000 to a private company to go through the Rafah Crossing.

"Bilal does not know she left," Hassan says.

"I saw her dad and the dog on the news last night," I tell him.

"They might seek family reunion with her cousins in Michigan."

I hear Hala say to her mother, "Your wedding ring!"

I wonder if it has been lost in the chaos.

Hassan assures Hala, "She gave it to Sabrine and Hanine as cash for the road."

I hear more ambulance doors slamming shut with new arrivals at Al Najjar Hospital. Overhead, the sound of drones and jets never ceases, punctuated by the sounds of bombs that can fall literally anywhere, north or south, even on a foosball table where children are playing.[43]

People in Gaza say that if you hear the bomb, you are lucky. The unlucky ones never know what hit them. The really unlucky ones die slowly, alone, under the rubble of what should have been their sanctuary in a difficult world.

The prospect of an Israeli invasion into a jam-packed Rafah hangs in the air, threatening human devastation beyond reckoning. But with bombs falling from the north to the south, with food and water barely reaching Rafah and even more difficult to find elsewhere, with bribes to leave via the Rafah Crossing costing thousands of dollars that most people don't have, there is nowhere to go to escape.

As for Naji and his family, I don't know their fate. But Israeli forces have destroyed virtually everything in the "buffer zone."

The area around Al Najjar Hospital has been bombarded relentlessly, but the hospital is one of a handful of Gaza's thirty-six hospitals that has not yet been blown up or invaded with the doctors, patients, and displaced people inside expelled, arrested, injured, or killed, often leaving behind mass graves and signs of field executions.

Hassan tells me about a surgeon he knows well who offloaded two children with amputations and a dead mother, only to realize the woman was his wife. She was killed by shrapnel to the head. Their two children lived, one with one leg and the other with two legs ripped off. The father had no option but operate on his children without anesthesia due to Israel's blockade on medical supplies.[44]

Thousands of children have lost limbs due to blasts, crush injuries, shrapnel, infection, and other causes related to the war and Israel's devastation of Gaza's medical system.[45]

Back in November, thirty-nine premature babies were removed from their incubators in Al Shifa Hospital, Gaza's most advanced medical center, due to Israel's blockade on fuel and electricity and its siege and raid on the hospital. Some of the babies weighed less than three pounds. They were kept side-by-side on ordinary beds, exposing them to infection and without adjustable temperature and humidity. Eight babies died within a week. The others made a perilous journey to Egypt for proper medical care after photos of the babies outraged the international community. Many of them remain unclaimed, their parents unknown and likely dead.

Not long after, a chilling tableau unfolded at Al Nasr Hospital's ICU ward after Israeli soldiers occupied it, kicked everyone out, and ransacked it. When a journalist was able to make the dangerous journey back to the hospital, the frail forms of four infants, some still tethered to wires and tubes meant to save their lives, lay motionless in their beds, their tiny bodies decomposing. Milk bottles and diapers rested untouched beside them. After ordering the evacuation of the hospital, knowing the babies were there, Israeli soldiers had abandoned them to their fate—to die slowly, alone.[46]

Al Shifa hospital has since been raided a second time and demolished completely, leaving behind mass graves that should be major worldwide headlines but have been virtually ignored.[47] Mass graves containing more than three hundred corpses were also found after Israeli forces occupied the Nasser Medical Complex in Khan Younis.[48] Many people, including medical personnel, remain missing.

In every possible guise, this is televised carnage unfolding in front of us. Some call it the world's first livestreamed genocide. Borders tightly sealed, meager humanitarian aid struggling to reach those in desperate need, and any moving target, whether journalist, rescue team, ambulance, or aid convoy falling prey to Israeli drones and warplanes. More than one hundred journalists, more than two hundred aid workers, and more than three hundred medical workers have been killed in Gaza. These are all historic, record-shattering numbers.

This includes people such as the eye surgeon who, on his Facebook page, expressed his determination that Gaza would not succumb to despair and pledged to continue saving lives in the hospital—an act that ultimately cost him his life.[49] Journalist Moamen Al-Sharafi tragically lost twenty-two family members, including his parents, siblings, and nieces and nephews. They were apparently killed simply for being linked to a journalist reporting Israeli atrocities on the ground.[50]

Where five hundred trucks once entered Gaza daily, now some days barely a dozen are allowed to venture forth. Even then, people may be shot by Israeli snipers or drones while trying to reach it, crushed by falling air drops with malfunctioning parachutes, or drowned in the sea as they swim for aid dropped into frigid and turbulent waters. Respected local people who try to coordinate aid distribution to prevent mobbing and looting are also targeted and killed by Israeli forces, contributing to further chaos.

Meanwhile, Israeli soldiers film themselves looting priceless artifacts, smashing neighborhood shops, burning life-saving aid, and gleefully detonating neighborhoods and universities. Then they proudly post it on TikTok and Instagram for all the world to see, knowing there will be no consequences.

In Khan Younis, a ground invasion unfolds. In addition to the killing, masses of people (including some children) are rounded up, stripped, and hauled off to brutal Israeli prison camps. More than ten thousand people have been kidnapped in this manner, including many doctors and medical staff, and held in inhumane conditions, beaten, starved, neglected, and denied proper medical treatment, with several having limbs amputated due to handcuff injuries. Others have been raped and several have died in Israeli prison camps, most held without charge or trial.[51]

Israel has steadfastly refused to let Western journalists enter the Gaza Strip, leaving many of their war crimes and genocidal acts nowhere near fully documented. More information will come out in time, although likely much too late to save many more victims. We can only hope it will be a wake-up call for all of humanity and that such things will never again be allowed. It will require a fundamental restructuring of world politics and power, and it is long overdue. Colonialism and genocide must end. An ethno-state that practices apartheid, ethnic cleansing, and genocide cannot be given a blank check any longer.

Even prior to this campaign of mass destruction, Gaza grappled with a high infant mortality rate.

Sally Abi Khalil, Oxfam's Middle East Regional Director, said: "Amongst the horror and carnage in Gaza, we are now at the abhorrent stage of babies dying because of diarrhea and hypothermia... In some cases, mothers are having to give birth in classrooms full of 70 people, with no medical support, dignity or even basic hygiene. I don't think there is anyone anywhere in the world that would disagree that is simply inhumane."[52]

Aya was three months pregnant when her husband, a schoolteacher, was killed in an Israeli artillery shelling in November. She fled barefoot with her wheelchair-bound deaf mother-in-law. They embarked on a twenty-five-mile journey along the once beautiful Salah El-Din Road, with Aya's hand raised above her head while she rolled the wheelchair with the other as instructed by Israeli soldiers. Sadly, no other family members survived. Six months later, the bodies of the dead remain unburied.

Aya is one of thousands of women giving birth prematurely amid the trauma and stress. Each breath is haunted by the threat of airstrikes that could hit the tent where she labors outside Al Najjar Hospital. In her worst nightmares, she never imagined she would give birth to her first baby in such inhumane conditions—faced with the agonizing choice between a bombed-out classroom or an ill-equipped tent, devoid of even a mattress. Aya would need a miracle to be attended to by doctors slammed with endless horrific trauma cases. The only hope she has for medical care is if she gets bombed while in labor. And what future awaits these newborns, born homeless in the midst of genocidal bombings and blockade?

Aya is left to confront life head-on, lacking diapers and baby clothes, with a premature baby she will have to raise as a single mother if she and the baby survive. Aya is starving and has little chance of being able to breastfeed. Her mother-in-law can only do so much to help. Being deaf and disabled, she remains unaware of the true extent of the situation. Unable to hear warnings or cries, she does her best to navigate the trauma and stress that surrounds them while her support person is in labor. She is facing heightened difficulties along with thousands of other disabled Gazans. There's not much in the way of accessibility in a war zone.

Meanwhile, menstruating women lack basic hygiene supplies and have been forced to use tent scraps as sanitary pads.

Another baby was born an orphan after Israeli airstrikes in Rafah killed 19 people, including thirteen children from one family and Sabreen Al Sakani, who was 30 months pregnant when she was killed.[53] Doctors delivered the baby via c-section and placed her in an incubator in a Rafah hospital. Her three-year-old sister, now dead, had wanted to name her Rouh, or Spirit / Soul. The newborn, with no immediate surviving family, died days later. This is just one of thousands of Gaza families wiped entirely from the civil registry.

A new acronym had to be invented in Gaza: WCNSF—Wounded Child, No Surviving Family—because this phenomenon is happening so commonly. UNICEF estimates that 17,000 children have been orphaned or separated from their parents.[54]

So many mothers and pregnant woman like Aya have received no proper prenatal care and lack a nutritious diet, clothing, birth plans, support systems, hospital bags, pain relief and postpartum care because of Israel's bombardments and blockade. Clean water and formula are at a premium, and all too often unavailable. Many babies have been born and died before they could even be registered, remaining officially uncounted in life or death.

My friend Ibrahim, Gaza's own Santa Claus, is making me proud. The Christians of Gaza are trapped in Israel's blockade like everyone else, and Ibrahim is starving, foraging, dodging, enduring, bracing, fortifying, persevering, fleeing, resisting, and worshipping all at the same time.

He is living in the Greek Orthodox Church of Saint Porphyrius, in the Zaytoun Quarter of Gaza's Old City, with hundreds of other displaced Christians and Muslims. It is the church whose campus was bombed in October 2023 by Israeli forces, killing 18 innocent civilians.

In the Holy Family Parish Church, also in Gaza City, two Palestinian Christian women were murdered by Israeli snipers. They targeted 70-year-old Nahida Anton as she was walking between buildings to go to the bathroom. When her 50-year-old daughter, Samar Anton, ran to help her, she was shot and killed by the same sniper.[55]

Others have died violently or due to prevention of medical treatment.

Ibrahim tells me about organizing a beautiful Easter, adorning the church with crosses, candles, images of Jesus Christ, palm branches, and lilies. He surveys the scene, with worshippers dressed in their Sunday best filling the wooden pews adorned with palm fronds for the service marking the start of Easter week.

I see hope when I hear a young man speaking from the pulpit, dressed in an ankle-length red robe, saying to those trying to survive starvation and airstrikes, "Palm Sunday is an opportunity for hope, goodness, and peace for us and for the entire world."

Solemn-looking altar boys in the front row listen quietly while parishioners with drawn faces after months of hunger and war fill the remaining pews. Their strength, steadfastness, courage, and kindness give me hope.

"This year, we don't have the heart to celebrate," says Sister Nabila Saleh, sheltering in the Holy Family Church. "It's true that we decorated, but we don't feel the joy of other years."

It's impossible to blame her. Gaza City has been bombarded relentlessly, and its Christians have not been spared. So much has been lost, with no end in sight. Many fear this could spell the end of the historic Christian presence in Gaza, dating back at least to St. Hilarion in the fourth century. And it's true that Christian Palestinians can much more easily get humanitarian visas anywhere. But what I hear from their actions is that Palestinians are not going anywhere, including Gaza's Christians.

"So that's Ibrahim," says Hassan when I tell him about it. "Make sure you amplify his voice to the world on every occasion. *Al hamdulillah*, history is repeating itself. Jesus could be any one of us."

Israel's destruction of Gaza's historical and educational fabric is incalculable. Nearly every location mentioned in this book bears scars of damage. Almost all universities have been destroyed, leaving tens of thousands of students displaced. Almost 90% of schools have suffered damage, leaving 625,000 students without access to education.

At the Basha Palace, valuable artifacts have been damaged or stolen. Marwan's museum lies buried beneath enormous piles of rubble. Jawdat Khoudary's stunning museum at Al Mathaf Hotel has been completely destroyed. Israeli soldiers posted videos of themselves playing around in the rubble.

The Gaza War Cemetery sustained severe damage after the caretaker family was driven out under threat of violence. It's unclear if the Jeradeh family will have anything to go back to, if they have survived, to continue their long family tradition of tending the hallowed grounds.

Gaza's seaport is no longer the crown of turquoise and jasmine flowers the city once boasted, a pride like the beautiful young women whose splendor poverty could not tarnish. It has been completely destroyed, like Rimal, Gaza City's commercial hub, and Khan Younis's beautiful old homes and public service buildings.

The blue waters tell you none of that matters. At least they couldn't erase the sea. On the way to the damaged boats, flowers blooming atop a heap of sand and debris created by a bulldozer weeks ago will call out to the world: Do not despair, Gaza—we have always proven that cities are made by souls, not stones, and as long as we are alive, nothing is impossible. Gaza will return more beautiful than any time before, *inshallah*.

"In general, the war in Gaza presents threats, but also opportunities to test emerging technologies in the field." This is according to Avi Hasson, chief executive of Startup Nation Central, an Israeli tech incubator.[56]

"Yes," Hassan tells me. "I am aware we are the world's testing lab for new military technology."

This shows up most ominously in the domain of Artificial Intelligence. Initially thought of as a benign force aimed at serving humanity, AI's involvement in warfare reveals its darker implications.

For example, the Israeli military developed an AI-based program called "Lavender" that played a central role in the targeting and bombing of Palestinians, especially during the early stages of the war. Its outputs were basically accepted at face value, with almost no oversight, as it marked tens of thousands of Gazans as 'suspects' to be assassinated, with soldiers bombing them with barely a glance at the underlying intel even though its decisions were known to be riddled with errors. The army also implemented an extremely lenient policy for killing the families of suspects as well as random bystanders.

Another automated system, grotesquely called "Where's Daddy?" is used to track people to their family's home so they can be bombed there.

"We were not interested in killing operatives only when they were in a military building or engaged in a military activity," an intelligence officer told +972 Magazine. "On the contrary, the IDF bombed them in homes without hesitation, as a first option. It's much easier to bomb a family's home." [57]

Thousands of women and children never involved in any fighting have been wiped out due to AI program decisions.

"This explains what we see around us," Hassan says. "We are being experimented on by automated AI killing machines. What an ominous reality. What a world."

"I know," I respond.

And it isn't just "operatives" who are targeted. People who shape public opinion and carry our people's hopes and history are regularly murdered along with their entire families. The Israeli military targets those who represent faith and connection to the land and share our stories with the world, whether they are artists, intellectuals, academics, university presidents, doctors, journalists, or even street vendors who hold meaningful ideas and have become pillars of our community. It is a way to "decapitate" our society, an attempt to destroy it as thoroughly as possible.

The list goes on. It's numbingly easy to tick off horrors without even scratching the surface: the assassination of poet and professor Refaat Alareer, the killing of *Reuters* reporter Issam Abdallah, the killing of *Al Jazeera*'s beloved Samer Abu Daqqa, the murder of young Hind Rajab and her family,[58] the Flour Massacre,[59] the destruction of Al Shifa Hospital. These stories may fade from view, but the haunting of the hearts of those left behind is beyond measure.

"Journalists, medical workers, professors, and hospital staff?" Hassan asks. "Tell me this is all just a terrible dream and that it will end when I wake up."

"I wish it was," I say.

"Where is the light?" he asks. "I can't see anything in here."

"In the sky," I answer. "We just have to keep striving toward it."

For too many in the West, these stories remain mere statistics, only obliquely mentioned in the news if at all.

But there are headlines, finally, when Israel targets an aid organization whose founder happens to be close to the President of the United States. In the anodyne language of military slaughter, it's called a "triple tap"—three successive strikes aimed at ensuring the complete elimination of a target. In this case, the target was the occupants of three vehicles in a humanitarian convoy that had just helped unload more than one hundred tons of humanitarian food to a warehouse in Deir Al Balah in central Gaza. After the first drone strike, survivors fled to the second car. When that was bombed, they scrambled to the third car, which was also blasted, killing all seven aid workers. One was from Australia, three from Britain, and one was Polish, along with a Palestinian and a man with dual American-Canadian citizenship.

On the day of the Israeli assault on the convoy, the US State Department approved the transfer of over 1,000 MK82 500-pound bombs, fuses for MK80 bombs, and more than 1,000 small-diameter bombs to Israel.[60] The US government has been steadfast in its arming and funding of the genocide, sending weapons worth tens of billions of US tax dollars and providing political cover by pretending to engage in good-faith ceasefire talks without pressuring Israel in any meaningful way, even as the Israeli government crosses every "red line" and assassinates its interlocutors.

The convoy had obtained permission from Israel to use this route and had coordinated everything with the Israeli military. The cars prominently displayed the organization's logo. They were targeted and slaughtered regardless.

An international uproar lasted for about a week. Then it, too, faded.

"Hassan, we went through harsh days; they were not as intense as this, but we managed to come through, and Gaza will eventually survive," I try to assure him in one of our calls.

"This time is different. Israel bombed international aid workers after giving them a safe route. These were nationals of the countries supplying the war machine."

"How do you know this?" I ask.

"Aseel showed me a photograph her friend sent her."

"And?"

"Is there no red line?" Hassan asks, exasperated.

Like him, with each fresh Israeli atrocity, I am tempted to think: This is the one, this is the one, now this is the one that will wake the world up. This is the one that will stop the flow of arms, this is the one that will finally end the massacres. But I have been saying this since I carried Rachel Corrie with the ambulance driver Abu Alaa to the same morgue and through the same metal doors over two decades ago. I'm either mad, or there's something wrong in this world, and it's mad.

"Reading Obama and Carter's memoirs, it made me realize any word these presidents say about Israel can bring down Congress," Hassan goes on. "Obama admitted he could not be loyal to his basic instinct, which was to be pro-Palestinian. So, the US can never be a solution. It will continue to fuel the war machine."

"The US just blocked a resolution for Palestinian statehood at the UN," I say tiredly.

"Are there any sensible Americans who can demand that things change?"

On that, at least, I have a little bit of hope.

"I know you haven't seen the news in several months," I tell him. "I know you are too focused on your own daily errands. But my friend, we are seeing unprecedented protests across the world, including in the US. Academics, students, artists, activists, and engineers are taking to the streets demanding a ceasefire. Many in the Jewish community in Europe and the USA are standing firm, shoulder to shoulder, demanding an end to this mass killing and destruction. The world is getting tired of this war machine, this endless profiteering while children are slaughtered. They can see everything on Instagram and TikTok. And they are horrified."

"But it is still continuing," he says. "Every single day I hear about scores of my lab clients hit by airstrikes."

"I know, Hassan. Believe me, I know. But the world is in uproar, every major city. They are not slowing down. In fact, universities all over the US and the world are revolting. The students and the faculty, too."

I'm sure it's cold comfort while he sleeps in a tent, scrounges for scraps of food, and dodges deadly bombings. But I believe Palestinian freedom is inevitable. No people will consent to live without freedom, with nothing but oppression and false promises, forever.

As Gaza grapples with starvation and mass killing, the US administration introduces a new project: constructing a pier off the Gaza coast to process food deliveries, aiming to alleviate the dire humanitarian situation as famine looms due to Israel's blockade. Palestinians never asked for this—it's far more efficient to transport aid over land. But instead of pressuring Israel to open border crossings sufficiently to prevent famine, much less calling for a ceasefire that would allow aid to be transported more safely, the US has decided to construct this pier, without asking the opinion of the people of Gaza.

I observe a seldom-told reality: the Palestinian transport company responsible for ferrying food trucks also transports the remains of demolished homes to build a jetty for maritime aid delivery. While trucks carrying food are bombed and aid workers and the starving population are killed, trucks transporting the rubble of our homes are allowed through.

"How can a colonial system differentiate between trucks, only to let construction trucks pass and then attack an aid convoy with international personnel aboard?" asks Hassan.

Of course, this jetty is more than simply the ruins of our demolished homes. The rubble carries the bones and flesh of our people. They bear the scent of our mothers, our memories, hopes, and aspirations—our exam schedules, vaccination cards, treasured toys and photographs, and certificates of life achievements.

The pier fails rapidly, in any case, due to weather and security concerns, and the people of Gaza continue to face forced starvation.

Ami Ayalon, former Israeli Security Agency (Shin Bet) director, was once asked to describe the reality of Palestinians. He replied, "It's a life of people who dream of freedom but don't see it. Whether we like it or not, we control the lives of millions."[61]

When questioned about what he would do if he were a Palestinian living in the West Bank or Gaza, he stated that he would fight against Israel to achieve his liberty and would do everything possible to attain it.

Palestinians will, too.

Right now, there are two Gazas. One is a minority whose desperation, rage, grief, or cynicism have turned them to the dark side. The rest, against enormous odds, maintain their sense of integrity, decency, and humanity, working tirelessly to improve conditions for the people and make social progress. Sadly, Israel's onslaught is likely turning at least some of the second camp into the first one. Most people who can see clearly know this is not good for anyone's security. We must have a ceasefire as soon as possible and human rights and freedom for all Palestinians, for the sake of everyone in the region and the world.

We can't afford to be complacent. At the same time the world is waking up, the forces that want to erase all of Palestine have more power than ever before in Israel. As the slaughter in Gaza continues, settlers rampage in the West Bank[62] while soldiers kill children with impunity there, too.[63] They are morally bankrupting and delegitimizing themselves with every new atrocity. The only question is how much more damage the Israeli occupation will be allowed do to my people and their homes and land until it finally destroys itself.

Gaza is wounded to its core. Its joys are overshadowed by grief. No one can truly understand it unless they are Palestinian. No one can truly relate to the horror of facing expanding settler-colonialism in the twenty-first century and suddenly waking up to the end of home, homeland, and family, not just as material and tangible things but even as ideas. By killings, this second Nakba dwarfs the massacres of 1948. In many ways, it is the inevitable sequel to that grave injustice.

Even when there's finally a ceasefire, the killing won't be over. Asbestos from pulverized buildings and heavy metals from vaporized bombs will leave a toxic legacy of cancer and birth defects for decades to come that may kill more Palestinians than those directly killed by bombs, bullets, infection, disease, and starvation during the active phase of the genocide.[64]

We have our sorrow, which cannot be soothed by the analysis of a world that hasn't experienced it. We have our loss, which others can only ponder in the realms of fiction and exaggeration. And we have our exile, in its abstract and pale meaning, where we are stranded as visitors, as perpetual refugees, with a crushed history, places that are no more, people you won't find, streets that have ended, and stones that fear we won't return.

No one in this world understands what it's like to die so silently, this glaring identity loss, the fact that we are susceptible to erasure with such offhand ease and audacity. It's not possible to understand this rare kind of grief without experiencing it firsthand. We don't blame those who don't share this sorrow with us, only those who refuse to see it.

Amid the devastation, the fight for Palestinian freedom continues. There is hope. There is always hope. In the stories of the NASA scientist Professor Suleiman Baraka, Sara at the ice cream factory, Kamal and his blind neighbor Hatem, Amira with her parkour skills, Ibrahim and his bag of gifts, Layla El-Masry connecting with her mother across the border, Hassan steadfast in his lab, Nermine with her eye for fashion, Samira Radwan up to her wrists in her native soil, and so many others, we saw the best in people under the most difficult circumstances.

We have experience in recovery and even more in resurrection. When the carnage finally ends, when the occupation finally ends, Gaza will recover. We will construct better schools, universities, hospitals, museums, mosques, churches, and playgrounds. We will raise our children to overcome the trauma Israel has inflicted upon them since before they were born, and we will become citizens of the world.

But the world as it is now may never fully recover from the scars of this human tragedy. Masks are falling off. A world system that allows tens of thousands of innocent children to be deliberately starved, killed, maimed, and orphaned while the world watches is a system that needs deep and fundamental changes.

There's a glaring double standard when human rights matter only for certain people, not for others. When international law is only applied to certain people, not to others. This is an unjust and unsustainable system.

The International Court of Justice's finding that Israel is plausibly committing genocide seemingly disappeared in a puff of smoke. The US vetoes any measures at the UN to hold Israel accountable for its crimes, no matter how many lies they tell or how many laws they violate. This dangerously undermines the very idea of human rights and international law, which were put in place to try to prevent more world wars and another Holocaust.

If Palestinian kids aren't safe and free, ultimately, no kids are safe. We are all in this together—or we should be. And we can be.

As we strive for a world where freedom, compassion, and justice reign, may this book serve as a rallying cry for humanity, in Gaza and beyond.

Acknowledgments

This book owes its life to the indomitable spirit of my people, the Palestinians of Gaza, whose voices echo through every page. To stand as your witness and advocate is a profound privilege. The courage it takes to survive—and to keep surviving—against unthinkable odds is both humbling and inspiring.

To my dear friend Hassan: I know the medical lab is no more. I know the blue plastic desks are now buried beneath the tread marks of tanks, and I know about the bulldozers obliterating what was left of blood samples and any fragile hope for diagnostics even after the "ceasefire deal." I know that you called me not just to tell me that you survived the unrelenting waves of killing, displacement, and loss, but also to talk about the thyme tea we used to sip, the postman who never returns, and Karam's father, who died still waiting for medical supplies.

My house is gone, too. My family is displaced. I stopped tallying everyone who was lost—family, friends, neighbors—because numbers feel obscene next to their faces, their stories.

But, my friend, we are building it again. Tea is brewing on the same land, with the same thyme that outlasts every occupation. Because, as you reminded me, you became a grandfather again, even in the darkest months of destruction. Yes, they bulldoze, they bomb, they destroy—but tell me: How can tyrants ever defeat us if, in the shadow of their violence, we keep living, and we keep welcoming new life? The demographic "war" they have chosen to fight is one they never stand a chance of winning.

And to give you something to laugh about: In one of my talks at the University of Texas, a young Israeli woman, visibly anxious, said, "I feel terrible about the pregnant women I delay, the students I turn away, and the humiliations we inflict at checkpoints."

When I asked her why she does it, she replied, "We are told the demographic war with Palestinians is one we can't afford to lose." Imagine that: Our tea, thyme, and grandchildren are seen as an existential threat. Well, history's math is always on our side.

To Dr. Helen Hintjens, I owe deep gratitude for your astute observations, especially your suggestion to thread Naji's story through the book as interludes. That decision greatly transforms and enriches the narrative. Your quiet humility and intellectual generosity are gifts to this book.

To Pamela Olson, whose sharp eye and precise editorial work make the story sharper and clearer—thank you. Your careful attention to the facts lends the work a vital accuracy and rigor, and for that, I am profoundly appreciative.

Finally, to my friends, comrades, and colleagues: your support, whether through encouragement, critique, or quiet faith, is the invisible foundation of this work. You understand that stories like these are not just a means of expression but a means of resistance, of endurance. Thank you for believing in the importance of this task and for helping me complete it.

We remain unbowed, because we have no other choice—and because hope, stubbornly, persists.

Endnotes

1   As of spring 2024, this pharmacy is famous as one of the few pharmacies serving over 1.5 million people crammed into Rafah.

2   Uncle Salah was sadly killed by tank shrapnel in December 2023 and left to bleed on his daughter's lap for eight days. By the time they got him on a donkey cart to Al Shifa Hospital, there were no doctors and no medicine. I called everyone I could, including deputy state secretary of defense in DC, but no one was able to help transport him from north to south, so he died from wounds he could easily have survived from with proper medical treatment.

3   Seven other camps and villages had the same conditions as the buffer zone before the settlements were evacuated in 2005. The rest of Gaza was slightly safer, although it remained ensnared in a state of closure and caught in a web of unpredictability. Of course, in the end, it is clear that no one was ever safe.

4   Many suspect that Israeli authorities keep vilifying and trying to defund or abolish UNRWA because they wish to end Palestinian refugees' status as refugees to try to force them to give up any hope of returning to the lands they were forcibly displaced from in 1948.

5   David Rose, "The Gaza bombshell," *Vanity Fair*, April 2008. https://www.vanityfair.com/news/2008/04/gaza200804

6   While Palestinian refugees are almost universally barred from returning to their homes in what became Israel, any Jewish person in the world can move to Israel and get instant citizenship.

7   They were not able to establish a school due to lack of funding. But they were able to teach, train, and inspire many children, many of whom were not even born yet when he got his first surfboard.

8   Unfortunately, this famous tower was obliterated by Israeli war planes in 2014.

9   Before the mass killing and destruction in Gaza that began in October 2023, there were seven space telescopes in Gaza, in large part thanks to Professor Baraka's efforts.

10 Like doctors and other public servants, teachers in Gaza were warned by the Ramallah-based Palestinian Authority (PA) to stay home following the coup attempt in 2007 or face penalties such as withheld salaries and dismissal. The *de facto* government in Gaza, aiming to maintain attendance in schools, threatened to terminate employees who participated in the strike. Employees were trapped between two forces: one that had the funds in Ramallah and another that administered employees in Gaza. According to the Gaza Ministry of Education, 55 percent of Gaza's teachers stayed home during the opening days of the academic year due to the strike. The resulting shortage of teachers prompted people like Ahmed to apply for teaching positions and be accepted. However, due to the economic blockade imposed on Gaza, the de facto authority struggled to provide full salaries. PA employees often received only 60% of their wages, and in some months, the Ministry of Finance lacked the resources to pay them at all. The de facto authority therefore accumulated debts to employees who took up positions in schools, hospitals, and other public service facilities. I reported on this many times and the PA protested, because donor countries protested paying for teachers and doctors to sit home. But the PA saw this as an extra burden that would force the *de facto* authority in Gaza to hand over power to the PA. Of course, this never happened, despite many national unity government visits to Gaza. Tens of thousands of employees went to work but didn't get wages while others sat home and got paid. It created intolerable injustice and pressure on people working with only sporadic pay as they tried to uphold the basic health and education of the people of Gaza.

11 This happens fairly often in Gaza, where one Israeli strike creates a crowd as people gather to try to help, and a second strike kills and injures many more. Palestinian paramedics know they have a greatly reduced average lifespan due to this and other tactics that target medical workers and facilities.

12 As of March 2024, Ibrahim remains trapped in the St. Porphyrius church with hundreds of others without adequate food and water, subject to airstrikes and sniper attacks from Israeli soldiers who have already killed around two dozen of the people sheltering there.

13 Within a span of five months prior to publication of the book, the Palestinian Football Association reported the killing of 157 Palestinian athletes, including 90 national and regional club football (soccer) players with their families. Mohammed Khattab, an internationally certified FIFA referee

renowned for officiating Asian and Arab Cup games since 2020, was killed along with his wife, mother, and four children in an airstrike on their home in Deir Al-Balah. Asian Football Confederation President Sheikh Salman bin Ibrahim Al Khalifa condemned Khattab's killing, calling it a significant loss for the global sports community.

14 "2018: Plight of Gaza fishermen after Israel's gradual destruction of their sector," B'Tselem, February 11, 2019. https://www.btselem.org/gaza_strip/20190211_gaza_fishermen_plight_due_to_israeli_restrictions

15 Conal Urquhart, "Gaza on brink of implosion as aid cut-off starts to bite," *The Guardian*, April 15, 2006. https://www.theguardian.com/world/2006/apr/16/israel "Israel forced to release study on Gaza blockade," *BBC*, October 17, 2012. https://www.bbc.com/news/world-middle-east-19975211

16 David Rose, "The Gaza bombshell," *Vanity Fair*, April 2008. https://www.vanityfair.com/news/2008/04/gaza200804

17 At least one lion and many birds and other animals were killed when Israel bombed the area with white phosphorus. The zoo was eventually shuttered. Most of the animals in Gaza's remaining zoo died of starvation after Israel's 2023-24 assault on Gaza.

18 Harriet Sherwood, "The KFC smugglers of Gaza," *The Guardian*, May 19, 2013. https://www.theguardian.com/world/shortcuts/2013/may/19/kfc-smugglers-of-gaza

19 It's possible the story of finding it in the sea was a fabrication, as the statue appears in better shape than it would have been if found underwater. This may have been to hide the true location of its origin, perhaps because it was on land that belonged to someone else or unearthed while building tunnels.

20 It was badly damaged in a recent Israeli air strike.

21 These figures come from this article: Tony Wright, "This is where war always ends, said the gardener of Gaza's graveyard," *The Sydney Morning Herald*, October 13, 2023. https://www.smh.com.au/national/this-is-where-war-always-ends-said-the-gardener-of-gaza-s-graveyard-20231012-p5ebsl.html

Another count is listed at the Commonwealth War Graves Commission: https://www.cwgc.org/visit-us/find-cemeteries-memorials/cemetery-details/71701/gaza-war-cemetery

22 In 2021, two Israeli missiles destroyed Samir Mansour's bookshop. The loss of more than 90,000 books, and the much-loved space, was a devastating blow to Samir and to the Gaza literary community. However, a global campaign followed with donations of funds and books from around the world that ended up rebuilding and tripling the size of the bookshop, demonstrating that strength of collective purpose and the significance of

literature as a force for shared solidarity and connection. Sadly, the bookstore was bombed again by Israel in 2023.

23 Built in the west of Gaza City, the cultural center was opened in 2004 with a theater, conference hall, library and digital library, research and study center, and computer labs. It also has halls to host fine art exhibitions.

24 During the 2023-24 onslaught, Dr. Abu Saif published numerous accounts in various mainstream publications such as *The New York Times* and *Slate*. They were collected into a book called *Don't Look Left: A Diary of Genocide*.

25 While the Mishal Center is known for empowering young artists, Gaza's most iconic hub of culture is Rashad Shawa Cultural Center, built in the 1980s in the affluent Al Rimal neighborhood. Through the years it has received world leaders like Nelson Mandela and Jacques Chirac. The Rashad Shawa Cultural Center was one of many Gaza landmarks targeted and leveled to the ground in Israel's assault that began in October 2023.

26 "Arab-Israeli" is what Israel calls Palestinian Israelis, the remnants of Palestinians left from the ethnic cleansing campaigns of 1948 and beyond.

27 TEDx Shujaiya, October 29, 2015. https://www.ted.com/tedx/events/16463

28 This school was destroyed by the Israeli military, and Israeli soldiers posted photographs of themselves smiling in front of the demolished building.

29 Professor Alareer was assassinated along with several family members after receiving threats from the Israeli military.

30 Reuven Pedatzur, "Why Did Israel Kill Jabari?" *Haaretz*, December 4, 2012. https://www.haaretz.com/opinion/2012-12-04/ty-article/.premium/reuven-pedatzur-why-kill-jabari/0000017f-ded6-db5a-a57f-defe58f00000, https://www.thenation.com/article/archive/report-gaza-under-siege

31 Rebuilding from this war was nowhere near complete when the next assaults took place in May 2021, August 2022, and October 2023 onward.

32 I had witnessed Leena and her husband's fertility struggles in the summer of 2001 during my final year of secondary school. A year later, I learned my Tawjihi exam results through the newspaper Hassan received before anyone else, thanks to his lab's convenient location next to the bookshop.

33 The Nakba is what Palestinians call the massive ethnic cleansing that accompanied the foundation of Israel in 1948. Zionist forces violently displaced the vast majority of Palestinians from their homeland inside what became Israel, massacred 15,000 people, and destroyed more than 400 Palestinian villages. Millions of Palestinians remain in forced exile. More than five million Palestinians in the West Bank and Gaza have lived under belligerent military occupation since 1967 without human rights, political rights, or freedom. Palestinians have attempted nonviolent

resistance to gain their freedom on countless occasions. Such efforts have always been either ignored or met with overwhelming deadly force, including the killing of more than 200 Palestinians (20% of them children) and injuring of more than 9,000 (most of them severely) in the Great March of Return in 2018-19. (Israeli soldiers openly bragged about how many kneecaps they shot during those demonstrations.) In 2023, even before October 7, more than 240 Palestinians were killed in the West Bank by Israeli settlers and soldiers.

A brief history of the conflict can be found here: https://pamolson.org/BriefHistory.htm

This article by Peter Beinart in *Haaretz* (the *New York Times* of Israel) explains how Israel frustrated and stymied attempts to jump-start the economy in Gaza after 8,000 illegal settlers were removed in 2005:

Peter Beinart, "Gaza Myths and Facts: What American Jewish Leaders Won't Tell You," *Haaretz*, July 30, 2014. https://www.haaretz.com/opinion/2014-07-30/ty-article/.premium/gaza-myths-and-facts-what-american-jewish-leaders-wont-tell-you/0000017f-e487-d7b2-a77f-e787e60c0000

Reprinted here with no paywall: https://fasttimesinpalestine.wordpress.com/2014/08/01/beinart-demolish-israeli-talking-points-gaza

For general analysis of how Palestinians think of the Hamas attacks of October 7, see: Muhammad Shehada, "How Palestinians look back on 7 October a year later," October 10, 2024. https://www.newarab.com/analysis/how-palestinians-look-back-7-october-year-later

Hilo Glazer, "'42 Knees in One Day': Israeli Snipers Open Up About Shooting Gaza Protesters," *Haaretz*, March 6, 2020. https://www.haaretz.com/israel-news/2020-03-06/ty-article-magazine/.highlight/42-knees-in-one-day-israeli-snipers-open-up-about-shooting-gaza-protesters/0000017f-f2da-d497-a1ff-f2dab2520000

34 He never mentioned that the reason Hamas took over in a coup was because Israel and the US tried to violently overthrow the democratic will of the Palestinian people in 2007.

David Rose, "The Gaza bombshell," *Vanity Fair*, April 2008. https://www.vanityfair.com/news/2008/04/gaza200804

He also neglected to inform the gathered press that Netanyahu facilitated the transfer of funds to Hamas and then ignored numerous intelligence warnings that an attack was planned.

Tal Schneider, "For years, Netanyahu propped up Hamas. Now it's blown up in our face," *Times of Israel*, October 8, 2023. https://www.timesofisrael.com/for-years-netanyahu-propped-up-hamas-now-its-blown-up-in-our-faces

Abdelali Ragad, Richard Irvine-Brown, Benedict Garman and Sean Seddon, "How Hamas built a force to attack Israel on 7 October," *BBC*,

November 27, 2023. https://www.bbc.com/news/world-middle-east-67480680

Michael Biesecker and Sarah El Deeb, "Hamas practiced in plain sight, posting video of mock attack weeks before border breach," *AP*, October 13, 2023. https://apnews.com/article/israel-palestinian-war-hamas-attack-border-wall-aa0b0f5f3613b6c6882cf37168e8e8ed

35   "Netanyahu's references to violent biblical passages raise alarm among critics," *NPR*, November 7, 2023. https://www.npr.org/2023/11/07/1211133201/netanyahus-references-to-violent-biblical-passages-raise-alarm-among-critics

Netanyahu's government has been the most right-wing and extremist in Israel's history.

See, for example: Jake Tapper, "Key members of Netanyahu's cabinet 'throwing fire on the flames'," *CNN*, November 16, 2023. https://www.youtube.com/watch?v=rFl2AuVhbMM

36   Omer Bartov, "As a former IDF soldier and historian of genocide, I was deeply disturbed by my recent visit to Israel," *The Guardian*, August 13, 2024. https://www.theguardian.com/world/article/2024/aug/13/israel-gaza-historian-omer-bartov

Owen Jones, "Israeli Dissidents Expose Genocidal Language," *YouTube*, December 15, 2023. https://www.youtube.com/watch?v=uxzcKiSuJQw

Chris McGreal, "The language being used to describe Palestinians is genocidal," *The Guardian*, October 16, 2023. https://www.theguardian.com/commentisfree/2023/oct/16/the-language-being-used-to-describe-palestinians-is-genocidal

37   Bethan McKernan and Quique Kierszenbaum, "'We're focused on maximum damage': ground offensive into Gaza seems imminent," *The Guardian*, October 10, 2023. https://www.theguardian.com/world/2023/oct/10/right-now-it-is-one-day-at-a-time-life-on-israels-frontline-with-gaza

38   Israel has an explicit policy, called the Dahiya Doctrine, of targeting civilian homes and infrastructure as a means of political pressure. This fits the definition of terrorism. See: "Dahiya Doctrine," *Wikipedia*. https://en.wikipedia.org/wiki/Dahiya_doctrine

Virtually all of Gaza City has been destroyed, an incalculable act of barbarity, collective punishment, and terrorism.

Yahya R. Sarraj, "I Am Gaza City's Mayor. Our Lives and Culture Are in Rubble," *New York Times*, December 24, 2023. https://www.nytimes.com/2023/12/24/opinion/gaza-city-palestine-war.html

Michelle Nunn, Tjada D'Oyen McKenna, Jan Egeland, Abby Maxman, Jeremy Konyndyk and Janti Soeripto, "We Are No Strangers to Human Suffering, but We've Seen Nothing Like the Siege of Gaza," *New York*

Times, December 11, 2023. https://www.nytimes.com/2023/12/11/opinion/international-world/us-government-gaza-humanitarian-aid.html

39 Irfan Galaria, "Opinion: I'm an American doctor who went to Gaza. What I saw wasn't war—it was annihilation," *LA Times*, February 16, 2024. https://www.latimes.com/opinion/story/2024-02-16/rafah-gaza-hospitals-surgery-israel-bombing-ground-offensive-children

40 Peter Beinart, "If Israel Eliminated Hamas, Nothing Fundamental Would Change," *The Beinart Notebook*, May 20, 2021. https://peterbeinart.substack.com/p/if-israel-eliminated-hamas-nothing

41 "3 hostages killed in Gaza by Israeli troops were shirtless and waving a white flag, official says," *PBS*, December 16, 2023. https://www.pbs.org/newshour/world/3-hostages-killed-in-gaza-by-israeli-troops-were-shirtless-and-waving-a-white-flag-official-says

42 Yaniv Kubovich, "Israel Created 'Kill Zones' in Gaza. Anyone Who Crosses into Them is Shot," *Haaretz*, March 31, 2024. https://www.haaretz.com/israel-news/2024-03-31/ty-article-magazine/.premium/israel-created-kill-zones-in-gaza-anyone-who-crosses-into-them-is-shot/0000018e-946c-d4de-afee-f46da9ee0000

43 Mohammad Al-Sawalhi, Kareem Khadder, Abeer Salman and Zeena Saifi, "At least 13 killed, including 7 children, after strike on Gaza's Al-Maghazi refugee camp," *CNN*, April 16, 2024. https://www.cnn.com/2024/04/16/middleeast/maghazi-refugee-camp-strike-gaza-intl-latam/index.html

44 Israel's brutal blockade of food, water, fuel, and medicine includes basic medical supplies like antiseptic, antibiotics, and anesthesia. Countless patients, including thousands of children, have undergone torturous surgeries with no pain medication whatsoever. One of the very few Western journalists who have been able to travel inside Gaza shows a few examples of the horrors found at Gaza's hospitals:

"CNN visited a Gaza hospital. This is what we saw," *CNN*, December 14, 2023. https://www.youtube.com/watch?v=SdlZmZr29L0

45 Jessie Yeung, Radina Gigova and Mohammed Tawfeeq, "More than 10 children losing legs in Gaza every day as dire health crisis grows, aid groups say," *CNN*, January 7, 2024. https://www.cnn.com/2024/01/08/middleeast/gaza-children-losing-legs-disease-intl-hnk/index.html

Eliza Griswold, "The Children Who Lost Limbs in Gaza," *The New Yorker*, March 21, 2024. https://www.newyorker.com/news/dispatch/the-children-who-lost-limbs-in-gaza

46 Miriam Berger, Evan Hill and Hazem Balousha, "Israel's assault forced a nurse to leave babies behind. They were found decomposing," *Washington*

Post, December 3, 2023. https://www.washingtonpost.com/world/2023/12/03/gaza-premature-babies-dead-nasr

Allegra Goodwin, Jomana Karadsheh, Abeer Salman, Florence Davey-Attlee and Mihir Melwani, "Infants found dead and decomposing in evacuated hospital ICU in Gaza. Here's what we know," *CNN*, December 8, 2023. https://www.cnn.com/2023/12/08/middleeast/babies-al-nasr-gaza-hospital-what-we-know-intl/index.html

Regarding the dozens of premature babies at Al Shifa Hospital:

Astha Rajvanshi, "The Race to Save Premature Babies in Gaza," *Time*, November 22, 2023. https://time.com/6338832/gaza-al-shifa-hospital-rescue-mission-babies

Matthew Mpoke Bigg and Samar Abu Elouf, "28 Premature Babies Evacuated from Gaza Arrive in Egypt. Others Never Had the Chance," *New York Times*, December 15, 2023. https://www.nytimes.com/2023/11/20/world/middleeast/premature-babies-gaza-hospital-egypt.html

47　Ruth Michaelson, "UN rights chief 'horrified' by reports of mass graves at two Gaza hospitals," *The Guardian*, April 23, 2024. https://www.theguardian.com/world/2024/apr/23/un-rights-chief-horrified-by-reports-of-mass-graves-at-two-gaza-hospitals

48　Abeer Salman, Ibrahim Dahman and Tim Lister, "More than 300 bodies found in mass grave at Gaza hospital, says Gaza Civil Defense," *CNN*, April 23, 2024. https://www.cnn.com/2024/04/22/middleeast/khan-younis-nasser-hospital-mass-grave-intl/index.html

49　His Facebook page was removed by Meta. There are hundreds like him, usually with mass followings on social media. Anyone who posted "Khan Younis, City of Love, we are immovable" was killed, or family members near their cellphone were killed.

50　"Israeli raid kills 22 members of Al Jazeera correspondent's family in Gaza," *Al Jazeera*, December 6, 2023. https://www.aljazeera.com/news/2023/12/6/israeli-raid-kills-21-members-of-al-jazeera-correspondents-family-in-gaza

51　Hagar Shezaf and Michael Hauser Tov, "Doctor at Israeli Field Hospital for Detained Gazans: 'We Are All Complicit in Breaking the Law'," *Haaretz*, April 4, 2024. https://www.haaretz.com/israel-news/2024-04-04/ty-article/.premium/doctor-at-idf-field-hospital-for-detained-gazans-we-are-all-complicit-in-breaking-law/0000018e-a59c-dfed-ad9f-afdfb5ce0000

Shaimaa Khalil and Mohamed Madi, "Bruises and broken ribs – Palestinian deaths in Israeli prisons," *BBC*, April 22, 2024. https://www.bbc.com/news/world-middle-east-68780112

Jonah Valdez, "Video of Sexual Abuse at Israeli Prison Is Just Latest Evidence Sde Teiman Is a Torture Site," *The Intercept*, August 9, 2024. https://theintercept.com/2024/08/09/israel-prison-sde-teiman-palestinian-abuse-torture

Joseph Massad, "Why raping Palestinians is legitimate Israeli military practice," *Middle East Eye*, August 12, 2024. https://www.middleeasteye.net/opinion/why-raping-palestinians-legitimate-israeli-military-practice

Prominent orthopedic surgeon Dr. Adnan Al-Bursh was one of many victims of torture and murder (and possibly rape) while in Israeli custody.

John Sparks, "'He was the light of my life and I lost him': How a famous surgeon died in an Israeli prison after being taken from Gaza hospital," *Sky News*, November 14, 2024. https://news.sky.com/story/he-was-the-light-of-my-life-and-i-lost-him-how-a-famous-surgeon-died-in-an-israeli-prison-after-being-taken-from-gaza-hospital-13253157

A personal story about Palestinian child prisoners: https://x.com/fadiquran/status/1728902006994022610

52 "Babies dying from preventable causes in besieged Gaza," Oxfam, November 23, 2023. https://www.oxfam.org/en/press-releases/babies-dying-preventable-causes-besieged-gaza-oxfam

53 Mohammed Salem and Nidal Al-Mughrabi, "Baby in Gaza saved from womb of mother killed in Israeli strike," *Reuters*, April 21, 2024. https://www.reuters.com/world/middle-east/baby-gaza-saved-womb-mother-killed-israeli-strike-2024-04-21

54 "Stories of loss and grief: At least 17,000 children are estimated to be unaccompanied or separated from their parents in the Gaza Strip," UNICEF, February 2, 2024. https://www.unicef.org/press-releases/stories-loss-and-grief-least-17000-children-are-estimated-be-unaccompanied-or

"What will become of Gaza's orphaned generation?" *Al Jazeera*, March 19, 2024. https://www.aljazeera.com/program/the-stream/2024/3/19/what-will-become-of-gazas-orphaned-generation

55 Chantal Da Silva, "Fears mount for Gaza's tiny Christian community after mom and daughter shot dead," *NBC News*, December 18, 2023. https://www.nbcnews.com/news/world/fears-mount-gazas-tiny-christian-community-mom-daughter-shot-dead-rcna130132

"Relative of two Christian women killed in Gaza church says they were shot by sniper," *Middle East Eye*, December 24, 2023. https://www.youtube.com/watch?v=tWaEZzRQZg8

56 "Israel deploys new military AI in Gaza war," *France 24*, February 10, 2024. https://www.france24.com/en/live-news/20240210-israel-deploys-new-military-ai-in-gaza-war

57 Yuval Abraham, "'Lavender': The AI machine directing Israel's bombing spree in Gaza," *+972 Magazine*, April 3, 2024. https://www.972mag.com/lavender-ai-israeli-army-gaza

58 Emine Sinmaz, "'I'm so scared, please come': Hind Rajab, five, found dead in Gaza 12 days after cry for help," *The Guardian*, February 10, 2024.

https://www.theguardian.com/world/2024/feb/10/im-so-scared-please-come-hind-rajab-six-found-dead-in-gaza-12-days-after-cry-for-help

59 "Flour Massacre," *Wikipedia.* https://en.wikipedia.org/wiki/Flour_massacre

60 "US this week approved transfer of thousands of bombs to Israel, official says," *Reuters*, April 4, 2024. https://www.reuters.com/world/middle-east/us-this-week-approved-transfer-thousands-bombs-israel-official-says-2024-04-04

61 "Ami Ayalon: The Missing Israeli Endgame," *Foreign Affairs*, November 28, 2023. https://www.youtube.com/watch?v=hUt0rV7Pl4M

62 Zack Beauchamp, "In the West Bank, Israeli settlers are on an anti-Palestinian rampage," *Vox*, November 9, 2023. https://www.vox.com/world-politics/2023/11/9/23945651/west-bank-israeli-settler-palestine-gaza-war-violence

63 Mona Chalabi, "Settler violence against Palestinians in the West Bank – visualized," *The Guardian*, April 22, 2024. https://www.theguardian.com/world/2024/apr/22/israel-settlers-violence-against-palestine-west-bank
    "CNN Discovers Israeli Settlers Are Ethnically Cleansing West Bank," *Majority Report*, December 21, 2023. https://www.youtube.com/watch?v=b1BDd1JWtGc

64 Nils Adler, "'Death sentence': Asbestos released by Israel's bombs will kill for decades," *Al Jazeera*, October 8, 2024. https://www.aljazeera.com/news/2024/10/8/death-sentence-asbestos-released-by-israels-bombs-will-kill-generations

Mohammed Omer Almoghayer was born and raised in Rafah in the southern Gaza Strip. He holds a PhD in sustainable development, awarded by Erasmus University Rotterdam, after completing the first-year theory of his doctoral studies at Columbia University. He has worked as a research fellow at Harvard University's Center for Middle Eastern Studies. Mohammed has held various roles at the UN, including Senior Advisor, where he provided crucial assistance to people in disaster-stricken regions. He later took on the role of Chief Executive Officer at the Global Partnership Hub in Geneva, with a passion for fostering sustainable development and international cooperation across developing countries.

In 2008, Omer Almoghayer was honored with the prestigious Martha Gellhorn Prize for Journalism. The award citation described him as "the voice of the voiceless" and called his reports a "humane record of the injustice imposed on a community forgotten by much of the world." He was awarded with the Ossietzky Prize in 2009 by the Norwegian branch of PEN International for his outstanding contributions to free expression. He received an honorable mention in Pulse Media's "20

Top Global Media Figures of 2009" and received the Lannan Cultural Freedom Award in 2011. He was named Best Youth Voice by New America Media in 2006 and ranked 398th on the Arabian Business Power 500 list in 2013.

He has reported for various media outlets, including *The New York Times*, *New Statesman*, *The Nation*, *Al Jazeera*, *Democracy Now!* and Norway's *Morgenbladet*. Omer Almoghayer is the author of *Shell-Shocked* (OR Books) and co-author of *The Oslo Accords 1993-2013: A Critical Assessment* (American University Press). His work has been translated into 27 languages including Arabic, Norwegian, Chinese, Japanese, Hindi, Spanish, French, Italian, Dutch, Swedish, Danish, Finnish, German, and Portuguese.